D1124048

CAMBRIDGE STUDIES IN PHILOSOPHY

Emotion

CAMBRIDGE STUDIES IN PHILOSOPHY

General editor D. H. MELLOR

Advisory editors J. E. J. ALTHAM, SIMON BLACKBURN
DANIEL DENNETT, MARTIN HOLLIS, FRANK JACKSON, T. J. SMILEY
BARRY STROUD

Emotion

William Lyons

Lecturer in Philosophy
University of Glasgow

Cambridge University Press

CAMBRIDGE

LONDON   NEW YORK   NEW ROCHELLE
MELBOURNE   SYDNEY

Published by the Press Syndicate of the University of Cambridge
The Pitt Building, Trumpington Street, Cambridge CB2 IRP
32 East 57th Street, New York, NY 10022, USA
296 Beaconsfield Parade, Middle Park, Melbourne 3206, Australia

© Cambridge University Press 1980

First published 1980

Set, printed and bound in Great Britain by
Fakenham Press Limited, Fakenham, Norfolk

British Library Cataloguing in Publication Data
Lyons, William
Emotion. – (Cambridge studies in philosophy).
1. Emotions
152.4 BF531 79–41378
ISBN 0 521 22904 9

TO
MY MOTHER AND FATHER

Contents

Preface

Recently a psychologist, Magda Arnold, wrote that 'the psychology of emotion is difficult enough for the researcher and theorist ... Because research is so prolific and results are so confusing, most psychologists working in this field either content themselves with an uncritical review of findings related to emotions, or restrict themselves to their own work and a short review of the findings of others in a very limited area ... without any attempt to relate these results to a connected theory of emotion' (introduction to Arnold, 1968). Even more recently Robert Solomon, a philosopher, wrote that 'emotion has almost always played an inferior role in philosophy, often as antagonist to logic and reason ... Along with this general demeaning of emotion in philosophy comes either a wholesale neglect or at least retail distortion in the analysis of emotion' (Solomon, 1977).

Even if one thinks that these judgments are a little harsh, it is probably true to say that nowadays emotion is a relatively neglected topic in philosophy. When it is discussed, the tendency is to concentrate on specific problems to the neglect of any attempt to show how these problems might be related to one another or how proposed solutions to these problems might affect our overall view of the nature of emotion. Indeed the tendency is to concentrate on one particular canonical set of problems or areas of discussion, namely the distinction between feelings and emotions, the connection between emotion and object, emotions and belief, the expression of emotion, and the justification of emotions. Besides giving some account of the more central of these areas, I have endeavoured to introduce some new or relatively unexplored topics such as the evaluative and appetitive aspects of emotion, the connection between physiological changes and emotions, emotions as motives, emotions and purpose, and blaming the emotions. And, while acknowledging that fear, the traditional paradigm case of emotions for philosophers and psychologists, is a useful model, I have deliberately made considerable use of love as an example, as it is an emotion which functions in many respects in an importantly different way, and, besides, it is interesting and important in its own right.

But my chief concern has been to give an overall rounded account of the nature of emotion, outlining the four major theoretical views about emotion and then showing how the theory I am espousing is to be seen as a version of one of these views, the cognitivist. Then, in the bulk of the book, I set out the detailed implications of this view with regard to the various facets and functions of emotion and, finally, I provide a summary of this view and its details in the final chapter. So, against the current fashion in both philosophy and psychology, I put forward a model or wholistic theory of occurrent emotional states, and approach individual aspects or problems concerning emotions as they serve to clarify the particular account of emotion I propose.

I hope, then, that this book will be of interest both to psychologists and to philosophers, though I fear that this topic is one that does really suffer from the doctrine of separation of disciplines which philosophers and psychologists adhere to, and that psychologists may find philosophical analysis too foreign to their methods. I have made considerable reference to and use of the relevant psychological literature but I have also argued, as philosophers do, from made-up cases. This does *not* mean that, in doing so, a philosopher is arguing *a priori*. He is not. His made-up cases are meant to be ordinary everyday examples reflecting facts which are basic and incontrovertible, and so do not stand in need of elaborate experimental support. We already know a great deal about human beings in emotional situations, and, when working at the fundamental level of trying to work out an acceptable theory or model of emotional states, we can and should draw first and foremost upon this knowledge. Sometimes, too, philosophers argue by reference to the way we use certain words. This again puzzles psychologists. R. S. Peters explains the point of doing this in the following way:

> The point of looking closely at ordinary usage, if one is a psychologist, is that it often provides a clue to distinctions which it is

theoretically important to take account of. We know *so much* about human beings, and our knowledge is incorporated implicitly in our language. Making it explicit could be a more fruitful preliminary to developing a theory than gaping at rats or grey geese [Peters, 1960].

Professor H. J. Eysenck said at a recent conference that 'both drug treatment and behavior therapy [for neurotic disorders] depend very intimately on a better understanding of the emotions', yet the author of the very first paper at the same conference asserted that 'an attempt to define emotion is obviously misplaced and doomed to failure'. One is tempted to say that the resulting situation must be like that of sallying forth to study rabbits while having no idea of what is to count as a rabbit. If one is seeking to understand the workings of something, one obvious way to proceed will be to concoct functional models. Definitions of emotion are nothing other than functional models put into words, and it is hard to see how anyone could proceed very far without attempting to formulate such definitions. Yet philosophers, who have a genuine claim to be involved traditionally and continually in the struggle to formulate definitions and adequate concepts for things, are often left out in the cold. The same conference, to which I have already alluded, included not one philosopher. Psychology and psychiatry inherited the study of emotion from philosophy but by and large philosophical work on emotions is now neglected by these other disciplines, so that models of emotion – such as the behaviourist one – which many philosophers, after considerable discussion, believe have been shown to be inadequate, continue to hold sway in these other disciplines. By contrast a cognitive model is still suspect to the majority who work in these other disciplines because it was and is primarily a philosophical theory or model. And, especially to psychologists yearning to be aligned alongside the experimentalists in the hard sciences, philosophy is thought of as metaphysical, which is a booword in their vocabulary and is taken to mean, more or less, magical. So my, probably vain, hope is that philosophers and psychologists in particular will work together on the emotions and, I am certain, for the benefit of both. This is already happening in some places but in most it is not.

I hope, finally, that this book is written clearly and simply enough to be understood by students who are just beginning to delve into the rich area of the emotions. However, excepting the first two chapters, it is not a survey of views in the area of emotion but an attempt to come to some explicit and fresh conclusions about the nature of emotion.

Acknowledgements

In the first place I should like to record my gratitude to Professor Terence Penelhum who provided both encouragement to me and kindly criticism of my first tentative explorations in the area of the emotions during part of a postgraduate year at the University of Calgary, and who helped me prepare some of the material for this book when it first appeared as articles. I also owe a considerable debt of gratitude to Professor G. P. Henderson of the University of Dundee who enabled me to do further work in the area of emotions as a graduate student in his stimulating department and who was unfailingly kind and solicitous for my welfare during my time in Dundee. But especially I should like to thank Professor L. C. Holborow, now of the University of Queensland, for his ever patient and penetrating criticism of my doctoral research; and my colleague John Skorupski, and Don Locke of the University of Warwick, who both gave me valuable advice and criticism during the preparation of the manuscript for this book.

From a reading of the text, it will be clear that I should acknowledge the immense help I gained from the work on the theory of the emotions of such philosophers as Alston, Bedford, Green, Kenny, Penelhum, Peters, Pitcher, Ryle and Wilson, and psychologists such as Arnold, Schachter, Singer, Leeper and Lazarus, whose writings on this topic are surely among the modern classics in the field.

Finally I should like to thank the editors and publishers of the *Canadian Journal of Philosophy*, *Philosophy and Phenomenological Research*, and *Ratio* for permission to reprint or make use of in a revised form material first published in their journals; and my colleagues David Campbell and George Weir for their generosity in assisting me with checking the proofs and references.

I

Three classical theories of emotion: the feeling, behaviourist and psychoanalytic theories

There are both philosophical and psychological theories which have contributed enormously to the study of the emotions. In this opening chapter I shall discuss three of these – the feeling, behaviourist and psychoanalytic theories – or perhaps more accurately three theoretical streams, as each stream comprises what might be called either several versions of a single theory or several theories which are related. There have been other theories which do not fit readily into these streams but, apart from the cognitive theory, which is outlined separately in the next chapter, I think it is fair to say that they have been less influential. The feeling and cognitive streams have been dominant in philosophy, and the behaviourist and psychoanalytic streams have dominated psychology. At any rate this and the next chapter do not make any claims to be giving an exhaustive account of theories of emotion but merely to be a discussion of these theoretical streams which could be said to be of such importance as to have the status of classical theories of emotion, and I will be confining my discussion of these theories to the classical philosophical and psychological literature on them, and the connections between them.

The point of this discussion is twofold. First, to provide the background or context into which I can place the theory whose details form the major part of this book, and thereby to make my account of emotion more comprehensible. In particular, I hope to make my discussions intelligible to psychologists, who often have difficulty in connecting up philosophical discussions of emotion with their own work in the same area. Secondly, I want to take serious note of theories which have not merely been influential but still are and so must be acknowledged as active rivals to any other theory. So, in

;iving my account of these rival theories, I shall also be outlining
vhat I believe to be the central difficulties in them.

The feeling theory

Some may wonder why I begin this account of some of the major
schools of thought concerning the emotions with the Cartesian
theory and why I do not begin earlier with the Greeks or at least the
Mediaeval philosophers. It is not because I am siding with Descartes
in his estimate of the contribution of 'the ancients' on this subject as
'slight' (Descartes, 1911–12, Part I, Art. I, p. 361); for while I think
it correct to say, as Kenny does, that 'it was Descartes' formulation
of the problems concerning the emotions which was to influence the
later history of philosophy and the early attempts to make psychology into an experimental science' (Kenny, 1963, p. 16), the ancient
Greek and the Mediaeval philosophers have directly or indirectly
influenced some of the important contemporary cognitive theories
of emotion in both philosophy and psychology. So I am merely
postponing discussion of the Greek and Mediaeval contributions to
the discussion in the next chapter of the fourth or cognitive theory
of the emotions, for that is where their influence lay. From the
seventeenth century to roughly the end of the nineteenth century,
with the odd exception, the Cartesian feeling theory was the ortho-
dox theory.

Descartes' account of the emotions or passions is contained in his
work *The Passions of the Soul*, Parts I and II.[1] Descartes begins this
account by telling us that we must first distinguish carefully the
separate functions of body and soul. The chief functions of soul are
thought; those of body are movement and heat: he then explains all
movement of the limbs in terms of movements of the animal spirits,
which are extremely minute material bodies and 'the most animated
and subtle portions of the blood' (Descartes, 1911–12, Art. x).

The soul's function, thought, he tells us, is of two sorts; its
actions or desires, and its passions. Desires are of two sorts; those
which are aimed at something immaterial, such as God, and those
which are aimed at moving our body in some way. Passions, the
soul's other function, are 'all those kinds of perception or forms of

---

[1] As this book arose out of Descartes' correspondence with Princess Elizabeth,
material on Descartes' account of the emotions can also be found in editions of his
correspondence.

knowledge which are found in us' (1911–12, Art. XVII). The sort of passions which we call fear, or joy, start with the perception of some object, such as, in the case of fear, a 'strange and frightful' animal approaching, which perception is then transmitted to the soul via the pineal gland. Once in the soul this perception is presumably compared in memory with a previous similar one and there is a realisation of some sort that this animal is liable to prove as harmful as previously experienced 'strange and frightful' animals did. But this process of realisation and comparison is surmise, for all that Descartes says on this point is that 'if this figure [of an animal approaching] is very strange and frightful – that is, if it has a close relationship with the things which have been formerly hurtful to the body, that excites the passion of apprehension in the soul and then that of courage, or else that of fear and consternation according to the particular temperament of the body or the strength of the soul' (1911–12, Art. XXXVI). But in point of fact, Descartes' account may be less cognitive than that, for he goes on to explain that the impression in the soul caused by the perception of the 'strange and frightful' animal, after being related in some unspecified way to previous experiences of such animals and, again in some unspecified way, judged in consequence to be of something harmful, 'disposes the brain in such a way that the spirits reflected from the image thus formed on the gland, proceed thence to take their places partly in the nerves which serve to turn the back and dispose the legs for flight, and partly in those which so increase or diminish the orifices of the heart . . . [that it] sends to the brain the spirits which are adapted for the maintenance and strengthening of the passion of fear' (1911–12, Art. XXXVI). And this maintenance, he explains, amounts both to a continuance of the flow of the animal spirits to the limbs used in flight and to a continuance of a flow of animal spirits to the pineal gland, which action causes the 'soul to be sensible of this passion' (1911–12, Art. XXXVI), that is, to be aware of these unusual activities in the body and, in particular, those in the heart.

Descartes then goes on to explain that 'the principal effect of all the passions in men is that they incite and dispose their soul to desire those things for which they prepare their body, so that the feeling of fear incites it to desire to fly, that of courage to desire to fight, and so on' (1911–12, Art. XL).

So, while at times Descartes writes as if the upsurges of animal spirits in brain, heart and limbs, and the consequent actions of the person concerned, are the passions, he is more often at pains to make clear that passion proper is a perception of the soul, and so part of thought. Passion is the reflective awareness of the commotions going on in the body. Fear, for example, is the awareness of the animal spirits causing or tending to cause us, say, to turn our back and run away, and is caused by these animal spirits. That is why, for Descartes, emotions are passive or passions. It is true that these motions and commotions themselves have been caused, usually though not always, by perceptions or presumed perceptions of the external world, and a comparison of these with previous experience; however, for Descartes, these are not part of emotion as such. Nor are the desires consequent to the instinctive motions following on the initial perceptions of the external world part of emotion as such.

Distinguishing the emotions becomes, for Descartes, a matter of distinguishing the different external objects – or different internal 'temperament[s] of the body or . . . impressions which are fortuit-ously met with in the brain' (1911–12, Art. LI), for this is Descartes' account of the generation of objectless and imaginary-object fears – which begin the whole causal process. Thus a certain reflective per-ception is labelled 'fear' because the commotions and motions it is reflecting on were caused by a 'strange and frightful' object. This perception, on the other hand, is to be called 'wonder' because the action in the brain – there is no general commotion in heart and blood with this one, he tells us – which is reflected on is caused by an object which is 'rare and extraordinary' (1911–12, Art. LXX).

But Descartes is clear that 'the objects which move the senses do not excite diverse passions in us because of all the diversities which are in them, but only because of the diverse ways in which they may harm or help us, or in general be of some importance to us' (1911–12, Art. LII). That is, Descartes has the beginning of what could be termed an evaluative aspect to his theory, though this would be a generous description. Indeed Descartes' causal account of the genesis of an emotion or passion contains all the elements which I believe are necessary for a full account of the emotions but, un-fortunately, he did not then state that this account was an account of emotion but only of the causes of emotion. He made emotion some-thing over and above all this. He made it a special perception in the soul which was caused in turn by the causal chain of perception, evaluation, physiological changes, desires and behaviour. Emotion was like an after-thought or epiphenomenon to the basic causal nexus from perception to bodily reaction and purposive action. He was led into this view of emotion, I think, because he had already committed himself to the view that anything important to humans must be found wholly in the soul, and that it must thereby be simple. The complex causal chain from perception to bodily reaction and purposive action could not be emotion because it is neither wholly in the soul nor simple. So he relegated his brilliant account of emotion to the preamble to emotion and invented a special epiphenomenon in the soul as the real emotion.

Now there are a number of difficulties with a view that makes emotion an experience in each person's soul of what is going on in his body. Descartes has it that the emotion is the subjective awareness of the activities of the animal spirits in the body. Thus fear will be a subjective awareness of our limbs being moved in flight and of, say, a constriction around the heart, or increased pulse rate, and so on. At any rate it will be a *sui generis* experience in the soul of this bodily activity.

The first difficulty is one that Kenny puts so well. It is to do with the inherent privacy of emotions if Descartes' view is correct.

Wittgenstein has shown that a purely mental event, such as Descartes conceived an emotion to be, is an *Unding* [An inconceivable and so inexpressible thing]. Any word purporting to be the name of something observable only by introspection, and merely causally connected with publicly observable phenomena, would have to acquire its meaning by a purely private and uncheckable performance. But no word could acquire a meaning by such a performance; for a word only has meaning as part of a language; and a language is something essentially public and shareable. If the names of the emotions acquire their meaning for each of us by a ceremony from which everyone else is excluded, then none of us can have any idea what anyone else means by the word. Nor can anyone know what he means by the word himself; for to know the meaning of a word is to know how to use it rightly; and where there can be no check on how a man uses a word there is no room to talk of 'right' or 'wrong' use (*Philosophical Investigations, passim*, especially 1 243–258) [Kenny, 1963, p. 13].

But perhaps Descartes' greatest problem stems from the fact that it makes emotion purely passive and sensation-like. Despite Descartes' referring to emotion as 'a passion of the soul' and to a passion as 'a form of knowledge', he goes on to give an explanation which makes emotion a feeling and without any cognitive element. Fear, for example, is just the subjective awareness of the animal spirits causing the limbs to make the body flee and causing the heart to constrict and so on. On his account, then, fear does not give us any know-ledge of the world or reflect our attitude to the world. It merely registers, as a feeling, our physiological changes and bodily move-ments. For Descartes, fear is not an awareness that something is frightening and that I am fleeing, it is the subjective concomitant feeling of my flight and of my being physiologically in a certain state.

This view of emotion as just a passive feeling, causes some diffi-culties not connected with how the word 'emotion' could enter the language. For example, it runs counter to the data that one can easily gather, that people can be in an emotional state and not be subjectively aware of it. For the following seems to be an uncon-troversial case of emotions: O'Reilly is so taken up by the discussion at the curriculum meeting that he does not realise that he is becoming very angry with Macdonald who is suggesting that the central texts in the first year course should consist only of the writings of the Existentialists. It is only later on, when Macdonald curtly remarks to O'Reilly that there was no need to get so heated, and he overhears MacFee wonder why he got so angry, that O'Reilly realises that he must have become very angry during the meeting. Yet, on Descartes' account, the above case is impossible, for to have an emotion is *ipso facto* to be aware of it, because for him an emotion is a feeling and one cannot have unfelt feelings. Feelings are subjective states in which one experiences (is aware of) whatever is the content of the feeling, say, a throb.[2]

Another difficulty stemming from Descartes' account of emotions as just feelings is that it cannot account for the fact that emotions give rise to behaviour and are, in consequence, cited as motives behind behaviour. It is not uncommon for someone to say some-thing like 'Jealousy caused Jones to stab his wife outside the bar.' Now, if we substituted the phrase 'a particular feeling' for 'jealousy'

---

[2] Alston makes a different but related point (Alston, 1967a, Vol. 2, p. 482): 'For, assuming that I cannot be mistaken about what I am feeling at the moment, if I can be mistaken about whether I am angry, then being angry cannot be just feeling angry.' That is, one can be in an emotional state but not know exactly what state one is in (Is it anger or fear? Remorse or shame?), but this is not true of feelings.

in the sentence – which we should be able to do without oddity if Descartes' view is correct – we get, 'A particular feeling caused Jones to stab his wife outside the bar', which begins to look odd. This oddity is compounded if we now substitute for the phrase 'a particular feeling' the phrase 'a feeling of throbbing and constriction around the heart'. For if we now transcribe the sentence as 'A feeling of throbbing and constriction around the heart caused Jones to stab his wife outside the bar' it becomes more or less absurd. For feelings by themselves don't lead to behaviour. They only do so if they are connected with wants or desires of some sort. A feeling of throbbing and constriction around the heart might lead me to do something if, say, the action to be done would relieve the feeling and I wanted the feeling relieved (perhaps I found it painful or at least uncomfortable). But, as such, feelings are, like sensations such as those of hot and cold, just neutral reactions. They do not by themselves connect up to behaviour. To say that I am hot is not to say that I want to do anything or am liable to do anything, much less that I will do anything. I might like being hot, I might not, I might be indifferent. It all depends on the weather, my health, the intensity of the heat, and so on.

I think Descartes himself realised that his theory was not able to make much sense of the connection between emotions and behaviour because, as we have seen, he does write that 'the principal effect of all the passions in men is that they incite and dispose their soul to desire those things for which they prepare their body, so that the feeling of fear incites it to desire to fly' (1911–12, Art. XL). But, as I have pointed out, his theory cannot really account for the connection, because feelings do not incite one to anything, and to write of them as doing so is to paste over a gap in the theory. As Ryle puts it, 'impulses, described as feelings which impel actions, are paramechanical myths' (Ryle, 1949, pp. 114–15).

Perhaps the most fundamental difficulty with Descartes' view of emotions is that it does not separate off what are commonly agreed to be emotions from what are commonly agreed not to be emotions. Given his theory, Descartes is forced to grant not merely that the subjective awareness of the bodily movements and physiological changes following on a perception of something such as a frightening animal, is an emotion, but also that the subjective awareness of the bodily movements and physiological changes following the injection of a drug or the onset of a disease, should merit the title 'emotion'.[3] For after all the perception of the external object is not central to Descartes' account of emotion nor even central to his account of the causal antecedents of emotion, for he does allow that some emotions, such as objectless and imaginary-object fears are caused entirely by 'temperaments of the body or ... impressions which are fortuitously met with in the brain' (1911–12, Art. LI), and there is no rubric laid down as to how these in turn must be caused. So it seems that there is nothing against a disease or drug causing them.

Bedford brings up another important difficulty for any Cartesian theory of emotion in the following way:

> I am inclined to think that if an emotion were a feeling no sense could be made of them at all. It may be said that an emotion is unjustified when a feeling is inappropriate or unfitting to a situation. But I find this unintelligible ... What reasons could be given for or against a feeling, or for or against its 'inappropriateness' to a situation? If someone were to say 'I felt a pang this afternoon' it would be meaningless to ask whether it was a reasonable or unreasonable pang [Bedford, 1967, p. 91].

Bedford's argument here seems to be that while emotions can be said to be unreasonable, unjustified or inappropriate, feelings cannot, therefore emotions are not feelings.[4] This seems to me to be a valid point, for if emotions can be judged in this way, they must include something which can be looked at to see whether it is backed up by reasons, and reasons which are appropriate to the circumstances, and so can be said to be justified in the circumstances. Now the usual claimants for such a role would be judgments or claims of some sort. What is clear is that a feeling *per se* is not a claimant.

But despite these difficulties with the Cartesian theory of the emotions, many followed Descartes in seeing emotion as a special feeling in the soul or the soul's perception from within of the body's changes and activities. The most notable exponent of his theory of the emotions was Hume. Though Hume's theory is overlaid with elements from his theory of mental activities, it is Cartesian none the

---

[3] See also Alston, (1967a, pp. 482–3).

[4] Pitcher (1965, p. 329) makes a similar point. He writes: 'For although we can speak of emotions in the ways indicated, we cannot do so of sensations. Certainly not of bodily sensations, at any rate: it makes no sense to ask for a person's reasons for having a tickling sensation in his throat, or to call a twinge or an itch justified or unjustified, reasonable or unreasonable.'

less. Hume's account of the emotions is contained in *A Treatise of Human Nature*, Book II, 'Of the Passions'. Here he tells us that the emotions or passions are 'secondary or reflective impressions' or imprints on the soul which 'proceed from some of these original ones [original impressions on the soul of sensations], either immediately or by the interposition of its idea' (Hume, 1978, Bk II, Part I, Section I, p. 275). That is, emotions or passions are second-order impressions, or impressions caused by other impressions (or their corresponding ideas), when associated in a particular way. They can be divided into two kinds, 'the calm and the violent' (p. 276). Calm emotions are the aesthetic ones, 'the sense of beauty and deformity in action, composition, and external objects' (Hume, p. 276). But the violent emotions are the passions proper, and include 'love and hatred, grief and joy, pride and humility', though he warns us that these so-called violent emotions 'may decay into so soft an emotion, as to become, in a manner imperceptible' (Hume, p. 276).

As to the details of how these paradigm emotions or passions arise, this depends on whether the emotion in question is direct or indirect. Direct passions, such as 'desire, aversion, grief, joy, hope, fear, despair and security' (Hume, p. 277) result from the direct association of pleasure and pain, good or evil, with some aspect or quality of some object. Joy, for example, is the immediate or direct impression of pleasure associated with something or other. Indirect passions, such as 'pride, humility, ambition, vanity, love, hatred, envy, pity, malice, generosity' (Hume, pp. 276–7) arise in a more complicated manner. They result from associating in a special way some pleasure or pain, which results from some particular quality or aspect of some object, with some quality or aspect of some other object. For example, pride results from associating the pleasure resulting from, say, the beauty of a house, with oneself in that one is associated with the house as its owner. It is in connection with these indirect passions or emotions that Hume is able to point out that the object of the passions often differs from its cause. It is the beauty of the house which causes the pleasure (which is the basic sensation part of pride), for that is what beauty naturally does to humans, but the object of pride is oneself or oneself as owner of the house (Hume, 1978, Bk. II, Part I, Section VIII, pp. 300–1).

How the associations or relations of ideas and impressions, and the resulting special impressions in the soul occur, may be a crucial point in Humean exegesis, but it does not much concern us here.

Suffice it to say that Hume's account appears to be that 'nature has bestow'd a kind of attraction on certain impressions and ideas, by which one of them, upon its appearance, naturally introduces its correlative' (Section v, p. 289). In short, his answer seems to be that we are programmed by nature to make these associations and combinations and so to produce the sensations which are the emotions.

For our purposes we now need only draw out from this rather complicated account Hume's general schema for the emotions. The essence of emotion, for Hume, is the peculiar or particular sensation in the soul which is caused by a particular combination or association of ordinary sensations or impressions and their corresponding ideas. Thus, 'any thing, that gives a pleasant sensation, and is related to self, excites the passion of pride' (p. 288). Pride, for Hume, is the peculiar second-level complex sensation in the soul resulting from a particular way of associating pleasure from something with oneself. The pleasure by itself is not the emotion of pride, though an essential part of it. The *sui generis* sensation in the soul resulting from feeling pleasure and making some association of a particular sort is the emotion.

At this point we should add to this general schema Hume's account of how the emotions give rise to action or behaviour. He tells us that 'DESIRE arises from good consider'd simply, and AVERSION is deriv'd from evil. The WILL exerts itself, when either the good or the absence of the evil may be attain'd by any action of the mind or body' (Hume, 1978, Bk II, Part III, Section IX, p. 215). That is, the will moves us to seek the good and avoid evil; this is 'an original instinct' (p. 215) or natural tendency. Now, if we realise that good and evil are 'in other words, pain and pleasure' (p. 215) and recall that 'the passions, both direct and indirect, are founded on pain and pleasure' (p. 214), then it is not difficult to see that the passions, being sensations resulting from associating pain or pleasure with people, things or events, will naturally incline us to seek out the source of the pleasure and to avoid the sources of pain. This is Hume's general picture concerning the relation of emotion to action, though he does explain that things such as custom or habit, and imagination, can facilitate or lubricate this link between emotion and action (Sections v and vi).

But it should be clear that Hume is very much a Cartesian. The emotion as such is still the sensation in the soul, and the rest, so much more meagre and obscure in Hume, is just the causal chain which gives rise to it, or results from it. As Kenny so pithily puts it:

> Like Descartes, he conceives his task to be to give a causal explanation of the origin of each emotion; though the explanations which he gives are in terms of associations of perceptions rather than bodily mechanisms, and his metaphors are drawn from chemistry rather than from clockwork. His differences from Descartes arise not from a disagreement about the nature of the passions, but from a disagreement about the nature of causality. [Kenny, 1963, p. 27].

Leaving aside the general difficulties with a Cartesian view of emotion as just feeling or sensation in the soul, which Hume is also heir to, Hume's account leads to a difficulty of its own in the one area where it significantly extends Descartes' theory.

Hume's version extends Descartes' theory by giving a fairly explicit account of the link between emotion and behaviour. Hume does see that an adequate theory of emotion must give some such account, and his account is based on the general psychological principle that we always act so as to gain pleasure and avoid pain, and on the claim that the peculiar sensation of the soul which is the emotion is always causally linked to a first-order or original impression of pain or pleasure. Thus, for example, the emotion of pride is the sensation in the soul which is caused by the sensation of pleasure together with the idea of the ownership of the object of pleasure.

The chief difficulty with this account is that it seems implausible with a good number of emotions, at least at times. It seems implausible to define all emotions at all times in terms of sensations of pain or pleasure. Is anger pleasant or painful, one might ask? A baffling question, for it seems impossible to give any definite answer. Some people may declare that they enjoyed the experience, especially if it was cathartic; some may even admit that they positively wallowed in it when the anger was righteous anger or anger denouncing injustice; and as we are told that revenge is sweet, so perhaps vengeful anger is as well. Others, on the other hand, may deplore any giving in to anger and declare that when they do they find it extremely unpleasant. Even a prime candidate for being a pleasant emotion, love, can surely be painful at times, when unrequited, frustrated or rejected. There may be some emotions which are paradigmatically, if not painful, at least unpleasant. It must be hard to find shame, remorse and disgust pleasant, yet I can imagine someone seeking to be in such emotional situations, and so giving us *prima facie* evidence that they find them pleasant (at least in a Humean sense where the test would be whether they seek out such emotions or not). They may thereby be candidates for psychiatric treatment, but that is another matter.

Because it was Descartes' view of emotion that came to influence the early attempts to make psychology into an experimental science, this resulted in some instances, as Kenny puts it, in the belief 'that the study of the emotions could be made scientific only by training introspectors in precise observation and accurate measurement of their interior states' (Kenny, 1963, p. 29). Indeed this tendency was checked only when Watson's behaviourism began to take hold. Ironically, it was an arch Cartesian, William James himself, who wrote that,

> The trouble with the emotions in psychology is that they are regarded too much as absolutely individual things. So long as they are set down as so many eternal and sacred psychic entities, like the old immutable species in natural history, so long all that *can* be done with them is reverently to catalogue their separate characters, points, and effects [James, 1890, Vol. II, p. 449].

And he deplored the fact that this cataloguing produced a 'descriptive literature of the emotions [which] is one of the most tedious parts of psychology' (James, p. 448).

I believe that William James thought he was changing the Cartesian doctrine of emotion in an important way, for James made it clear that, while he still saw emotions as feelings, these feelings were of the physiological changes and disturbances that went on during an emotional occurrence. I think that his hope was that, at least eventually, psychology would be able to distinguish emotions from one another, and from non-emotions, by reference to these observable physiological changes. If we do look upon James' account in this light, it is not so difficult to see behaviourism as one of its offspring, particularly if one recalls that Watson's behaviourism was in terms of physiological patterns rather than operant behaviour.

What I think is uncontroversial is that James' theory of the emotions has been one of the reasons why many psychologists nowadays fasten almost exclusively upon physiological changes, and the feelings resulting from them, as being the essence of emotion. Quite likely too it was James' distinction between the 'coarser emotions', such as rage, grief and fear, and the 'subtler emotions' such as love, indignation and pride, and his own almost exclusive concern with the former, which has influenced psychology in its preference for studying these emotions with their marked physiological and feelings aspects, and in its preference, for the most part, for seeing emotion as non-cognitive and essentially physiological or behavioural.

The fullest account of James' theory of the emotions is contained in his classic *Principles of Psychology*, Vol. II, Chapter xxv.[5] There James begins his account of emotion by distinguishing it from instinct. Though he allows that objects which arouse emotions in us usually arouse instincts in us as well, this is not always so, and emotions must be clearly distinguished from instincts to behave in certain ways.

The core of his theory of emotion is that *'bodily changes follow directly the perception of the exciting fact, and that our feeling of the same changes as they occur* IS *the emotion.* Common-sense says, we lose our fortune, are sorry and weep . . . The hypothesis here to be defended says . . . that we feel sorry because we cry' (James, 1890, 449–50). In his well-founded insistence that a concept of emotion without reference to physiological changes should be unthinkable, James almost totally passes over any reference to any cognitive aspects of emotion. The causal sequence for him is perception of the object (the only cognitive aspect he mentions), then the physiological arousal, then the feeling or subjective awareness of the arousal. Indeed, as we have seen, he makes emotion to be just our feeling of these physiological changes. Even the minimal cognitive element, perception, is not given a place in emotion proper, it is only a causal antecedent of emotion. As James puts it:

> What kind of an emotion of fear would be left if the feeling neither of quickened heart beats nor of shallow breathing, neither of trembling lips nor of weakened limbs, neither of goose-flesh nor of visceral stirrings, were present, it is quite impossible for

[5] One might also like to refer to the earlier paper on which this chapter is based, 'What is an Emotion?', *Mind*, Vol. 9, 1884.

me to think . . . For *us*, emotion dissociated from all bodily feeling is inconceivable. The more closely I scrutinize my states, the more persuaded I become that whatever moods, affections, and passions I have are in very truth constituted by, and made up of, those bodily changes [James, 1890, p. 452].

So, for James, emotions are really just internal bodily sensations, that is, the feelings or subjective sensible aspects of physiological occurrences caused by perceptions. Ordinarily, says James, sensation is 'an object-simply-apprehended', emotion, is 'an object-emotionally-felt' (James, 1890, p. 474).

It is only after he has given this central account of emotion, in terms of what he calls the 'coarser emotions', such as rage, grief and fear, that James turns to what he terms the 'subtler emotions', such as love, indignation and pride. He argues that these emotions are either to be explained in the same terms as the 'coarser emotions', that is, as sensations, or else as, at most, etiolated examples of emotion in so far as the feeling content in these 'subtler' emotions is less than in the 'coarser' ones.

An immediate attraction of this view, as we shall see, has been the fact that it clearly makes sense of such cases as electrically stimulating the cortex and causing physiological changes which the subject says gave him or her feelings of, say, rage. For a view such as that of James, such a case is clearly a case of a fully-fledged emotion, not an artificial simulation of the physiological part of emotion. For James gives just such an explanation when writing of objectless emotions; 'the emotion here [an objectless emotion] is nothing but the feeling of a bodily state, and it has a purely bodily cause' (James, 1890, p. 459).

Another clear advantage of the Jamesian emotion-as-physiological-change-and-feeling school was that emotion was clearly amenable to objective quantitative measurement and scrutiny. So James might be seen as one of the fathers of modern psychology of the emotions in that he, among others, turned this field into a branch of physiology. If one was to find differences in the emotions then they must amount to differences in physiological changes, either in quantity or quality. Indeed the different emotions could only be distinguished by different quantities or types of physiological changes. This is, I think, peculiar to the James version of the Cartesian theory of the emotions, for only he suggests that the

feeling which is the emotion is merely the feeling of the physiological changes involved. He took the feeling out of the soul and
put it into the purely bodily arena, for his feeling was just the
subjective side of the physiological changes involved, so that if the
feeling was different for each emotion it was because the physiological changes accompanying each emotion must be different as
well.

Unfortunately, as I shall discuss in more detail in a later chapter
(and briefly refer to again later on in this chapter), the wealth of
experimental evidence about the physiological aspects of emotions
has yet to confirm the possibility of distinguishing emotions by
reference to physiological changes alone. This, of course, does not
mean that in the future new evidence might not come to light which
does enable us to distinguish emotions purely by reference to the
physiological changes involved. But there are clearly some who
think that the evidence so far available is already very extensive and
points the other way.[6] But it should be mentioned also that there are
others who believe that they have had some success in distinguishing some emotions, or some emotions in certain experimental
circumstances,[7] by reference to physiological changes, and this
might be seen as some hope for future confirmation of the James
version of the Cartesian theory. But perhaps a fair general conclusion to be drawn from the evidence to hand, might be such as
N. L. Munn gives: 'In the above experiments . . . the physiological
records alone did not tell the whole story [when one sought to
differentiate the emotions]: These had to be interpreted in terms of
the situations which produced them and also the verbal reports of
the subjects' (Munn, 1961, p. 325).

Other than this point about physiological changes, which is
peculiar to the James version of the Cartesian theory, I do not think
there is any other difficulty which is peculiar to his version. It is
perhaps the clearest and most uncompromising of the Cartesian
views and so perhaps the easiest for seeing why a Cartesian theory
is too meagre to encompass all that we find in connection with
emotions, but I do not see any point in rehearsing again the basic
difficulties with Cartesian theories.

[6] Frankenhaeuser (1975); Mandler (1975a, Ch. VI); Pátkai (1971); Schachter (1970,
Ch. 7); Goshen (1967); Schachter and Singer (1962); Cantril and Hunt (1932);
Cannon (1927b).
[7] Izard (1972, Ch. I); Ax (1971); Stanley-Jones (1970, Ch. 2); Plutchik and Ax (1967);
Funkenstein (1955); Wolff (1950); Wolf and Wolff (1943).

But it is worth mentioning briefly at this point a celebrated refutation of the James–Lange theory which contains one fallacy. Soon after the James–Lange theory became established, it came under fire from Cannon in his famous paper, 'The James–Lange Theory of Emotions: A critical Examination and an Alternative Theory'.[8] One of Cannon's arguments was that the James–Lange theory of emotions was false because it stated that an emotion was a feeling, yet this could be shown experimentally to be false. Cannon then went on to cite experiments, such as those of Sherrington (1900) which claimed that when the experimenter 'transected the spinal cord and the vagus nerves of dogs so as to destroy any connexion of the brain with the heart, the lungs, the stomach and the bowels, the spleen, the liver and other abdominal organs – indeed, to isolate all the structures in which formerly feelings were supposed to reside', nevertheless 'these extensively disturbing operations had little if any effect on the emotional responses of the animals' (Arnold, 1968, p. 45). But, as I shall discuss at greater length in the next section of this chapter, Cannon's argument cannot count as a refutation of the James–Lange theory because it begs the question. For only if one accepts a behaviourist position – and I shall argue in the next section that there are good reasons why one should not – will behaviour alone be sufficient evidence for the presence of an emotion, and so sufficient evidence that Sherrington's dogs underwent emotions while not undergoing feelings. Cannon, of course, did bring forward other evidence which does seriously cast doubt on the James–Lange theory, for Cannon brought forward experimental evidence to suggest that 'the same visceral changes occur in very different emotional states and in non-emotional states' (Arnold, 1968, p. 46) and so are not a very good basis for distinguishing emotions, and that 'visceral processes are fortunately not a considerable source of sensation' (p. 51) so that, even if distinctive changes did occur, they would probably not be mirrored in feelings.

But the Cartesian theory did not die with James and still has its adherents. Consider for example this account of emotion: 'Emotion is beyond reasonable doubt a primary state of consciousness depending, in some way not yet understood, upon the cerebral mechanisms concerned with the general regulation of somatic and vegetative activities' (Zangwill, 1950, p. 133).

[8] Cannon (1927), reprinted in part in Arnold (1968); page references will be to this reprint.

The behaviourist theory

In his book, *Psychological Explanation*, J. H. Fodor writes that, 'if there is a received view about psychological explanation among Anglo-American Philosophers and experimental psychologists, it is surely that one or another form of behaviorism is true' (Fodor, 1968, p. 49). So it is clearly important to consider the behaviourist account of emotions.

The behaviourist theory of the emotions, like behaviourism itself, is a product of that period when psychology was breaking away from philosophy and seeking to establish itself as a natural science. J. B. Watson, usually accorded the title 'founder of behaviourist psychology', begins his classical text of behaviourism, *Psychology from the Standpoint of a Behaviourist*, with this ringing manifesto: 'Psychology is that division of natural science which takes human activity and conduct as its subject matter. It attempts to formulate through systematic observation and experimentation the laws and principles which underlie man's reactions' (Watson, 1919, p. 1). But probably one of the least successful parts of Watson's *Psychology* is the attempt to give a behaviourist account of the emotions, and, as we shall see, Watson himself seemed to realise this.

Watson placed the emotions among those behaviour patterns which he believed were inherited rather than acquired, and he desired to establish this by conducting experiments on newly-born babies. Not unnaturally (at least from the parents' point of view),[9] he did not receive much cooperation in this enterprise and was unable to really gain much evidence that the behaviour patterns termed 'emotion' were hereditary. Because of this, and the belief that even if they were hereditary they would very soon become overlaid with acquired characteristics, he suggested that 'the separation between hereditary reaction modes and acquired reaction modes can thus never be made absolute' (Watson, 1919, p. 194). Indeed, because, as we shall see, he found it difficult to establish anything very definite about emotions by his methods, he was

---

[9] When one realises what experiments he wanted to conduct on the newly-born infants – '(1) To suddenly remove from the infant all means of support, as when one drops it from the hands to be caught by an assistant [the child is "held over a bed"] ... (2) by loud sounds; (3) occasionally when an infant is just falling asleep or is just ready to waken, a sudden push or a slight shake is an adequate stimulus' (Watson, 1919, p. 199) – one can see why his enterprise did not elicit much cooperation.

content to state that 'hard and fast definitions are not possible in the psychology of emotion, but formulations are possible and sometimes help us to group our facts' (p. 195).

So, armed with these disclaimers, he suggested that,

A formulation which will fit a part of the emotional group of reactions may be stated as follows: *An emotion is an hereditary 'pattern-reaction' involving profound changes of the bodily mechanism as a whole, but particularly of the visceral and glandular systems.* By pattern reaction we mean that the separate details of response appear with some constancy, with some regularity and in approximately the same sequential order each time the exciting stimulus is presented [Watson, 1919, p. 195].

Thus an emotion differs from an instinctive reaction in that 'when the adjustments called out by the stimulus are internal and confined to the subject's body, we have emotion, for example, blushing; when the stimulus leads to adjustment of the organism as a whole to objects, we have instinct, for example, defense responses, grasping, etc.' (Watson, 1919, p. 197). But straight away Watson tells us that this account

fits only the more stereotyped forms of emotional response as seen, for example, in the states popularly called blushing, anger, fear and shame. When we take into account the whole group of phenomena in which we see emotional manifestations in adults, a pronounced modification is necessary. Apparently the hereditary pattern as a whole gets broken up. At any rate it largely disappears (the parts never wholly disappear) except under unusual conditions (Watson, 1919, p. 197).

So Watson's behaviourist account becomes self-refuting. Watson has told us that an emotion is a 'pattern-reaction', chiefly of physiological changes, which is found in its unadulterated form only in the new-born child, though it is difficult to get clear evidence of this. Since he admits that this 'pattern-reaction' is adulterated or becomes etiolated, or both, soon after infancy, he is admitting in effect that with adults one cannot distinguish one emotion from another, or emotional reactions from other sorts of reactions, by means of a behaviourist account. Indeed, given the admitted paucity of his evidence concerning emotional reactions in the new-born, one can doubt his claim to be able to do this even with infants.

I think, in fact, that Watson has been shiningly honest. He seems to be admitting that one cannot distinguish one emotion from another, or emotions from non-emotions by reference to behaviour patterns, particularly in the case of his own particular version of behaviourism which equated emotional behaviour patterns with patterns of physiological changes. As we shall see in a later chapter, where I discuss in some detail the relation between physiological changes and the emotions, the claim that there are patterns of physiological changes peculiar to each emotion is at best supported by conflicting evidence and at worst should be considered falsified.[10]

Watson himself realises that the evidence is wanting, and tries to explain this by suggesting that 'if this formulation is to fit the facts, the general condition of the organism must be such that the stimulus can produce its effect' (Watson, 1919, p. 195). In other words, the predicted pattern only occurs when everything is *just right* concerning the external stimulus conditions and the internal physiological response mechanisms. But, in saying this, Watson gives us no grounds for accepting that the reaction pattern which he dubs 'the emotion' is the norm and other reactions pathological cases or deviations from the norm. Indeed with a behaviourist theory no behaviour pattern should be considered more central or paradigmatic than another, unless there is firm evidence that some particular pattern occurs more frequently than others in the given conditions. Prior to that, all behaviour should be given equal consideration, and what distinctions there are to be made should be made without any assumptions as to which behaviour is basic or normal and which not. Watson, of course, realises that if he were to accept all putatively emotional behaviour, which occurs with more or less equal frequency, at face value, the number of the emotions would be in the millions, for probably no two emotional behaviour reactions are the same. In restricting the behaviour to be considered to purely physiological reactions and to reflex ones at that, and isolating these in so far as they are noted in new-born infants, he may have cut down on the number of reactions to be noted; but in making this move he runs into the opposite difficulty that all the emotions now appear to be roughly the same. Similar variations on the activation or discharge of the central nervous system and basic reflex reactions seem to occur with a great many of the emotions, and any pattern one settles on as, say, the fear pattern, or the love pattern, is quite

[10] See also p. 15, nn. 6 and 7.

likely to occur in a situation we intuitively regard as, say, one of shame or anger or grief.

Watson's three 'original and fundamental' emotions discovered in his studies of new-born infants were '*fear, rage*, and *love* (using *love* in approximately the same sense that Freud uses sex)' (Watson, 1919, p. 199). Leaving aside a person's sexual reactions, which are not usually considered an emotion, this leaves only two basic patterns, those for fear and rage. If only physiological changes are considered, it is difficult to see how Watson can derive a very thorough-going theory of the emotions from just two patterns (given, of course, that he can even distinguish two definite patterns for these two emotions in a newly-born infant).

Leaving aside the lack of distinguishing patterns on the response side, Watson can still look to the stimulus situation as a way of distinguishing emotions. But here Watson again runs into difficulty. For the same situation seems to cause different emotions in different people. The big dog can frighten the little boy but delight the dog-breeding father, or vice versa. The ride on the roller-coaster can thrill one person and frighten another. Watson should say that, if the physiological reactions are more or less the same, and the situation is the same, then the emotions undergone are the same. Watson's critics would say they are different because of how the persons concerned view the situation. As the little boy believes the dog is going to eat him, his reaction must be put down as fear. The father's reaction, because, say, he views the dog as a particularly fine specimen of Doberman pinscher, would probably be classified as one of delight. But Watson cannot refer to beliefs, or to anything else which is not immediately observable without inference.

Finally it is not clear that Watson can distinguish emotions from non-emotions without making unargued and ungrounded assumptions. If an emotion is just a pattern of physiological changes resulting from some external stimulus, why is not a person's physiological reaction of becoming comatose after being hit on the head with a mallet, or being given a whiff of gas, an emotional reaction? Watson has to say either that the stimulus is the wrong sort or the reaction is. He cannot say the reaction is because a new-born child will exhibit both when 'stimulated' by both stimuli, which seems to be his sole criterion for acceptable reactions. So the distinction must be found in the stimulus or environment. But why is a big dog an acceptable stimulus for an emotional reaction but a whiff of gas not? Clearly Watson has to appeal to some intuition as to what is to count as an emotional stimulus situation, but in doing this he is either making the kernel of his theory to be found in a non-behaviourist account, or being purely arbitrary.

In our own day B. F. Skinner is the best known exponent of 'behavioural science' or 'the experimental analysis of behaviour' (Skinner, 1974, p. 7) and, in his most theoretical book on behaviourism, *About Behaviourism*, Skinner tells us that 'the environment performs the functions previously assigned to feelings and introspectively observed inner states of the organism' and 'what an organism does will eventually be seen to be due to what it is, at the moment it behaves, and the physiologist will someday give us all the details' (Skinner, 1974, pp. 248–9). In other words the explanation of behaviour is to be found in terms of two factors alone, physiology and the environment or external stimulus.

But Skinner's behaviourism, at least in the area of the emotions, differs from Watson's account. Skinner looks, not to physiological changes and reflex behaviour for the pattern reactions which are the emotions, but to operant behaviour or, in non Skinnerian language, behaviour that produces a desired result and so tends to be repeated because of this. Perhaps the clearest and simplest expression of Skinner's view of emotions occurs in his book of 'programmed instruction', written with Holland, and entitled *The Analysis of Behavior:* 'Under different emotional conditions, different events serve as reinforcers, and different groups of operants increase in probability of emission. By these *predispositions* we can (do) define a specific emotion' (Skinner and Holland, 1961, p. 213). Thus, 'An *angry* man may pound the table, slam the door, or pick a fight. The angry man is predisposed (more likely) to emit certain operants rather than others' (Skinner and Holland, 1961, p. 214). That is, anger is the behaviour of pounding tables, slamming doors, picking fights and, presumably, other pieces of behaviour, because it is the behaviour that is reinforced by, and so tends to increase in frequency in, the 'emotional conditions' of anger. These behavioural responses are reinforced because, when performed in such circumstances, they tend to bring about desired results, such as, say, the offending person's behaviour (the behaviour which caused the angry response) not being persisted in or repeated. The behaviour which defines an emotion, on Skinner's view, is just that behaviour which is produced and found to bring about some desired change in the environment, and so tends to be reproduced whenever that environment reoccurs.

The difficulty is that while an angry man *may* 'pound the table, slam the door, or pick a fight', he may not. He may stand stock still, go red in the face, tense, purse his lips, and then go out with studied calm. In short it is an impossible programme to find a list of behavioural items, some or all of which must be present if the behaviour in question is to be dubbed angry behaviour. Even to try poses a baffling question, namely 'How does one know which behaviour counts as angry behaviour?' Is picking one's nose angry behaviour? Is moving one's arm swiftly in a circle angry behaviour? Is going red in the face and shouting angry behaviour? Only the latter, you might reply. But how did you decide that only the latter was to count as angry behaviour? The situation, Skinner must say, the 'emotional situation' as he puts it. But there's the rub. All the weight is now moved to the stimulus situation, the environment that calls forth the operant behaviour of going red in the face and shouting. But how is one to decide, if only situations or external environments are now considered, what is an emotional situation? Is a sunrise an angry situation? Or a train passing? Or someone insulting you? The latter, you, and Skinner, would say. But why? Because, Skinner must say, it calls forth going-red-in-the-face-and-shouting behaviour or pounding-the-table-and-slamming-the-door behaviour. But this becomes a circular definition of anger. The behaviour is identified as angry behaviour because of the stimulus situation, and the stimulus situation is identified as one of anger because of the behaviour it stimulates. This circularity is an indication that neither the behaviour nor the situation gives one grounds for ultimately identifying a reaction as one of anger.

Skinner's behaviourism, finally, much more than Watson's version, is open to the difficulty that many instances of some emotions, and most instances of others, exhibit little or no operant behaviour. Grief, especially when it is about something irretrievably lost or dead, does not lead to much, if any, operant behaviour, because no behaviour can bring about any desired results. For the desired result – that what is dead be brought back to life or what is irretrievably lost be found – is clearly impossible to achieve. But even angry people can be angry and not show it in operant behaviour. That is, some people just are controlled, undemonstrative

people. They may still admit to being very angry and emotional
but they do not show it in non-reflex behaviour. Watson's behaviourism, with its accent on reflex reactions and physiological
changes, can better cope with this difficulty, but his theory, as we
have seen, has its own difficulties.

At this point it should be mentioned that there is a considerable
body of experimental data about the production of rage or anger in
decerebrate and decorticate animals, which is thought to provide
empirical evidence in favour of behaviourist accounts of emotions.
In regard to these experiments Philip Bard, in his paper 'On
Emotional Expression after Decortication with Some Remarks on
Certain Theoretical Views', writes that, 'It is a well established fact
that a decorticate cat or dog, in the chronic condition, is capable of
displaying a type of behaviour which is commonly regarded as
expressive of anger or rage' (Bard, 1934, Parts I and II, p. 309). He
then went on to describe the experiments of Goltz and Rothmann
where decorticated dogs exhibited 'emotional expression ... confined to a reaction consisting of barking and growling, with vigorous attempts to bite' (Bard, p. 309) and Dusser de Barenne's experiments where decorticate cats 'displayed energetic movements of
defense and those reactions so characteristic of the angry cat –
spitting, growling, erection of hair' (pp. 309–10). Bard also describes how, when Schaltenbrand and Cobb's decorticate cat was
given a light pinch on its tail, it exhibited 'hissing and biting with
lowering of the head, arching of the back and vigorous clawing of
the surface upon which the animal rested' (pp. 309–10). Then he
explains that his own lengthy experiments confirmed those findings.

Bard went on to describe experiments with decerebrate animals
(where not merely the cortex but the whole cerebrum was removed)
conducted by Woodworth and Sherrington, where again there was
obtained 'certain responses, expressive of affective states' though
this behaviour 'never amounted to an effective action of attack or
escape' (Bard, 1934, p. 316). And, summing up, Bard explains that
in all these experiments 'it seems reasonable to believe that after
removal of the higher parts of the brain, including the cerebral
cortex, there is an absence, or at least a profound modification, of the
conscious aspects of emotion' yet 'one may, however, speak with
assurance of its *expression* of emotion. The activity under discussion
is termed rage because it unmistakably "simulates the expression of
anger seen in the normal cat"' (Bard, 1934, p. 320).

The difficulty with such experiments is that they beg all the theoretical questions if they are used to support a behaviourist theory of the emotions. Only a behaviourist would be tempted to say that 'hissing and biting, and lowering of the head, arching of the back and vigorous clawing' is rage and all that rage ever is rather than reflex or residual rage behaviour, or behaviour similar to that exhibited during rage, and only a behaviourist would be adamant, on merely observing this behaviour, that it is definitely rage rather than, say, fear. Indeed only someone who believes that observing behaviour is sufficient evidence for discovering emotions would be prepared to say quite definitely that here we have behaviour related to emotions rather than something else, such as spasm reaction after an electric shock or (where the hypothalamus is left intact) after a prodding of the hypothalamus. Indeed the tendency is for behaviourists to say that the decerebrate and decorticate animals exhibit rage because it is like 'normal rage' or 'rage in the normal cat', but this presupposes that one has already an independent criterion for deciding what is normal rage or rage in a normal cat. Now if this independent criterion is a behaviourist one, it runs into the immense difficulties I mentioned when discussing Watson's and Skinner's theoretical accounts; if it is not a behaviourist criterion, then behaviourism would turn out to be propped up by some non-behaviourist account and so would not be behaviourism at all.

It is not surprising, then, that the sorts of experiments conducted by Bard and others have been criticised, not as experiments, but as grounds for saying that the decerebrate and decorticate animals were in emotional states or at least identifiable ones. Harlow and Stagner pointed out that the behaviour said to be rage could as easily be interpreted as being fear (Harlow and Stagner, 1933) and Elizabeth Duffy pointed out that, even if it is considered to be rage-like behaviour, it differs significantly from normal animal rage in that it is undirected or else misdirected (Duffy, 1962, p. 12).

All that such experiments can be taken to show is that behaviour, reasonably similar to that shown when animals are afraid or enraged, can be stimulated in decorticate and, to a much lesser extent, in decerebrate animals and, as some of the experimenters went on to do, that the reactions and activities forming this behaviour seem to be controlled from the hypothalamus. Nothing of a theoretical nature can be deduced except in regard to theories, though I doubt if anyone has ever held them, which deny that such activities and reactions can occur in decerebrate and decorticate animals, and deny that such activities are controlled by the hypothalamus.[11] It would prove such theories false.

By way of conclusion to this section on Behaviourism, I might mention that it is not uncommon now for textbooks of psychology, which are still for the most part more or less of the behaviourist persuasion, to declare that '"emotion" is a term that refers to some very different conditions, apparently little related',[12] and indeed, sections on emotions in textbooks of psychology often give a purely descriptive account of the observed physiological and behavioural aspects of particular emotions without even making any attempt to show why such behavioural or physiological patterns are to be grouped together as emotional, or are to be identified as this or that emotion.[13] So one of the marked influences of this most influential of theories in this area has been to curtail attempts to give a theoretical structure to the reactions we ordinarily call emotional, and to curtail attempts to give answers to the question 'Why do we say this group of behavioural responses are emotional ones?' and 'Why do we even group these responses together?' The failure of the behaviourist account of emotions has led in some quarters to a total abandonment of the attempt to make sense of emotion.[14]

The psychoanalytic theory

The classical source for the psychoanalytic theories of emotion is the works of Freud. But Freud had no single or systematic account of emotion or 'affect' as he called it, but tended to restrict himself to giving accounts of the workings of particular emotions, particularly anxiety. To understand why this was so, it is important to realise, as Wollheim has put it, that 'psycho-analysis originated in therapy' and that 'the application of psycho-analysis, or psycho-analytic therapy, consists, essentially, in the handing on by the analyst to the patient of these explanations [of his neuroses], (Wollheim, 1971, pp. 150–1).' If we realise, too, that Freud claimed to find the source of

---

[11] For further experimental material of this sort, one might consult Lashley (1938) and Delgado, Rosvold and Looney (1956).

[12] Hebb (1966, p. 235); on this point, see also Elizabeth Duffy (1941).

[13] See, for example, Munn (1961; Ch. 13).

[14] See, for example, George Mandler (1975b), where he writes that 'it is my opinion that an attempt to define emotion is obviously misplaced and doomed to failure' (p. 10).

our neuroses in unconscious and unfulfilled wishes, impulses and drives, then one can see that explanations which were of interest to the psychoanalyst were likely to be explanations which make reference to unconscious repressed drives and wishes. It is no wonder, then, that what seems constant in Freud's references to affect is his insistence that they are the symptoms or signs of blocked drives and repressions. To put it another way, Freud's clinical interests were clearly bound to be centred on the emotions of disturbed persons, so it is no surprise that he most frequently refers to emotions such as anxiety and fear, and often to these in their extreme manifestation in hysteria, nor that he explains these as generated by blocked drives and unfulfilled wishes. Thus, in Lecture xxv of *Introductory Lectures on Psycho-Analysis*, entitled 'Anxiety', Freud writes:

> An affect includes in the first place particular motor innervations or discharges and secondly certain feelings; the latter are of two kinds – perceptions of the motor actions that have occurred and the direct feelings of pleasure and unpleasure which, as we say, give the affect its keynote. But I do not think that with this enumeration we have arrived at the essence of an affect. We seem to see deeper in the case of some affects and to recognise that the core which holds the combination we have described together is the repetition of some particular significant experience. This experience could only be a very early impression of a very general nature, placed in the prehistory not of the individual but of the species [Freud, 1959a, Vol. xvi, pp. 395–6)].

Here Freud sees emotions, such as anxiety, as the reaction to traumatic events, but these events were not undergone by the individual but are merely part of the individual's inherited, unconscious, repressed memories. The actual emotion is a resurrection of the original traumatic emotional state triggered by some present event which stirs that memory. As Freud himself puts it: 'Affective states have become incorporated in the mind as precipitates of primaeval traumatic experiences, and when a similar situation occurs they are revived like mnemic symbols.'[15] (Freud, 1959b, p. 93). And in his 'Postscript' to *Group Psychology and the Analysis of the Ego*, Freud gives an account of affectionate emotion as being the overt symptoms of repressed sexual drive for either the object of that emotion

---

[15] Jung followed Freud in the matter of affective states and gives a similar account in Jung (1960, pp. 346–7).

or someone whom the object represents in the mind of the subject of the emotion.

Psychoanalysis, which illuminates the depths of mental life, has no difficulty in showing that the sexual ties of the earliest years of childhood also persist, though repressed and unconscious. It gives us courage to assert that wherever we come across an affectionate feeling it is successor to a completely 'sensual' object-tie with the person in question or rather with that person's proto-type (or *imago*) [Freud, 1971, p. 90].

For good or ill, Freud's clinical explanations of emotions such as anxiety and fear have been worked up into full theories of emotion by later psychoanalysts and psychologists. A good example of this lies in the work of David Rapaport which spanned both disciplines, psychoanalysis and psychology.

The [psychoanalytic] theory of affects, the bare outlines of which seem to emerge, integrates three components: *inborn affect-discharge channels* and discharge thresholds of drive cathexes; the use of these inborn channels as safety valves and indicators of drive tension, the modification of their thresholds by drives and derivative motivations prevented from drive action, and the formation thereby of *the drive representation termed affect charge*; and the progressive 'taming' and advancing ego control, in the course of psychic structure formation, of the affects which are thereby turned into *affect signals* released by the ego [Rapaport, 1967, p. 508].

In less tortured language, this theory can be expounded in the following way. When the energies of instinctual strivings or drives, which reside in the unconscious, are unable to be discharged in the normal way into appropriate instinctual behaviour, because of some inhibition, repression or other block, they are discharged via a safety valve. This safety valve is emotional occurrences or affects, and they release the pent-up psychic energy through the physiological disturbances or discharges of the central nervous system which form their core. In so far as a person's ego can control such discharges, then such discharges are converted into 'affect signals' or purposeful behaviour and other meaningful expressions of affects.

An interesting variation of the psychoanalytic theory of emotions has been put forward by the philosopher Jean-Paul Sartre in his *Sketch for a Theory of the Emotions*. While he endorses the psychoanalytic theory of the emotions in so far as it invests emotional reactions and behaviour with significance of a teleological or goal-seeking sort, he cannot go along with this theory in finding the point or significance of the emotions in the unconscious. However, he does go along with the psychoanalytic theory in holding that the point or significance of the emotions is not to be found in ordinary perceptual consciousness of the world. Rather than in the unconscious, he finds the significance in an imaginary or 'magical' view of the world which we adopt or project onto the world when we cannot cope with it as it really is.

> We can now conceive what an emotion is. It is a transformation of the world. When the paths before us become too difficult, or when we cannot see our way, we can no longer put up with such an exacting and difficult world. All ways are barred and nevertheless we must act. So then we try to change the world; that is, to live it as though the relations between things and their potentialities were not governed by deterministic processes but by magic [Sartre, 1971, p. 63].

Thus Sartre sees emotion as a failure to cope, as a reaction which does not help us adapt to the world as it is but helps us put our head in the sand or in the clouds and 'see' a more manageable but unreal world. As Sartre himself illustrates:

> Take, for example, passive fear. I see a ferocious beast coming towards me: my legs give way under me, my heart beats more feebly, I turn pale, fall down and faint away. No conduct would seem worse adapted to the danger than this, which leaves me defenceless. And nevertheless it is a behaviour of *escape*; the fainting away is a refuge. But let no one suppose that it is a refuge *for me*, that I am trying to save *myself* or to *see no more* of the ferocious beast. I have not come out of the non-reflective plane: but, being unable to escape the danger by normal means and deterministic procedures, I have denied existence to it. I have tried to annihilate it . . . I have annihilated it so far as was in my power. Such are the limitations of my magical power over the world: I can suppress it as an object of consciousness, but only by suppressing consciousness itself [Sartre, 1971, pp. 66–7].

His account of how our emotional reaction in 'active fear' is also an escape into the 'magical' tends to bring into sharp focus the implausibility of this approach: 'We do not take flight to reach shelter:

we flee because we are unable to annihilate ourselves in unconsciousness. Flight is fainting away in action; it is magical behaviour which negates the dangerous object with one's whole body' (Sartre, 1971, p. 67). So with fear as with all the emotions, 'all ways out being barred, the consciousness leaps into the magical world of emotion, plunges wholly into it by debasing itself' (Sartre, 1971, p. 78).[16] Thus, says Sartre, 'we have to speak of a world of emotion as one speaks of a world of dreams or of worlds of madness' (1971, p. 81).

On one level the Freudian account of affect or emotion is quite Cartesian, for Freud writes, as we have seen, that 'an affect includes in the first place particular motor innervations or discharges and secondly feelings' and he then goes on to tell us that the feelings are 'of the motor actions that have occurred' and 'of pleasure and unpleasure'. That is, emotion is physiological changes and bodily movements and the subjective registering of these in feeling; plus a Humean addition of an overall tone of pleasure or the opposite. Where it departs from the Cartesian picture is in its peculiar causal explanation of how the affect occurs and what, in consequence, is its significance. Unlike the Cartesian, or the Behaviourist accounts for that matter, the Freudian account sees the external stimulus as acting only as remote cause of emotion. Events in the world cause us to react emotionally only in so far as they first stir up in us some instinctual drive or impulse, and in so far as this drive or impulse is repressed or blocked. Emotion is the safety valve that lets off psychic steam when the repression or blocking of the normal outlets becomes unbearable.

So the Freudian, and the Psychoanalytic theories in general, will be liable to the general difficulties inherent in adopting a Cartesian view, but there is no point in going over these difficulties once again. What is of interest to us here are the peculiar difficulties of the psychoanalytic and Sartrean theories. The most obvious of these is that, in the pure psychoanalytic version, emotion is no longer a reaction to the world but to something in our unconscious. In anxiety I am anxious, not because the situation is difficult or threatening, but because it triggers off some unconscious repressed desire which I find threatening or difficult to cope with. This, of course, is

---

[16] It should be noted that Sartre points out that, with some emotional occurrences, the person involved does not so much invest the world with magic as find it already so clothed. For example, the world may present itself via 'the disturbing impression of a landscape, of certain objects, or of a room which retains the traces of some mysterious visitor' (1971, p. 87).

a possible account of some anxieties, and maybe it even fits best the sort of chronic or neurotic anxieties which psychoanalysts are most likely to meet with in their clinical work. But it clearly cannot be an account of all anxieties and all emotions. For example, all the evidence might point to the fact that Jane is anxious about her final degree examinations next week. She tells everyone that she feels she cannot pass them, yet she knows it is essential that she does. For keeping the job she has, which enables her to maintain her children (she is divorced), is conditional on her eventually getting a degree. At any mention of the examinations she becomes tense and unsettled. All her activities are centred around preparing for the examinations, even to the point of losing sleep and not eating properly. In the face of all these pointers to the fact that Jane is anxious about her forthcoming examinations, the psychoanalytic theory must suggest that she is anxious because the prospect of the examinations stirs up a repressed drive which, being stirred up, must explode into anxiety behaviour which, presumably, ought to signal or reveal the suppressed drive or unfulfilled wish which it is releasing. In short, the psychoanalytic theory is forced to adhere to an account which fits the facts less well than the commonsense account.

Another facet of the psychoanalytic account is that it seems more readily to fit violent disturbed emotions such as anger, anxiety of certain sorts, and fright, rather than calm or subtler emotions such as awe, joy, and sadness.[17] Further, since all emotions, on the psychoanalytic account, involve the sudden release of pent-up feelings, like the sudden release of steam from a safety valve, emotional states which are not short term and sudden but last a long time, such as certain cases of grief and remorse, would not fit the theory very well. On the psychoanalytic theory, the emotional disturbances related to repressed drives and unfulfilled wishes should only occur when directly and unavoidably triggered, for at other times they are of course repressed, but one can grieve for days though the original stimulus or trigger be no longer present, and adequate emotional 'steam' be already let off.[18]

With Freud's theory the extrapolation from the model of affect, which might fit some cases of anxiety, to positing the same model

[17] On this point, cf. Leeper (1948).
[18] These points would also tell against another view, which seems to be derived from psychoanalytic theory, and which might be called the disturbance theory as it depicts emotions as interrupted or disturbed basic motivations. See Munn (1961), Woodworth (1940), Young (1943).

for all cases of affect is seen at its weakest in his notorious account of affection as repressed sexuality. Leaving aside the difficulty of seeing affection as always explosive and like a safety valve in action, it looks bizarre, for example, as an account of a mother's or father's love for a week-old child. How could the affection for the child seriously be seen as a repressed sexual drive in connection with the child suddenly triggered when the child is born? Besides, if hormonal secretion and glandular swellings of a certain kind are the observable marks of sexual interest, one could easily observe whether any emotional show of affection towards the week-old child had a sexual tone or not. Or is it that the repressed sexual drive would not be revealed in any way? But if that is so, why say it is operative in such a case?

Sartre's adaptation of the psychoanalytic theory has its own peculiar difficulty. For this view commits him to interpreting all emotional reactions as involving essentially misdirected or pointless behaviour if viewed at face value, because the emotional behaviour results, not from an accurate view of some event in the world and an assessment of what is to be done about it, but from a failure to cope with some event in the world, which failure generates an illusory view of the event. On Sartre's account, emotional behaviour only fits in with the illusory view of the event, and so must appear pointless, misdirected or counterproductive when viewed in relation to the event seen in a non-illusory or objective light. But this is contrary to the facts. While it is undoubtedly true that some emotional behaviour is disorganised and counterproductive, it is equally true that some of it is very useful indeed.[19] The frightened man may run faster that he ever has before to get away from the man with the gun; the mother who sees her child about to be run over by a truck may be stirred up by fear and love to hurl herself in front of the truck and save the child. That is, much emotional behaviour is clearly generated by a sound and swift assessment of the situation.

Indeed Sartre's theory is in a way self-refuting, as it becomes most implausible when he tries to account for what he calls active fear. The person fleeing out of fear, he tells us, is 'fainting away in action'. A curious form of fainting! Of course, he is compelled to give this account of active fear because he took as his paradigm of fear the person who is incapacitated by it, and swoons. Clearly such swooning does occur, but equally clearly it is absurd to use it as the

[19] For psychological material on this point see Lazarus (1966).

paradigm, not merely for all fear, but for all emotional reactions. I even doubt whether Sartre's account of the fear that makes a person faint is correct. I see no evidence that leads one on from the fact that X faints when confronted with something extremely frightening, to the explanation that X sees the world in a magical or illusory light, and is intent on debasing himself. A much more plausible explanation would stop short of talk about the magical, and refer only to Sartre's second stage of suppressing the frightening object from consciousness by fainting. But even this seems implausible in that it seems too purposive. One cannot cause oneself to faint at will in this way. The process of fainting is not basically purposive or voluntaristic but physiological. So the most likely explanation is that the physiological disturbances occasioned by the extreme fright disrupt the mechanisms maintaining consciousness.

So all in all I think that the psychoanalytic theories are a case of taking a model which fits certain cases of certain emotions and blowing it up into a general theory of emotion, without taking a hint from the growing implausibility as the theory is extended in this way.

2

A fourth classical theory: the cognitive theory

The prime source for cognitive theories of emotion is Aristotle, and, ʌia Aquinas, his account has given rise to the best known contemporary cognitive theory of emotion, namely that of the psychologist Magda Arnold in her two-volume work *Emotion and Personality* and elsewhere.

Aristotle's account of emotion is not, as one might expect, to be found in the *De Anima* but in the *Rhetoric*, for Aristotle was interested in the emotions in so far as they could be manipulated and so be a means by which orators, politicians and others, might manipulate people. As Aristotle remarked, 'the emotions are all those feelings that so change men as to affect their judgments' (Aristotle, 1941, Bk II, 1378a, p. 1380); thus, to change their emotions will be, at the least, very often to change their views. (Quite useful knowledge indeed for orators and politicians!)

But Aristotle's account is a cognitive account, not because he believed emotions affected our judgment, but because he also believed that judgments or cognitions were central to emotion. In general, a cognitive theory of emotions is one that makes some aspect of thought, usually a belief, central to the concept of emotion and, at least in some cognitive theories, essential to distinguishing the different emotions from one another. Aristotle suggested that the best way of studying an emotion was to analyse it under the following three headings:

> Take, for instance, the emotion of anger: here we must discover (1) what the state of mind of angry people is, (2) who the people are with whom they usually get angry, and (3) on what grounds they get angry with them. It is not enough to know one or even two of these points; unless we know all three, we shall be unable to arouse anger in anyone. The same is true of the other emotions [Aristotle, 1941, p. 1380].

Aristotle is saying that, if you can work out how an angry person views the world and, more specifically, what he thinks of the people he is angry with (for anger is directed primarily at people), and why he thinks that, then you have discovered the *cause* of anger and so will have the knowledge necessary for causing anger in others. Aristotle is not saying that emotions are just a way of looking at the world, for he makes it quite clear that emotions (emotional states) include feelings and impulses, but the feelings and impulses are caused by what we think of the world. Thus he writes that: 'Anger may be defined as an impulse, accompanied by pain, to a conspicuous revenge for a conspicuous slight directed without justification towards what concerns oneself or towards what concerns one's friends' (Aristotle, 1941, p. 1380). That is, anger is to be defined as a belief that we, or our friends, have been unfairly slighted, which causes in us both painful feelings and a desire or impulse for revenge. For Aristotle, and cognitive theories in general, the primary cause of the feeling and physiological aspects of emotion is belief. That this was Aristotle's view is clear from comparing this account of anger with his account of fear. 'Fear may be defined as a pain or disturbance due to a mental picture of some destructive or painful evil in the future' (Aristotle, 1941, Bk II, 1382a, p. 1389). Fear is caused by 'a mental picture of some destructive or painful evil in the future', that is, by a belief that something terrible is about to happen to us. Indeed fear differs from anger, not as regards its feeling side, for feeling slighted and feeling frightened are both painful, but they differ as regards the beliefs which give rise to these feelings and as regards the different impulses or desires that are thereby generated. But because the impulses or desires are related as effects to the cause, beliefs, and also have a rational connection with the beliefs, the beliefs are prior and more basic. Thus such theories are called cognitive theories, for accounts of knowledge or cognition will usually include reference to a belief which is true.

This picture of emotions, I am going to suggest, is by and large the correct one. I say 'by and large', for I think that the emphasis should be placed less on beliefs than on evaluations, though Aristotle's phrase, 'the state of mind' of the subject of emotion, should be interpreted, most probably, as including the concept of evaluation as well as belief. For Aristotle does not merely say that the angry person believes that someone has said something or done something, he believes that what he or she has done is to be viewed or evaluated as a slight. Moreover one can discern in Aristotle's account that the evaluative aspect of emotion is not of a disinterested or dispassionate sort, such as a magistrate might make when deciding that what Brown said was indeed to be construed as a slight, but is of a subjective and involved nature. Indeed how could it give rise to a passion or emotion if it were not passionate and partial? The angry man evaluates something as a slight *to himself*. It is this relating of events to ourselves, or to our quasi-selves, our friends or loved ones, that generates emotion. If we didn't we would not be moved. We would be just calm and dispassionate adjudicators and evaluators of passing events.

So my quarrels with Aristotle are comparatively slight. His phrase 'state of mind' is too vague and loose. The belief part of the emotional person's state of mind needs to be separated in analysis from both the evaluative and appetitive (or wants) aspects, and the emphasis needs to be placed firmly on the evaluative rather than on the belief or appetitive aspects. This latter is very important, for different emotions can be generated by the very same factual beliefs. I can believe that the mortality rate for free-fall parachutists is very high and so infer that the prospect of a free-fall parachute drop ending in death is highly probable. My companion might hold the same belief and make the same inference. Now if we both decide to make a free-fall parachute drop, or are ordered to, I might be in a state of fear but my companion in a state of excitement. For my mind might be dominated by the evaluation of the situation as dangerous *to me*, while my companion's mind, while allowing that what he is about to do might be dangerous, is taken up by the realisation that here is a challenge worthy of him.

Unfortunately Aristotle's account of emotion was interpreted by his most famous mediaeval commentator, Thomas Aquinas, less as a cognitive account than as an impulse or conative account of emotion. Where Aristotle wrote of anger as a feeling and impulse caused by a state of mind, and, in the *Rhetoric* at any rate, put the emphasis on the state of mind component, Aquinas put the emphasis on the impulse or desire component. There are, of course, passages in Aristotle's work, particularly in the *De Anima* (Aristotle, 1968, Bk I, Ch I, 403a 29, pp. 4–5) which do seem not merely to emphasise the impulse or desire component but which seem to forget all about any belief or evaluative aspects.

At any rate, as I have already mentioned, Aquinas' account of emotion was in terms of impulses or desires, and the accompanying physiological changes and feelings, rather than in terms of cognitions and evaluations.[1] As Aquinas puts it: 'So passion, and therefore emotion, is seated in the orectic rather than in the cognitive part of the soul' (Aquinas, 1967, 1a 2ae, Q22, Art. 2, p. 11). The orectic part of the soul is, as Eric D'Arcy explains in his glossary, 'that power of the soul concerned with tendency, desire and behaviour, in contrast with the cognitive side which is concerned with knowledge, belief or perception' (Aquinas, 1967, p. 139). One should not be misled by Aquinas' reference to the soul here. He had a basically Aristotelian, though rather more dualist, view of the soul. Thus the soul's orectic or appetitive functions could be either physical and sensory, or mental and intellectual. In fact Aquinas placed emotions first and foremost in the sensory orexis (Aquinas, 1967, 1a 2ae, Q22, Art. 3, p. 15).

So Aquinas is quite clear that, for him, emotion is firstly a felt tendency, that is, a desire which is, in the first instance, physiological and set into motion by perception alone, unmediated by beliefs or evaluations. Aquinas held that there were two basic types of emotion: the primary ones which remain wholly grounded in the sensory orexis, and the secondary ones which begin in the sensory orexis but have cognitive overtones (Aquinas, 1967, 1a 2ae, Q23, Art. 1, p. 21). These secondary emotions include and build on the primary ones. Thus fear is an impulse to run away from some perceived evil or threat together with a realisation that the evil or threat will not be easy to avoid. But if the evil or threat is avoided, joy, a primary emotion, ensues. If the evil or threat is not avoided – and one is not dead! – sorrow ensues. So we can see now that Aquinas differentiates the emotions solely in terms of the object as perceived, and the impulse that results. Sorrow differs from joy in that its object is a perceived evil and one seeks to avoid it, while joy's object is a perceived good which attracts one to it. Fear differs from sorrow in that its object is an evil perceived both as an evil and as difficult to avoid, and which one seeks (has an impulse) to avoid.

The difficulties of such a theory derive from its jettisoning of the cognitive–evaluative aspects of emotion, in regard to primary emotions at least, in favour of a pared-down causal chain from object to perception to impulse and its physiological accompaniments. Aquinas must ultimately account for the difference between,

[1] The bulk of Aquinas' work on the emotions is contained in his *Summa*, Q 22–30.

say, love and hate, in terms of impulse alone. For, if MacGregor perceives Rover, the dachshund, and loves him, but MacKay also perceives Rover, in exactly the same circumstances, yet hates him, Aquinas can only explain the different emotional responses by saying that MacGregor was drawn towards Rover but MacKay wasn't. But to say this is not really to give an explanation at all. It is not to say *why* MacGregor was drawn towards Rover but MacKay wasn't. Genuine cognitivists, on the other hand, would be inclined to suggest that MacGregor must not merely perceive that Rover is a dog but must *evaluate* Rover, or dachshunds, or dogs in general, as good; and, similarly, MacKay must not merely passively perceive Rover but must view him in a disapproving way. MacGregor may relate Rover to his general strong approval of dogs as 'man's best friends and silent steadfast companions through life's arduous highways and byways'. MacKay might perceive Rover and immediately place him in that category of 'machines for fouling pavements, frightening children, and putting car-drivers into a frenzy'.

On reading Aquinas' account, one wonders why the sensory appetite is drawn to some things but not to others. It cannot be because those it is drawn to are good, because this would imply that there has taken place some process by which it has been decided that or judged that it is good. This, we have seen, is not the case. On the other hand, if Aquinas says that, in so far as something attracts the sensory appetite it is good, then he has given no explanation of *why* it should be so. He has merely repeated *that* it is so.

Another set of emotions which the Thomistic impulse-towards-perceived-good-or-evil account cannot accommodate are the backward-looking emotions. Sorrow at a loss, such as the death of a best friend, does not impel a person towards or away from anything, or even to do anything at all. After all one cannot do anything. One cannot bring back the dead. Action is irrelevant, and so must be any impulse to action. One might wish that the dead person could be brought to life, but such wishful thinking does not issue into impulses to action. This is one way in which wishes differ from wants.

Spinoza's account of emotions is, in so far as anything could be said to be clear in Spinoza, clearly a cognitive account. But his account is, historically, a maverick one. It is not in the Aristotelian–Thomistic stream at all and, though it has some affinity with the Cartesian account of emotion, the fact that it is basically a cognitive account signifies that it is a clear departure from the Cartesian tradition as well. Spinoza's account has not generated many disciples but it is worth discussing, if for no other reason, because it has been recently claimed that his account of emotion should be considered 'the best and most systematic representative' of the cognitive accounts of emotion (Neu, 1977, pp. 1 and 152).

Spinoza's account of emotion is in *The Ethics* (Spinoza, 1883). Here Spinoza writes that, 'By *emotion* I mean the modifications of the body, whereby the active power of the said body is increased or diminished, aided or constrained, and also the ideas of such modifications' (Spinoza, 1883, p. 130). Thus, for Spinoza, the term 'emotion' is much wider than our present use of the term. His use covers any modification of or motion in the human person, but especially those caused by some external object, that is, passive modifications or passions. The three basic modifications or emotions are thus desire, pleasure and pain. What we mean by the term 'emotion' today – items such as love, anger, embarrassment, fear – would usually be, in Spinoza's terminology, passive emotions, and more complex than the three basic first-level emotions of desire, pleasure and pain, upon which they are based. For example, Spinoza tells us, '*Love* is *nothing* else but *pleasure accompanied by the idea of an external cause: Hate* is nothing else but *pain accompanied by the idea of an external cause* (Spinoza, 1883, p. 140). That is, undergoing the emotion love is experiencing pleasure *and* believing, rightly or wrongly, that something, in this case presumably, that some person or quasi-person, is the cause of the pleasure. Conversely with hate. Essential to love and hate, on this account, are the beliefs about what is the cause of the pleasure and pain ingredients (the feeling and physiological changes ingredients) of occurrent states of love and hate. Thus Spinoza's theory could be pigeon-holed as belonging in general to accounts of emotion which include thoughts as an essential ingredient, or, in different terminology, as a classical example of a cognitive theory of emotion.

Where Spinoza's theory differs from most other cognitive theories is in not linking causally the idea or belief aspect of emotion to the pleasure or pain aspect (i.e. the feeling and physiological changes aspects). The idea or belief concerning the external cause is said only to *accompany* the pleasure or pain, not to be its cause. The cause of the pleasure or pain is something external. The thought or idea or belief is merely *of* this cause, and comes after or accompanies the effect of this cause, the pain or pleasure. The belief itself, though

about the external cause, seems to have no explicit causal role. However, for Spinoza, the idea or belief is still *essential* to emotion, because the different emotions are defined mainly in terms of the
different accompanying ideas or beliefs. Besides, it is the beliefs
which make emotions object-directed and so lift them to a level of
complexity above that of just isolated feelings or sensations. The
thought or belief makes the pleasure into love because it directs the
pleasure to someone who then becomes the beloved. So, for Spinoza,
emotions are thought-directed rather than thought-dependent; they
are also feelings, directed – usually at any rate – outward to whatever
is believed to be the cause of the feelings. Indeed, Spinoza tells us,
we often generate false beliefs about the causes of our feelings and so
end up hating those we should not, and loving those who do not
deserve to be loved.

A difficulty with this version of the cognitive theory of emotions
is that it seems to be too catholic in regard to the emotions. Every
pain or pleasure is in line for being counted as an emotion given that
the subject has an accompanying thought about the cause of the
pleasure or pain. So, on this account, a headache, being tickled, and
having pins and needles, all become emotions if the subject experiencing them concomitantly has some belief, whether mistaken or
not, about their cause. And since we usually do have some belief,
however inadequate, as regards the cause of our headache, tickles,
and pins and needles, on this view we would have to say that our
headache, tickles, and pins and needles are emotions. It might be
suggested that the sense of feelings involved in Spinoza's account of
emotion is less localised and less physical than that of pins and
needles, headaches and such like.[2] But such a move does not erase
the basic difficulty. For, if one takes a drug which gives one a
generalised feeling of 'being down in the dumps', that is, gives one a
feeling of pain in a more generalised sense, and if one has the
accompanying belief that it is the drug which is causing the feeling,
then, on Spinoza's account, this is an emotion. So Spinoza's account
cannot separate off what we intuitively think of as emotions from a
host of other feelings which we cannot think of as emotions.

Spinoza's view of emotions also makes it difficult for him to explain how emotions can be motives. What characteristic sort of
behaviour does the drug-induced feeling of being down in the
dumps lead to? There is nothing in the Spinozan model of emotion

[2] As does Neu (1977, p. 76).

which could lead directly to behaviour of any particular sort. Spinoza's emotions cannot of themselves generate behaviour because they are just feelings plus beliefs about their causes. There is no evaluative aspect to them, and so nothing to make the subject of such 'emotions' want to do anything. In a richer theory of emotion, there would be some account of how, for example, typical love behaviour, say behaviour aimed at pleasing or caring for the beloved, is generated by the basic components or aspects of an occurrent emotional state of love, or love in a dispositional form.

When discussing Hume, I suggested that there were difficulties for an analysis that always interprets emotion as involving a feeling of either pleasure or pain. I suggested that such an analysis could not account for the fact that love is sometimes pleasant, sometimes painful, and that one could say the same about hate, anger, and many other emotions. The twin categories of the pleasurable and the painful seem a poor basis for differentiating the emotions, or even for isolating all the manifestations of any single emotion. This criticism applies to Spinoza's theory as well, but there is no need to rehearse these difficulties again.

An early cognitive theory in psychology was that of Alexander Shand in his classic of emotion theory, *The Foundations of Character*.[3] He writes:

> 'Emotion' for us will connote not feeling abstracted from impulse, but feeling with its impulse, and feeling which has essentially a cognitive attitude, however vague, and frequently definite thoughts about its object. The thoughts of anger and fear are quite familiar to us: we have only to hear someone express them in order to know that he is angry or afraid [Shand, 1914, Bk II, Ch I, p. 178].

But the thoughts or cognitive aspect is not central to Shand's account of emotion. As with Spinoza's account, the thoughts merely accompany the central aspect of emotion, they do not have any major causal role in the generation of emotion, nor conceptual role in the definition of emotion. But Shand's theory differs from Spinoza's in that it does not give feeling a central place. Shand's account makes the kernel of emotion to be *sui generis* impulses,

---

[3] Shand (1914). The theory put forward in this book acknowledges a considerable debt to McDougall's *An Introduction to Social Psychology*, Methuen, 1908. Indeed the impulse or motivational theory is often called the Shand–McDougall theory.

hence it is often referred to as an impulse or motivational theory rather than a cognitive theory. For Shand, external objects cause the different emotions in so far as they excite particular innate impulses which are the conscious side of an aroused instinct or pattern of instincts. This impulse and its instinct (or instincts) give the characteristic tone to the other distinguishing aspects of the emotion in question.

> It [the emotion] is penetrated throughout by an impulse that organises it, which accepts certain thoughts and rejects others, and directs them to its pre-determined end. Thus anger excludes 'reasonable' thoughts and 'kindly' thoughts about its object, and possesses its feeling in support of its impulse, which is innately organised to work toward a certain result or end, the injury or destruction of its object [Shand, 1914, Bk II, Ch I, p. 179].

Thus anger is a particular innate impulse in man to injure or destroy, which is excited by certain objects in certain definable situations. This impulse gives rise to visceral and motor responses which are mirrored in consciousness by a particular feeling or feelings which come to be characteristic of anger, and also give rise to certain thoughts which come to be characteristic of anger, and issues externally into behaviour, such as fighting, or other aggressive displays, which also come to be associated with anger. The impulse and instincts which are anger, like all such impulses, are ultimately to be viewed as a force derived from the primary innate tendency in man to achieve self-preservation in all circumstances. So the particular impulse which is the core of the emotion anger can be seen as aimed at self-preservation because, in the circumstances, fighting or some other aggressive behaviour aimed at injuring or destroying can be seen as useful to self-preservation. It might, for example, ward off a dangerous attack. The particular impulses at the heart of the different emotions are related to this primary tendency to self-preservation in that they are this tendency adapted to the particular situation in hand.

Now the most immediate difficulty with such a theory is in individuating the emotions and so in differentiating them from one another. Emotions do not issue forth into behaviour of a sufficiently constant sort, particularly in human beings, such that one can say, 'Ah yes, running, that must be fear' or 'Sobbing, that must be grief'. Shand, of course, realised this and explained at some length that, even in animals, fear gives rise to a variety of behaviour, namely behaviour expressive of the 'instincts of flight, of concealment, of silence, of clinging or keeping close to something, of shrinking or starting back, of immobility or simulation of death, of crying for help' (Shand, 1914, Bk ii, Ch ii, p. 207). And Shand went on to admit that the patterns of behaviour that express the impulse of fear are further diluted in man by acquired tendencies directed to ends other than self-preservation, for these acquired tendencies mingle with and subvert his innate instinctual or animal tendencies (Shand, 1914). But if, as he admits, practically any behaviour could be fitting as an expression of fear on some occasion, and that the fear of getting fat will give rise to very different behaviour from that derived from fear of the dark or fear of losing face, then it is difficult to see how Shand can maintain that what is central and distinctive of each emotion is an impulse. For he has described this impulse in such a way that, while the chief evidence for its presence will always be external behaviour, this evidence is too diluted and confused in man to be of any help at all, at least by itself.

Perhaps Shand could suggest that introspection on each occasion reveals that the varied behaviour is to be related to a single impulse. If Shand were to make that move, then the emotion, fear, becomes a purely introspectible item, which is not mirrored in the external behaviour it gives rise to and cannot be inferred by scrutinising the external behaviour. As with Cartesian feeling theories, the impulse theory now runs into the difficulty that the word 'emotion' labels an internal item, an impulse, the access to which and the signs of the presence of which lie solely with the person who has the impulse.

Shand's theory, like so many in psychology and philosophy, fits emotions other than fear and anger less well. Take, for example, the emotion of grief. As it is most often backward-looking, it is not easy to see, in the first place, how it could be related to any characteristic impulse to action, and, in the second place, how any such impulse could be construed as ultimately aimed at self-preservation.

Shand does not avoid this obvious difficulty in his theory, and feels compelled to admit that 'of all the primary emotions sorrow is the most difficult to interpret' for 'what variety of instincts can we expect to find in its monotonous and depressing system?' (Shand, 1914, Bk ii, Ch ix, p. 301). His attempt to find an impulse which is the emotion of grief or sorrow is summed up in the following passage:

From this survey of the facts we conclude that sorrow is a system which possesses a characteristic impulse, first manifested in the infant's instinctive cry for help, a little later by watching for its approaches; the cry itself becoming more distinctive of sorrow, and joining itself to articulate language, appealing for relief, distraction, sympathy; and finally, on the frustration of all hope of help from men, turning to Heaven [Shand, 1914, Bk II, Ch IX, p. 316].

Leaving aside that this account, at least in part, looks more like an account of frustration or despair, rather than sorrow or grief, sorrow is often backward-looking and caused by some loss such as a death, which cannot be reinterpreted as a frustration of some forward-looking impulse. And in the cases of sorrow concerning a death, say the death of a friend, far from seeking assistance, one might be more likely to want to be left alone. There is nothing any-one can do, so there is no point in seeking assistance. Assistance would only be an intrusion. Sorrow and grief are often non-active, still emotions; in extreme cases, even catatonic.

Finally it is not easy to see how emotions such as grief, shame and embarrassment could be said to be derived from a primary instinct to self-preservation. Shame and embarrassment, in so far as they are related to the preservation of anything, are related to the preserving of our self-concept (the view of ourselves which we like to present to others or, in other versions, the view of ourselves which we derive from the way others view us),[4] not to the preservation of life. Most animals would not display such emotions as shame and em-barrassment, as they are incapable of any self-concept. A frog, for example, showing shame seems inconceivable. Yet Shand's account of the emotions as impulses which are ultimately subservient to a primary one of self-preservation is derived from a study of animals and their impulse systems, including emotion systems. This, I think, has misled him into making emotions such as fear and anger the touchstone, and subsequently into analysing emotions in their pure unadulterated state as related always to self-preservation.

Sorrow and grief are also difficult to analyse as related to self-preservation. How could my grief over the loss of a dear friend be related to self-preservation? It is clearly not related to my

---

[4] A healthy self-concept is brought about when we come to accept the more or less objective view of ourselves which we derive from knowledge of what others think of us. See Wylie (1968).

self-preservation if I did not depend economically or emotionally upon this friend. If it is related to the dead friend's self-preservation, then it is too late to be effective!

Impulse accounts, as we have already seen when discussing Aquinas' account, also have difficulty in giving an account of the contemplative emotions like awe, wonder and surprise. But there is no point in rehearsing these difficulties again here.

The Shand–McDougall impulse theory of the emotions was superseded by the behaviourist theories, which dominated psychology right up to the 1940s if not later. With the behaviourist veto on reference to internal conscious phenomena of any sort, the terms 'impulse' and 'instinct' were no longer employed, though the behaviourist theories of emotion were little more than impulse theories shorn of the impulse. It is, then, not surprising that, during the reign of behaviourism in psychology, there were no cognitive theories of emotions put forward. There were a few nods and winks in the direction of cognitivism, but they were at best veiled, hesitant and apologetic.[5] In 1948, in his now famous paper, 'A motivational theory of emotion to replace "emotion as disorganized response"'[6] Robert Ward Leeper briefly returned to a Shand–McDougall impulse or motivational theory. But he has, since, adopted a full-blooded cognitive theory.[7]

But it has really been left to Magda Arnold, almost single-handedly, to revive the cognitive theory of emotions in psychology. This she did in her superb study, *Emotion and Personality* (1960). She acknowledges there the debt her theory, and any cognitive

[5] For example, F. Kreuger in 'Das Wesen der Gefühle', *Archiv für die gesamte Psychologie*, Vol. 65, 1928, trans. and abridged by Arnold (1968, p. 100) asserts that 'feelings [of affective sort] are always related to what goes on in *experience* at the same time or immediately before'. And Dumas (1948b, p. 112) an excerpt trans. by Y. Bégin and M. B. Arnold from *La Vie Affective*, Presses Universitaires de France, 1948, and reprinted in Arnold (1968), writes that 'these emotions ... are complex states composed psychologically of excited, depressed, embarrassed, demented, rebellious *attitudes*, sometimes followed by impulsion, as happens in anger and fear, but always accompanied by organic changes' (Italics mine in both quotations).

[6] *Psychological Review*, Vol. 55, 1948; reprinted in Arnold (1968) in abridged form.

[7] In 'The Motivational and Perceptual Properties of Emotions as Indicating their Fundamental Character and Role' in Arnold (1970, p. 156) Leeper wrote: 'What I want to propose is, in brief, that emotions are perceptual processes. I mean this, furthermore, not in some odd and marginal sense, but in the full sense of processes that have definite cognitive content, or are rich in informational terms as well as in terms of their motivational properties ... I am proposing that emotions are basically *perceptions of situations* and that, commonly, *they are long-sustained perceptions of the more enduring and significant aspects of such situations.*'

theory, must owe to the classical Aristotelian and Thomistic versions. She seems to lean particularly towards the Thomistic version and so her theory, not surprisingly, is strongly motivational as well. 'Emotion seems to include not only the appraisal of how this thing or person will affect me but also a definite pull toward or away from it' (Arnold, 1960, Vol. 1, p. 172). Arnold goes on to explain that by the term 'appraisal' she means a direct and immediate evaluative judgment of an object as 'good or bad, pleasurable or dangerous for us', though this evaluative judgment can be reflective as well (Arnold, 1960, Vol. 1, p. 175). She rightly sees the appraisal or evaluative aspect as distinct from the perception of the object or situation, and as important in tracing the link between perception of the situation and behaviour appropriate both to the situation and to the emotion.

> To know or perceive something and to estimate its effect on us are two distinct processes, and appraisal necessarily presupposes perception ... Following upon perception and completing it, appraisal makes possible an active approach, acceptance or withdrawal, and thus establishes our relationship to the outside world.
>
> [Then] the intuitive appraisal of the situation initiates an *action tendency that is felt as emotion*, expressed in various bodily changes, and that eventually may lead to overt action [Arnold, 1960, Vol. 1, pp. 176–7].

Yet, despite, as I will argue later, getting all the pertinent aspects of emotion right, Arnold ruins her account by suggesting that 'does not the emotional *quale* consist precisely in that unreasoning involuntary attraction or repulsion' which follows after the appraisal? (Arnold, 1960, Vol. 1, p. 172). That is, for Arnold, emotion as such is an action-tendency felt subjectively as a characteristic emotional feeling and displayed objectively as a characteristic pattern of physiological changes and, sometimes, behaviour. The felt tendency is not identical with the pattern of physiological changes because, she says, there is a time gap between them. The felt tendency comes first and then causes a characteristic pattern of physiological changes.

When discussing both the behaviourist and the motivational accounts of emotion, we saw some of the difficulties that such a view must contend with. There is a strong body of opinion, for example, which suggests that there are no convincing empirical data to show that one can differentiate emotions by reference to patterns of physiological changes.[8] But it should also be conceded that the evidence is confused and conflicting, and that there are experimental psychologists who believe that there is some indication that, at least with fear and anger, one might be able to distinguish emotions by reference to physiological changes.[9] What does seem clear is that it cannot be done now, and, even if it could be done, it could only be done by physiologists. But since we do refer to and differentiate between the different emotions, fairly confidently, there must be another way to do it other than by reference to alleged patterns of physiological changes. It may be that Arnold, though seemingly a convinced cognitivist, is a victim of the behaviourist influence on psychology, such that she hankers after some item more tangible than cognitions or evaluations as the basis for differentiating the emotions. Indeed, though she criticises the behaviourists, it turns out that her own account of emotions in terms of impulses manifested in patterns of physiological changes is not all that different from J. B. Watson's behaviourist account of emotions in terms of physiological changes of a reflex kind.

Anthony Kenny's account of emotion can be gleaned from his modern classic of philosophical psychology, *Action, Emotion and Will*. His account is to be gleaned rather than simply examined, because he nowhere declares explicitly what for him is an emotion. In so far as his view can be pieced together, he appears to be putting forward an essentially Aristotelian–Thomistic cognitive account of emotion overlaid with a preoccupation – derived from the Wittgenstein of the *Philosophical Investigations* – with how we might come to know the meaning of emotion terms. Kenny shares with the later Wittgenstein, and with linguistic analysis of the 1950s and 1960s a shyness over naked theorising of a general sort, and so his discussion of emotion tends to range over a series of problems, such as how emotion differs from sensation and perception, how it is related to its object, how its object differs from its cause, and how it can be a motive for behaviour. His other major concern, as regards the emotions, in *Action, Emotion and Will*, is to mount a powerful attack on the feeling theory of emotion.

Perhaps the most revealing and characteristic passage on the nature of emotion in *Action, Emotion and Will* is the following:

[8] See p. 15, n. 6.
[9] See p. 15, n. 7.

The concept of each emotion is linked with non-emotional concepts in three ways. The concept, for example, of *fear* stands on three struts:
- (a) fearful circumstances
- (b) symptoms of fear
- (c) action taken to avoid what is feared.

Just as the verbal expression of fear must be learnt in the context of these factors, so it can be understood only in the context of one or other of them. In the standard case, which is both the paradigm for learning and the most easily intelligible, all three factors will be present. The man-eating lion advances roaring; the defenceless planter screams, pales, and takes to his heels. His later report 'I was terrified' is as fully intelligible as such a report can be. But the verbal expression of fear remains intelligible when one, or even two, of these factors is absent but the third remains [Kenny, 1963, p. 67].

Realising that this three-strut analysis is in danger of being circular, Kenny tells us a few pages later that 'fearful circumstances' could be replaced by 'dangerous circumstances', 'symptoms of fear' by 'a purely physical description', and that 'action taken to avoid what is feared' could be 'explained purely in terms of intention' (Kenny, 1963, p. 70).

Now the difficulty here is in knowing precisely what Kenny is giving us with his three-strut analysis. Kenny apparently is not giving us an account of the concept of fear (and he nowhere does) but only of the conditions under which we may come to learn the meaning of the term 'fear'. Yet, there is a suggestion that Kenny may want to hold that to learn the meaning of the term 'fear' is to grasp the concept of fear. But even so, to list the conditions or grounds or struts by means of which one attains to the concept is not to list the parts or aspects of the concept. Besides which, I am inclined to think that one can understand the meaning of the term 'fear' without being able to grasp the concept. The concept of something is the quite technical rendering of the necessary and sufficient conditions for something being that thing (given that it is amenable to such technical conceptual analysis). For most people, consistent and correct use of the term 'fear', even in novel situations, is grounds for saying that they understand that term, but it would not be grounds for saying that they have grasped the concept of that thing referred to or captured by the term. Most of us understand the term 'X-ray' but few would claim a grasp of the concept X-ray.

More importantly, Kenny's three struts are not sufficient conditions for being in an emotional state of fear, if that is what his three struts are meant to be. I could, twenty yards away from a man-eating lion, happen to exhibit certain fluctuations of breathing rate and other physiological reactions sometimes associated with fear, emit screams, and take to my heels with the lion in pursuit, *but not be afraid*. I might be a veteran lion-handler and be tense and excited, though not afraid, by my role in leading the lion into a trap. Alternatively I might not be in any emotional state but just be simulating one for the purposes of a film, for the physiological reactions – the most difficult to simulate – might be induced by drugs or certain stressful exercises or clever fakir-like manipulation.

So while Kenny's three-strut analysis does not shed much light on the concept of fear, his other way of discussing emotions does, though here again he is tantalisingly unclear. His way into the concept of emotion, this time, is via its identification and differentiation. He tells us that 'It is not in general possible to identify an emotion without identifying also its object; and where, *ex hypothesi*, an emotion takes the form of a feeling which is not acted upon, the connection with the object can be made only by the thoughts which surround the sensation' (Kenny, 1963, p. 64). On one interpretation, this is just wrong. To identify the object of an emotion will not help one to identify the emotion itself, or not very easily. I might realise from the context that the emotional state which is clearly engulfing you is directed towards the woman to your left in the group you are in. But this does not help very much. For it is not revealed thereby whether you are in love with her, embarrassed by her presence, afraid that she will be indiscreet about something, or in the grip of some other emotion. Emotions are not specified by their objects or targets but by what the subject of the emotion *thinks of* the object or target. Your emotion will be fear if you believe that you are in danger of being exposed by this woman as a thief and a liar and this belief causes your emotional reaction. It will be embarrassment if you believe that the woman knows that you are the one who rejected her application for compassionate leave, and in consequence you believe the situation to be one of extreme awkwardness, and this belief causes your emotional reactions. Your emotion will be love if the reaction is caused by your belief that this woman is the most perfect person you have ever met and could possibly meet.

But, on a generous interpretation of Kenny's position, by 'object' Kenny means 'intentional object' or object-as-thought, that is, as displayed in the examples above, the object considered under that particular description which is generated by the beliefs which you have about the object. That is, the situation must be one of at least *putative* (or *believed*) danger if I am to say that you are afraid of the woman rather than, say, embarrassed or in love with her. You must at least believe, rightly or wrongly, that you are in danger of being exposed as a thief and a liar. That this is Kenny's view is lent further weight by his discussing the notion of 'formal object'. Kenny rightly implies that to claim that a person is in such and such an emotional state is to claim by implication that the person must view the object in a certain light, and that the general category summing up this particular view for any particular emotion is the 'formal object' of that emotion.

> Emotional attitudes, like other mental attitudes, have formal objects . . . If the emotions were internal impressions or behaviour patterns there would be no logical restrictions on the type of object which each emotion could have. It would be a mere matter of fact that people were not angered by being benefited, nor afraid of what they already know to have happened [Kenny, 1963, pp. 191–2].

Kenny is annoyingly loose about the notion of a formal object. It is not really a restriction on the type of object or target of an emotion but a restriction on how the subject of the emotion views the object. But Kenny's philosophical heart is in more or less the right location. The key to the differentiation and specification of emotions does lie in the notion of formal object properly understood; though I will suggest later on that the term 'formal object' is something of a misnomer which does more harm than good as it leads one all too easily into thinking that emotions are specified by their objects and not by the evaluative categories under which their subjects' particular evaluations of the object fall. Sometimes I feel that Kenny has been misled in just that way. For, of course, one can be afraid of what in fact has already happened, if, say, one falsely believes that it has not yet happened or of what one knows has already happened, if one simply believes that the past can haunt us.

To be fair to Kenny, he does not set out to give an account of the concept of emotion as such or the concept of any particular emotion. He is more interested in the Wittgensteinian task of working out how we might learn how to use words like 'fear' and 'anger', and so how we come to learn their meaning. So, while he does hint that central to each type of emotion is a specific category of belief about an object or target, Kenny does not in fact carry us far enough in this direction for it to become clear that emotions are not differentiated by means of the object or even the subject's factual beliefs about the object but by means of the subject's evaluative beliefs about the object. For your emotion is, say, not one of embarrassment unless you evaluate or view the situation as awkward or unpleasant. If you were thick-skinned and did not mind in the least meeting people whom you had rejected or failed in some way, then you would not evaluate such meetings as awkward and unpleasant, and so would not be embarrassed in such situations.

However, the last cognitive theorist I will consider did stress the evaluative aspect of the emotional subject's beliefs when giving an account of emotion, and my own account is closer to his view than to that of any other cognitive theorist. I refer to the theory put forward by the philosopher R. S. Peters in his paper 'The Education of the Emotions',[10] which has been almost entirely neglected by his fellow philosophers, partly no doubt because it appears in a collection of papers of which the vast majority are by psychologists, and philosophers do not often read the relevant work of psychologists, nor psychologists that of philosophers.

In this paper, delivered to an audience mainly composed of psychologists, Peters asserts uncompromisingly that, central to the concept of each emotion, is a cognition of an evaluative sort:

This brings me to my second reason for omitting to delve into empirical work done by psychologists on emotion, which is that the concept of 'emotion' employed by many psychologists fails to do justice to what I would regard as its central feature, namely its connection with a certain type of cognition. If we ask ourselves

[10] In Arnold (1970). I also owe a good deal of the impetus for my causal–evaluative theory to the briefly sketched 'comprehensive view' of emotions suggested by William Alston in his fine article 'Emotion and Feeling' in *The Encyclopaedia of Philosophy*, P. Edwards (ed.) Macmillan and The Free Press, 1967, Vol. 2, pp. 485–6, though, ultimately, Alston himself believes that the concept of emotion can only be given a loose 'family resemblance' analysis.

what we might naturally call 'emotions' we would give quite a long list which would include fear, anger, sorrow, grief, envy, jealousy, pity, remorse, guilt, shame, pride, wonder and the like. What sort of criterion underlies this selection? Surely, the connection between emotions and the class of cognitions that are conveniently called 'appraisals'. These are constituted by seeing situations under aspects which are agreeable or disagreeable, beneficial or harmful in a variety of dimensions. To feel fear *is*, for instance, to see a situation as dangerous; to feel pride *is* to see with pleasure something as mine or as something that I have had a hand in bringing about [In Arnold, 1970, pp. 187–8].

And Peters, rightly, stresses that we cannot identify what particular emotion is present in any situation without either knowing or guessing correctly at the appraisal of the situation which the subject of the emotion is making (In Arnold, 1970, p. 189).

The other main feature of Peters' account of emotion is his rejection of the motivational version of the cognitive theory of emotion and his emphasis on the passivity of emotion: while both motives and emotions are to be explained by reference to the subject's appraisals, '"motive" is a term we employ to connect these appraisals with things we *do*, emotions with things that *come over us*' (In Arnold, 1970, p. 191). An appraisal is said to be an emotional one if it is connected with physiological reactions but a motive if it is directly connected to action. Peters then goes on to explain that some emotions, such as certain cases of fear and anger, do not issue into anything more than reactions, while some other emotions, such as grief, sorrow and wonder, rarely issue into action (In Arnold, 1970, pp. 191–2).

But I think that Peters, while by and large correct, has overplayed his winning hand when making the distinction between motives and emotions. For it is not true to suggest that we only speak of motives in connection with actions that take place, and it is also incorrect to say that a motive must produce an action. To take an example; the Resistance leader might say of his group, 'We all had a good motive for killing the Chief of the Gestapo but none of us dared to.' Everyone in the group had a motive yet none of these motives was causally operative. Besides, while it is true that some emotions, as Peters notes, do not have any direct link with action, certain emotions, arguably the majority of them, are strongly motivating, at times ungovernably so. Emotions such as rage, fear, love, hate, revenge, jealousy, vanity, shame, pity, compassion, and others, are of this sort.

This is not to deny that emotions and motives differ; rather it is to suggest that the difference lies elsewhere. For to suggest that the situation is one of emotion is primarily to imply that physiological changes, of a speeded-up or unusually calmed down variety, have taken place at some stage in connection with the view of the situation of the person concerned. For emotions are psychosomatic, pure motives are not. For example, his killing the stranger who entered his house at night was motivated by fear if, say, it was the case that he believed that the stranger was going to attack him and that he was in danger of his life, *and* this belief so affected him that his physiology was stirred up and he was moved to rid himself of the danger by shooting the stranger. On the other hand, his killing the stranger was the result of a pure non-emotional motive, if it was the case that he coolly decided that strangers ought not to enter people's houses at night and needed to be taught a lesson.

It is not so much that emotions are always passive, and motives active, as Peters seems to suggest, but that emotions are appraisals that affect us physiologically while pure or non-emotional motives are appraisals that do not. Appraisals that are motives are, of course, connected to the possibility of action, because they generate wants of certain sorts, but the appraisals that are emotional can and most often also are motives for the same reason that they generate wants or desires to act. Admittedly emotions like sorrow, grief, wonder, awe, surprise do not generate wants or desires to act, but it should not be concluded from this that emotions differ from motives in being passive. They can be passive in this sense, but need not be. They are always passive in the sense that the appraisals central to emotions affect the subject of the appraisal's physiology. But then motives can as well, and in so far as they do they become emotions. Emotions and motives overlap.

3

The causal–evaluative theory of emotions

Against the background of this brief survey of the classical theories of emotion in philosophy and psychology I want to introduce and outline a version of the cognitive theory of emotion which, for obvious reasons, owes a good deal to the work of the key figures in the long history of the cognitive theory. This version, for reasons which will become clear, I call the 'causal–evaluative theory of emotion'. This theory will be discussed in relation to the following propositions:

(1) That this account is of occurrent emotional states rather than of emotions considered dispositionally;

(2) That the concept of emotion as occurrent state involves reference to an evaluation which causes abnormal physiological changes in the subject of the evaluation;

(3) That it is by means of the evaluative aspect that we differentiate the emotions;

(4) That the concept of particular emotional states may include desires as well as evaluations and physiological changes;

(5) That the central evaluative aspect gives rise to emotional behaviour via a rational, and causal, link with desires;

(6) That making evaluation to be central to emotion does not mean that emotions are intangible and non-objective.

Occurrent emotional states vs. emotions considered dispositionally

It will have become clear, during my survey of the four classical theories of emotion, that theories of emotion are generally couched as theories of occurrent emotional states rather than as theories about emotions considered dispositionally, though the distinction is never in fact alluded to. So this distinction, between the occurrent and the dispositional, needs to be outlined and then related to emotions, if the following account is to be understood.

The occurrent–dispositional distinction as such is not difficult to grasp. We can refer, for example, to a person as vain, and mean this either occurrently or dispositionally. That is, the term 'vain' can refer to an actual display of vanity on the part of that person, say the person is actually boasting, or it can refer to that person's disposition to be vain, that is, his or her proneness to do vain things, such as boasting, whenever the opportunity occurs.

Similarly, in the emotional context, a term such as 'anger' can be used occurrently or dispositionally.[1] If I say that my father is angry with me for taking the car and crashing it into a wall, this could mean either that my father is actually in the grip of the emotion anger, such that it shows in his raised tone of voice, his shaking fists, red face and his jumping up and down on his hat. This would be the occurrent use of the term 'anger' as it would refer to an actual emotional state. On the other hand, I might say that my father is angry with me for taking the car, but he may not be in any emotional state at this very moment, as he may be watching the cricket on the television or feeding the cat. What I mean here is that my father is liable or prone to get into actual emotional states of anger, at least in a truncated or etiolated form, or to behave in a manner that is traceable to some former occurrent state of anger, from time to time. My father's disposition to be angry with me may be activated in the following form: if I mention the car, he may go very quiet and steely, and say in a piqued tone of voice, 'I wouldn't mention motor cars if I were you.'

In making this distinction between the occurrent and dispositional sense of emotion terms, one is shedding light on the vocabulary we employ about emotions. The dispositional account of emotions, being an overall summary type of claim, will explain why we can refer to emotions as 'vacillating' or 'desultory' or 'constant'. The occurrent sense of emotion terms, referring to an actual here-and-now bodily state, usually involving feelings, will allow us to speak of emotions as 'hot', 'throbbing', 'burning', 'flaming' or 'palpitating', indeed as 'passions' or 'emotion'.

---

[1] It is worth noting that there are philosophers, such as Bedford, who seem to deny that there is an occurrent sense of any emotions. See Bedford (1962, p. 110) where he writes that 'my argument . . . is meant to show that an emotion is not any sort of experience or process'.

But one must be careful about studying emotions via the study of emotion terms. One could easily give an analysis of various emotion terms, such as 'anger', 'love' and 'rage', and think that one was studying the same thing in each case. This would not be so. While a disposition is a proneness in someone or something to do or react in a certain way, a claim that someone has a disposition labelled '*x*' does not imply that there must be occurrences also labelled '*x*', though the dispositional use of a term, being the attribution of a liability or proneness, does imply that the person in question is liable to reactions or episodes of some sort.[2]

A belief is, I think, a disposition. To say Smith believes in God is a claim that Smith will do or say certain things which imply that he considers that God exists. There may be no mental act or occurrence which could be labelled 'believing in God', instead there may be only Smith's acts of worshipping God, praying to Him, saying that he believes He exists and so on, all of which can be summed up as his belief in God. Rather than having to say each time that Smith worships God, prays to Him and, when asked, admits to believing in Him, one can simply sum up this general behaviour pattern as a belief in God. From this it will be clear that some terms only have a dispositional use.

In regard to emotions, while, as we have seen, the term 'anger' seems to have both an occurrent and a dispositional use, and so does 'fear', the term 'love' seems to be a term which only has a dispositional use. When we say '*X* loves *Y*' we are referring to a proneness of *X* to do certain things and react in certain ways to *Y*, especially the former. If we are referring to emotional love, we will probably imply that, among those ways in which *X* is prone to act or react, there are emotional states, but I do not think that we would ostensively label such emotional states with the term 'love', though it is not clear what term one would use. On the other hand we could refer to these states as emotional states *of* love, for they must be caused by love, otherwise why associate them with love at all. By contrast the term 'rage' has only an occurrent use, labelling actual occurrent emotional states of anger of a very strong and tempestuous sort.

To complicate matters further, there are two sorts of dispositions and two sorts of dispositional terms associated with some emotions. Associated with anger, for example, are both the disposition referred

[2] This was more or less the burden of my paper, Lyons (1973b, Vol. 24).

to by the term 'angry' and that referred to by the term 'irascible'. To say someone is angry is to say that he or she is liable to act or react in an angry way about something fairly specific, say the breaking of that person's favourite possession. 'Anger', when used dispositionally, implies a focussed disposition. On the other hand, to say someone is irascible is to say that he or she is liable to act or react in an angry way about many or even most things. It is an unfocussed disposition; practically anything will activate it. Moreover it is a second-order disposition, for to be irascible is to be liable to be angry. So it should be clear that to study emotions via emotion terms is liable to be a very confusing business.

As has been the habit in psychology and, until this century, in philosophy, I will be expounding my account of emotion chiefly as an account of occurrent states of emotion. Besides the continuity this has with the accepted practice in psychology, and the classical accounts of emotion in philosophy, an important reason for this is that the occurrent emotional state, and not the disposition, is the full or paradigm case. Consider the case, first, of a non-emotional disposition, the disposition to be seasick. If a medical scientist studies your proneness to be seasick, he will be trying to discover what it is in you that reacts with the motion of ships at sea so as to produce seasickness. Though he may from time to time observe actual cases of vomiting at sea, he is chiefly concerned with discovering in you some structural basis, in this case presumably some physiological factor, which would seem likely to be the cause of your proneness to be sick at sea. Yet, though the scientist is studying the factor which is the basis for your disposition to be seasick, the actual occurrent state of being seasick is the full paradigm case of seasickness. For here we have, not only the factor the scientist is interested in, but also its actual occurrent effects.

It is the same with emotions. Whatever factor it is which remains dormant in the person still disposed to be angry about something, will also be present when it is operative. Now it is most fully operative as emotion, when it causes not merely motivated behaviour, but affects someone emotionally, that is, physiologically, stirring up feelings, and generating wants or desires to do certain things. So, in this outline, I will be giving an account of a full occurrent emotional state, though, clearly, when later I discuss particular emotions, I will need to point out whether this or that emotion typically fits the full paradigm case or not. Fear, for example, is a fairly obvious paradigm of emotion as it unequivocally can occur both as a disposition and as an emotional state which we would readily label as 'fear', and for that reason it will feature centrally in any account of emotion. But it is also important to consider emotions, such as grief or love, which deviate from the full paradigm, if one is attempting to give a general account of emotion, for there is no claim being made that the paradigm emotional state is the typical case, only that it is the fullest in that it displays all the aspects or components which are found in occurrent emotional states.

Thus, according to this causal–evaluative theory of emotions, the fullest paradigm case of an occurrent emotional state will include the person's beliefs about his or her present situation, which may or may not be caused by a perception of some object or event, but which are the basis for an evaluation of the situation in relation to himself or herself. This evaluation in turn causes the wants or desires which lead to behaviour, while the evaluations and wants together cause abnormal physiological changes and their subjective registering, feelings. To take a simple case of fear, the sight of a ferocious dog might cause Fred to evaluate it as threateningly dangerous to him, such that he wants to run away and escape, and so he takes to his heels. And the combination of the evaluation of the situation as threateningly dangerous, plus his urgent desire to escape, stirs up his physiological processes, increasing his adrenaline output, his blood flow, and respiration rate, so that he feels his heart thumping, the sweat on the palms of his hands and down the small of his back, a constriction around the chest, and a dryness in his mouth.

It is the workings and interrelations between these components found in occurrent emotional states that I will be discussing, here in outline and, in later chapters, in detail.

The concept of emotion as occurrent emotional state involves reference to an evaluation which causes abnormal physiological changes

The notion of a full paradigm case of occurrent emotional states is different from the concept of occurrent emotional states as such. The concept of something is the list of necessary and sufficient conditions – where this is possible – for something's being that sort of thing. Now the causal–evaluative theory gets its name from advocating that X is to be deemed an emotional state if and only if it is a physiologically abnormal state caused by the subject of that state's evaluation of his or her situation. The causal order is important, emotion is a psychosomatic state, a bodily state caused by an attitude, in this case an evaluative attitude. Just to believe that one is in danger but not to be thereby physiologically affected, is not to be emotional. If I overexercise and confuse myself, such that I start babbling nonsense; or if I drink too much and fall over, I am not being emotional. But if I think you have made a fool of me, and this upsets me, upsets me physiologically, and I start babbling and falling over, then I am being emotional.

So, for X to be an emotional state, X must include an evaluation which causes abnormal physiological changes. Both the evaluation and the physiological changes are necessary conditions for X being an emotional state, but neither are separately sufficient. Jointly they are.

That the evaluation causing a physiological upset alone is sufficient to constitute an emotional state can be seen by considering a deliberately pared down example of emotion in which only these are present. A bird lover out birdwatching sees a golden eagle in full flight. She thinks it marvellous, rare and beautiful, and this strongly affects her physiologically, it stirs her up physiologically. But it does not lead her to want to do anything. She doesn't say anything, and nothing unusual shows in her expression and she makes no gestures. To an observer she would appear merely as a woman gazing at a bird in flight. It may even be that she is so taken up with the sight that she does not advert to her own emotion. She may feel nothing because she is so absorbed. Yet we would clearly call this a case of emotion, an emotional state of awe or excitement.

Now as regards the sort of attitude which is essential to emotion, it must be evaluative, for only such an attitude is sufficient explanation for why we are physiologically stirred up. If I perceive a dog and describe it as so high, and grey, and correctly label it as a wolfhound, there is so far no reason why this should cause me to get worked up. But if I tell myself that the dog is liable to take a large piece out of me, and that it is giving every indication that it will, and if I would prefer that it did not, in a very strong sense of prefer, that is, if I evaluate the dog's approach as threateningly dangerous, then I have reason to get worked up about the situation, and my beliefs have become the plausible cause for any ensuing physiological upset such as a sudden discharge of my sympathetic nervous system and a speeding up of my metabolic processes. The evaluation central to the concept of emotion is an evaluation of some object, event or situation in the world about me in relation to me, or according to my norms. Thus my emotions reveal whether I see the world or some aspect of it as threatening or welcoming, pleasant or painful, regrettable or a solace, and so on.

Now this evaluation need not be a mental occurrence, even when an account of it is given in relation to emotions as occurrent states. On the other hand, if evaluations play some causal role in occurrent emotional states, there must be some occurrent aspect to them. If, as I think one should, one gives a dispositional analysis of evaluations, then one must posit some factor, psychological or physiological, which is in me in some real sense. For, just as the structural or, as it is sometimes called, categorical (in contrast to hypothetical or non-actual) base for my disposition to be sick at sea will most likely turn out to be some physiological factor, say, an imbalance in the fluids in my inner ear, or something like that, which interacts with the motion of boats at sea to cause vomiting, so the structural or categorical base for my (dispositionally analysed) evaluation will be either a physiological factor or a psychological one. For this factor must be real and occurrent if it is to cause me to say and do certain things, or be physiologically disturbed and feel certain things, on certain occasions.

On the other hand, I do not want to deny that, at least on some occasions, evaluations should be given an entirely occurrent analysis. For sometimes my evaluation of the situation as dangerous will involve my actually murmuring, out loud or under my breath, the words 'Now I've had it. I'd better say my prayers', or something similar which amounts to or implies an actual declaration that I believe that I am in danger.

Considered epistemologically, evaluations are not really cognitive at all. Etymologically, 'cognitive', from the latin *cognoscere*, implies perception, knowledge or, in general, becoming acquainted with. But to evaluate is not to gain knowledge but to relate something already known or perceived to some rating scale. In the context of certain emotions, such as love, for example, this scale seems to be of a very personal and subjective sort, for what is lovable is very much in the eye or mind of the lover. With other emotions, such as fear, the scale will turn out to be reasonably objective, for what is rated as dangerous is more or less what it is or has been shown to be in the past. Yet even here the rating of the perceived situation as dangerous is done with a personal twist. The situation is seen in relation to me, as primarily one which is threatening me (or those close to me), where I am the final arbiter of whether it is really threatening or not. Hence a good proportion of fears are rated by others as phobias.

As regards the physiological condition for something being an emotional state, this reflects well the etymology of the word 'emotion'. 'Emotion' is from the latin *movere* meaning 'to move'. To be emotional is to be literally moved, in a bodily sense. The older expression for the psychologist's technical term 'physiological changes' was 'bodily motions'. Yet it is interesting to note that the current meaning of the word 'emotion' as listed in the Concise Oxford English Dictionary is 'agitation of mind, feeling; excited mental state'. The sense of *bodily* changes or motions seems to have dropped out entirely, probably, I suggest, under the influence of Descartes' view of emotion as being just the experience in the soul or just the mental state, for this view came to dominate philosophical work on the emotions.

By physiological changes in relation to emotion, I obviously mean unusual ones. Physiological changes are always going on in our bodies, so, if we remark that someone is emotional, and are referring to their physiological state, we must be remarking that their physiology appears abnormal or remarkable. Abnormally speeded up or slowed down. It must be that the emotional person is literally exhibiting a set of physiological changes which would not be listed in a medical textbook under the description of the normal stable state. Of course emotions are normal to humans, and in that sense the changes are normal but in the sense that the physiological changes resulting from physical strain or excessive exercise are normal. Emotional states involve a stretching or dampening down of our more usual physiological processes and states.

Not all physiological changes which are caused by evaluative attitudes will be relevant. Emotion involves primarily the physiological changes associated with adrenaline flow, blood circulation, respiration, muscular tension, gastro-intestinal activity, temperature, secretions, in short, those changes associated with the central nervous system, and, of course, their manifestation in our facial colouring and expression, and in our reflex behaviour. While such physiological changes are always open to scrutiny by a physiologist, most often they will also be abundantly evident to the ordinary observer via their manifestation in facial appearance and gesture.

These changes may cause permanent physiological changes but are not themselves permanent.[3] Thus a psychosomatic disease, say a skin condition caused by extreme shyness or a twitch brought on by a sense of failure, are not emotions. On the other hand the physiological state resulting from a discharge of the sympathetic nervous system, which has been caused by a sense of failure, is an emotional state. Of course such a state may have the side effect of turning one's hair white, bringing out spots and producing a twitch, but these physiological states are not part of the concept of an emotional state as such. Why, you might ask? First, because they are not the physiological changes which psychologists have found to be present more or less consistently when they have examined cases of what are generally accepted to be emotional states. Secondly, hair turned white, spots and twitches do not seem to be part of the life of the comparatively transitory emotional states themselves, for they develop much too slowly to be so.

At this point it is relevant to ask how one can even establish any causal link between an evaluation and physiological changes. One cannot establish the link by strict Humean methods. That is, there is no constant conjunction between evaluative attitudes and the physiological changes associated with emotion. Diseases, drugs and many other things can cause physiological changes at least roughly similar to those associated with emotion, and evaluative attitudes can occur without any ensuing physiological changes.

Why then should one ever suggest that an evaluation is the cause of physiological changes? For modified Humean reasons. If it is known, as it is, that physiological changes of the type we are concerned with do often follow on the generation or activation of some evaluative disposition in a person, and if in a certain case the physiological changes follow quite directly the evaluation, and if it is known that there is nothing else present in or near the person who is undergoing these physiological changes which might be associated with the appearance of these changes, then one has good reasons for claiming that the evaluation is the cause of the physiological changes. It is quite simply a matter of the evaluation being the best claimant

[3] See for example Woodworth and Schlosberg (1955, Chs 6 and 7).

in the circumstances for being the cause of the observed physiological effects.

I do not think it is a weakness in this or any other theory that I cannot give an account of *how* an evaluation can cause physiological changes. As I am not forced by the theory to consider evaluation as mental in a Cartesian sense, this theory is not landed with the difficulty of explaining how mental substances cause or interact with physical ones. If pressed on the mind–body problem I would hold some version of a double-aspect theory, speculating that the mental and the physical are aspects of the human organism which are not causally incompatible in the way that the Cartesian account of the mental and physical seems to make them.

The differentiation of the emotions by their evaluative aspect

When considering the attempts by behaviourists to differentiate emotions in terms of physiological changes or behaviour, we found that these attempts did not succeed. Similarly with motivational or impulse accounts, which either collapse into behaviourist accounts by suggesting that the different impulses peculiar to each emotion are reflected in behaviour or physiological changes, or they fail to give a convincing account of emotions which, since they never give rise to appropriate behaviour, seem to involve no impulses at all. Others have tried to differentiate emotions in terms of their objects, but unless this term 'object' is interpreted as 'formal object' – which is really a crib for object-as-evaluated – then this doesn't work either. Two different emotions can certainly have the same material object. I can fear something which you love.

By a process of elimination this leaves us with the so-called cognitive factors, the beliefs and evaluations. I have already argued that the factual beliefs will not do the trick, as they amount to just the object as neutrally described, and one has the same problems in differentiating the emotions by reference to descriptive beliefs as one has in trying to differentiate them by reference to the object as such.

But this is not to say that the evaluative account is of use. It must be shown that the evaluative factor can positively differentiate the emotions.

Let me show that it does work, that the evaluative factor does differentiate the emotions, by means of an example. I am standing talking with a man at a party when a third person, a woman, joins us. The man gets edgy, shifts from foot to foot, fidgets with his glass, flushes and is suddenly much brusquer in manner and tone of voice. He doesn't reveal in his conversation or expression what is upsetting him, except that it is associated with the woman's suddenly joining us. It could be that he hates the woman, or is in love with her, or is angry with her, or afraid of her, or embarrassed. I cannot tell what emotion he is undergoing till I work out how he sees, that is, evaluates, the situation. If, afterwards, I learn that she was his ex-wife, I'm still not much the wiser. But if I learn that he believes that she betrayed him to the Gestapo during the war, I would be fairly safe in assuming that he probably despises her utterly and so his emotion is hate. If I learn, on the other hand, that he believed that she was going to reveal that he had stolen the silver, then his emotion was most probably fear because he probably believed that he would be publicly shamed. If I learn, however, that she has just rejected his offer of marriage, then I would guess that his emotion was embarrassment, as he probably considered the situation to be very awkward.

The point is that, to work out what emotion is in question, I seek clues as to what is this person's view of the situation, that is, how he evaluates it. Behaviour, facial expressions, gestures, words, the interplay of persons in a group, may all function as clues to differentiating the emotions, yet they are not themselves the differentiator. They are clues to how the subject of an emotion evaluates his situation, and this is the differentiator proper. When we jump straight from observing behaviour or gestures or facial expressions to concluding that such and such an emotion is in question, it can only be because the behaviour or gesture or expression is typically the manifestation – the deliberate sign or reflex symptom – of some evaluative attitude.

The concept of a particular emotion may include desires

Now the concept of any particular emotion may include reference to factors not mentioned in the concept of emotion as such, for this latter concept is the concept of the minimum required, the smallest list of conditions (if it can be put in that form) for something's qualifying as an emotional state. It will not, of course, include factors not mentioned in the paradigm case of an emotional state, for this was a model of the full list of factors involved in an emotional state and of the connection between these factors.

Certain emotions cannot be said to be present unless the subject of the emotion admits to having certain wants or desires. These emotions are ones that are behaviour oriented. Love is a clear case. One could not claim to be in love, that is, to love emotionally, if one did not admit to wanting to be near the beloved or to please the beloved or to wish him or her well. There are probably other wants to be included here, but these will do for our purposes now. If you said that you loved your wife but you never wanted to be in her company, and couldn't care less whether she were dead or not, I'd say that you must be mistaken or lying when you said you loved her. For X to love Y, then X must not merely evaluate Y as appealing (this formal object would need to be refined but will do for the present), but X must want certain things in regard to Y as well. X must want to be with Y, to please Y, to cherish Y, to want Y to return the love, to want Y to think well of him. Thus evidence that X does not love Y or has ceased to, would be evidence that X does not behave towards Y in a manner that is in keeping with these wants associated conceptually with love, in the absence of mitigating circumstances.

In saying that wants are part of the concept of some emotions, I am not saying that some emotions are to be given a behaviourist treatment. Fear is to be defined as an evaluation of the situation as dangerous plus a want to avoid or be rid of the danger, which combination affects the subject physiologically. But the subject might be outstandingly brave and never in fact give in to the want to avoid or be rid of the danger, yet still frequently have these wants. It would only be if this person becomes inured to danger and no longer ever wanted to avoid or be rid of danger that we would say that he or she is never afraid.

Of course, too, the concepts of certain emotions include no wants at all. Backward-looking emotions, such as grief, do not, though one might argue that they give rise to wishes that things could be otherwise than they are. Grief of some sorts, for example, might be defined simply as evaluating something as a great loss and that this affects the person physiologically.

*Behaviour arises, rationally and causally, from the evaluative aspect
via desires*

In my survey of the classical theories of emotion in philosophy and
psychology, I mentioned that the feeling theory in particular had
difficulty making sense of the fact that emotions are linked to behaviour in an intimate way, being often cited as the motive for
behaviour. The causal–evaluative theory has no such difficulty. The
evaluation of the object, event or situation, which the subject of the
emotion makes, leads one both rationally and causally to certain
specific desires, which in turn lead to behaviour in suitable circumstances. For example, the fearful person's evaluation of the object as
dangerous gives that person a good reason for wanting to avoid or
be rid of the object. A feeling does not of itself provide one with a
good reason for wanting to do anything and so for action. An
evaluation does, particularly the evaluation involved in emotion, for
such an evaluation, being of the world or some aspect of it in relation to the subject's needs, interests or values, generates desires to
change the situation *vis-à-vis* the subject, or else to prolong it.

The strength of an evaluative theory in comparison with a
motivational one is that it can explain how the very different behaviour resulting from the fear of getting fat, the fear of dogs and the
fear of being found out, can all be accommodated under the one
emotion, fear. A purely motivational account is forced to say that all
fear behaviour stems from a single innate impulse or action-tendency. But what single action-tendency could give rise to eating no
sugar out of a fear of getting fat, putting up a wire fence around the
house out of a fear of dogs, and going to America out of a fear of
being found out? Action-tendencies or impulses, with their paradigm case, instinctual drives, are too closely related to particular
sorts of behaviour to be able to explain emotional behaviour. Wants
are much less tied to particular sorts or patterns of behaviour. Thus
an evaluative theory can explain that not eating, putting up defences,
and running away can be the appropriate action or piece of behaviour for one all-embracing desire given the circumstances. They
can all be seen as appropriate to a desire to avoid or be rid of the
danger, given the circumstances and the danger in question.

The evaluative aspect of emotions provides a reason for the
emotional behaviour in question, the appetitive aspect provides a

proximate cause, and together they can show that practically any behaviour can be appropriate to some emotion in certain circumstances. So the causal – evaluative theory makes sense of the fact that there are no tight or set patterns of behaviour to be associated with a particular emotion, something the behaviourist theory could not come to terms with.

The tangibility of emotions

I have argued that an account of emotion should be primarily of occurrent emotional states, for dispositional attributions will be parasitic on there being some evidence that some emotional states, associated with that emotion, have taken place. Being primarily occurrent emotional states, emotions have at least the tangibility that they include bodily changes and, very often, facial expressions, gestures, utterances and motivated behaviour. But this will not allay the doubts of a psychologist, for what will worry a psychologist will be the fact that the causal–evaluative theory proffers a mental item, an evaluation, as the differentiator of the various particular emotions. Fear differs from anger and love, not as psychologists would hope, in terms of clearly observable patterns of visceral changes or behaviour, but in terms of something rather 'airy fairy', evaluations. Further, in arguing via an example that the evaluative aspect was the differentiating factor, I described a case in which it was abundantly clear that clues or evidence for what evaluation the subject of emotion had made were very difficult to come by. It seemed to be a matter of gathering clues and acting on hints and hunches as best one could. In such a case, there was no clear-cut, infallible, unambiguous way of immediately deciding what emotion was in question.

This is an important and real worry, and I want to suggest that evaluations are as tangible as behaviour or physiological changes but perhaps in a different way.

It will be recalled that I argued that evaluations are most probably to be given a dispositional analysis in the way that belief is but that, even so, one must posit a very real categorical or structural base. To say that this piece of Venetian glass is brittle is to make a dispositional claim, it is to claim that this piece of glass would break if let fall or struck even lightly. In explaining such a claim, one would eventually have to refer to the physico-chemical structure of

Venetian glass as being what makes the glass break up when brought into sudden contact with something hard. It will be the same with evaluations as with dispositions. One will have to posit some structural or categorical basis for claiming that the liability or prone-ness is still operative. With Venetian glass, there is no risk in claim-ing that this piece is as brittle as the next, or as brittle this week as it was last week. We have no reason to think that the composition and structure of Venetian glass alters from one day to the next. With evaluations the matter is less certain. Today I might evaluate labrador dogs as dangerous and be afraid of them. Tomorrow I might read an article in the authoritative *Dog Lover* which claims that they are the most tranquil of dogs and that there is no known instance of their biting or attacking anyone, and so not be afraid of them. Evaluations come and go more readily. Nevertheless, given that I have reason to believe someone still evaluates something in a certain way, though nothing occurrent is taking place at this moment, I must posit something real, residing in that person, which could trigger off something occurrent, such as behaviour or utter-ance, in suitable circumstances.

It may be that we will find out that there is a one-to-one correla-tion between the categorical or structural basis of evaluations and brain states. If this is so, then an evaluative account of emotions is reducible to something akin to a behaviourist account, for one could distinguish emotions by means of physiological changes: not visceral ones, as behaviourists like Watson have looked to, but brain states. Physiologists may eventually be able to differentiate emotions for us, if evaluations become open to such direct scrutiny. Whether this correlation between the structural or categorical basis of evaluations and brain states is possible or not, is a contingent empirical matter to be decided in the future. It certainly cannot be done now. But because it cannot be done now is no reason to reject an evaluative account of the differentiating factor for emotions.

It is worth referring at this point to the following passage from an article by Robert Leeper. The context is a discussion of the fact that, traditionally, psychological theories have placed emotions and cog-nitive–evaluative factors in separate and mutually exclusive cate-gories because of alleged physiological facts.

Indeed, this older psychological thought assumed also that emotions are lower-order processes, partly because emotions were pictured as dependent on subcortical mechanisms and the autonomic nervous system, whereas perceptions and cognitive activities generally in the higher vertebrates were pictured as dependent on the neocortex and on the somatic nervous system.

However, any such neurological dichotomy can be dismissed fairly surely. The new discoveries about the influences of the brainstem reticular formation were merely part of the evidence showing the interdependence of cortical and subcortical functioning both in cognitive activities and in emotional processes[4] . . .

Indeed, since emotional functioning is most developed in creatures like man and chimpanzees, less in dogs, and still less in chickens, it may even be that the neocortical part of the brain has been as crucial for emotional characteristics as for traditionally recognized sorts of perception, learning, and thinking [Leeper, 1970, pp. 156–7].

So, if Leeper is right, the most obvious candidate for a physiological correlate for the structural or categorical base for the evaluative aspect of emotional states would be some part of the neocortex connecting with the limbic region of the brain, such as the amygdala and hippocampal gyrus, which are intimately connected with the thalamus and hypothalamus, for this would be in keeping with the considerable empirical data in psychology which shows that emotional reaction and behaviour are controlled from this area of the brain.[5] But there has been no experimental work as yet on isolating an evaluative centre in the brain, partly no doubt because the theory underlying the experimental work on emotions is generally behaviourist and so does not recognise the function of evaluation in emotion.

However, it could be that it is correct to point to evaluations as the differentiating factor, even if there is no correlation between their categorical base and brain states or anything else of a physiological nature, and if the categorical base is irreducibly mentalist or psychological and so not directly observable. But this would not mean that this theory of emotions becomes non-objective. One cannot directly observe or contact even such incontrovertibly

---

[4] At this point Leeper refers to R. A. McCleary and R. Y. Moore, *Subcortical Mechanisms of Behaviour*, Basic Books, 1965.

[5] For example, Lashley (1938); Delgado, Rosvold, and Looney (1956); Stanley-Jones (1970); Izard (1972, Ch. 1); MacLean (1975); Sigg (1975); and Lader and Tyrer (1975).

physical entities as electrons; one sees their traces in Wilson cloud chambers or on the screens of oscilloscopes. One sees their footprints. It could be that we can only posit the existence of an evaluation on the basis of the footprints it leaves, that is, the behaviour, expressions, gestures, utterances and other items which bear its imprint. So such purely psychological theories, which posit irreducibly mental items, are not thereby non-objective, for there are objective observable grounds which are the basis for positing them.

At any rate, in the matter of the causal–evaluative theory of emotions, as regards its evaluative aspect, the matter is still wide open. There may turn out to be a physiological correlate, there may not. If there is, the theory will be strengthened. If there is not it will not be thereby falsified, for the theory does not claim that there must be such a correlate. It merely hopes that there might be.

In the chapters that follow, I will endeavour to go into, in some detail, the part played by the various factors in the full paradigm case of an emotional state, that is, the cognitive or belief aspect, the evaluative aspect, the appetitive aspect, the physiological changes, the feelings and the behaviour. I will also discuss the various interpretations of the phrase 'object of emotion', in what sense emotions are purposive, what sort of control we can exercise over our emotions, and so if and when we might blame people for having them.

4

The cognitive and evaluative
aspects of emotion

In this and the next chapter I propose to discuss the core part of the emotions. With some emotions this seems to be a reasonably easy task, and fear is the one that springs easily to mind as an example of an emotion which has been defined more or less to the psychologist's and philosopher's satisfaction. Fear is usually defined as an emotional reaction resulting from the apprehension that there is danger about and the consequent desire to avoid or be rid of the danger. In other words this core part of an emotion, the evaluative aspect of which I have suggested is what actually distinguishes this emotional reaction as being of such and such an emotion, has three parts, the cognitive part which will involve factual judgments which give rise to belief or knowledge, the evaluative part which will involve objective evaluations or subjective appraisals, and the appetitive part which will involve desires stemming from the cognitive and appetitive aspects. In the next chapter I will suggest reasons why, in addition to the evaluative aspect, the appetitive aspect seems to be part of the very concept of certain emotions.

But in this chapter I want to make an attempt to clarify the cognitive and evaluative aspects of the emotions, and in the course of this and subsequent chapters it will become clear why I speak of these aspects, together with the appetitive, as the core parts of emotional states. As we have seen, it has sometimes been held that an emotion is a completely non-cognitive state, that it is a matter of feelings or animal attraction or instinctual behaviour.[1] At the opposite end of the spectrum, some philosophers have held that some emotions at any rate, such as love, involve a special somewhat

---

[1] Besides those works already referred to in the discussions of the feeling, behaviourist and psychoanalytic accounts of emotion, see also Titchener (1902, pp. 229–34), Wundt (1901, pp. 371–7), and Freud (1971, cf. pp. 29–31, 55–6) where he says that love is just aim-inhibited sex.

mysterious type of knowledge. In the case of love, this has been called 'unitive knowledge' or 'knowledge by participation' and is said to give the lover knowledge of the uniqueness of the beloved.[2] I would like now to argue in some detail that the true picture is to be found somewhere between these two extremes, which is to say that an emotion is partly cognitive but that this part is not so much a source of knowledge about the world as an evaluation or appraisal of some part of the world *in relation to oneself.*

So in this chapter I shall argue:

(1) That generally speaking an emotion is based on knowledge or belief about properties;

(2) That, however, there are some caveats and possible exceptions to be noted;

(3) That the properties mentioned above are to be thought of in terms of a specific sort of viewpoint, namely an evaluative one;

(4) That, on the other hand, certain emotions seem to involve a subjective appraisal rather than an objective evaluation;

(5) That the evaluative aspect is central to emotions and the standard objection to this view is not fatal;

(6) That the objection, that some occurrent states of emotion do not include evaluations, is not fatal;

(7) That the backward-looking/forward-looking and approval/disapproval distinctions between emotions are based on the evaluative aspect.

Generally speaking an emotion is based on knowledge or belief about properties

The emotions presuppose certain judgments, correct or incorrect, cursory or well-considered, irrational or rational, as to what properties something possesses. It would be contradictory to claim, for example, both that one loved X or was angry with X but knew nothing about X. So saying 'I am angry with X' or 'I love X' implies that at some time or other I have apprehended or believe that I have apprehended certain qualities in X. (I should add that there do seem to be exceptions to this view, though they are rather maverick ones. But these will be sufficient to warrant my adding the phrase 'generally speaking' to my thesis.)

[2] See Huxley (1946, pp. 95ff.), Johann (1954, pp. 28ff., 45) (he claims to derive his view from Aquinas), Murdoch (1970, pp. 28–30), Fromm (1957, pp. 29ff.).

For instance, Fred's anger in regard to President Ford might presuppose the judgment that Ford pardoned Nixon for his Watergate
misdemeanours and the judgment that this pardon was illegal.
John's love for Frieda might be based, at least partly, on the judgments that she is shy and that shy people are by and large more kind
and affectionate than extroverts.

It needs to be emphasised that these judgments are ordinary ones
and do not give rise to any sort of special or privileged knowledge,
for these are just as likely to be mistaken or self-deceiving as any
other judgments. Further, it should be stated that these judgments
are not peculiar to emotions or to particular emotions. The same
judgment, for example, that Frieda is shy, can form the basis for any
number of different emotions, which fact points to the conclusion
that such a judgment is not part of the concept of any particular
emotion. At one time John might be angry with her because she is
too shy to tell the shopkeeper that he has shortchanged her; at
another time John might be embarrassed in her company because
her shyness makes it difficult to converse freely with her about
certain topics; finally, John might love her because he finds her shyness appealing. So this judgment, that Frieda is shy, cannot be said
to be integral to or part of the concept of anger, embarrassment or
love.

But while these purely cognitive or factual judgments may not be
part of the concept or definition of any particular emotion, they do
play a fundamental part in the generation of emotional states, so that
what we think of these judgments – how we evaluate them – will be
reflected in the way we think of the emotions themselves. Thus, if
one were to give grounds for saying that John's judgment that
Frieda is shy is superficial, irrational or mistaken, then this would be
grounds for saying that John's anger, embarrassment or love generated, at least in part, by this judgment is superficial, irrational or
mistaken.

There are, of course, other grounds for impugning emotions
because of factual judgments associated with them. The intensity of
an emotion already generated can cause a judgment, made under the
influence of that emotion, to be superficial, irrational or mistaken,
and this judgment can then influence the further course of that
emotion. A man who is filled with hate for his neighbour may be led
by his hate into making irrational judgments about his neighbour.
He may judge that by waving a greeting to his wife the neighbour

is flirting with her, and this may increase the hatred he feels to such an extent that one could say that his emotion had become irrational.

Emotions can, of course, be labelled as superficial, irrational or mistaken for reasons not associated with the factual judgments or cognitive aspect of emotions at all. An emotion can be branded as, say, superficial or irrational because the evaluative judgment integral to it is superficial. But this will be made clearer below (see p. 78). An emotion might also be branded as irrational because the behaviour stemming from it is irrational, even though this irrationality is not based on any judgment, cognitive or evaluative, which is associated with the emotion. The person concerned might be so overcome by the emotion that he neglects his job and his health. Here the emotion, but not the judgments integral to it, has led him to be irrational.

Some caveats and possible exceptions to the above

So far I have been arguing that a claim that someone is in an emotional state in regard to X implies that at some time or other this person must have apprehended or believed that he apprehended certain qualities in X. Now these phrases '... at some time or other ...' and '... apprehended or believed that he had apprehended ...' need careful elucidation.

The judgments that form the basis for an emotional reaction do not have to be repeated for each occurrence of the emotion. If John loves Frieda because he believes that she is shy, and that shy people are generally speaking more kind and affectionate than extroverts, then he does not have to keep re-making these judgments in order to maintain his claim to love Frieda. It is sufficient that he once made them. He need not even remember now that he once made them. For, when discussing the basis for referring to emotions dispositionally, it seemed clear that the initial cognitive judgments, as well as the evaluations and wants, certainly need not and probably are not made explicitly on each occasion that an emotional state is generated. The judgments probably endure subliminally in some physiological memory bank but exercise a causal influence whenever suitable circumstances occur. The endurance or persistence of these judgments, and especially of the evaluations and desires, whether subliminally or not, make up the enduring psychological or physiological structure. On this is based the dispositional claim that so-

and-so is liable or prone to have a particular emotion in particular circumstances.

Thus John might melt with love when he meets Frieda on her return from a visit to her parents in America. In order to melt with love on this occasion, he does not have to recall that he found her appealing because of her shyness. He does not even have to recall that he found her appealing. When the original judgments, evaluations and wants were formed such that they made him react emotionally in such a way as to be called 'love', a pattern – physiological or psychological or both – was set. The pattern would be said to be upset if on such an occasion as Frieda's return after a long absence, or her being struck down with a serious illness, he does not react with emotion. If this happened one must assume that wittingly or unwittingly, at some time or other, he had grown cold towards her.

The judgments that form the basis for an emotional reaction do not have to be correct ones. They may be false. John might judge that Frieda is shy and come to love her for her shyness whereas there may be incontrovertible evidence, known to his friends, that she pretends to shyness in his company because she knows he likes shy people but is in fact a raging extrovert. In such a case what John loves is an imaginary quality in Frieda, an imaginary woman, but his love itself is not imaginary. A genuine, full-fledged emotional state can be generated from such a false belief.

The judgments that form the basis for an emotional reaction, even those of a very personal emotion, such as love, do not necessarily pick out properties which are unique to the person, thing, action or situation which is reacted to. John might love Frieda for her shyness but many people are shy and there is no reason to believe that, if this were his only reason for loving Frieda, he would not be prone to falling in love with shy people in general. For surely my finding Ferguson intensely irritating because he belches constantly will be evidence that I will quite likely be irritated by anyone who belches constantly.

Of course there is a respect in which certain emotions probably tend to penetrate to the unique or more or less unique qualities or set of qualities in the object. Presumably one loves this person but not these hundred others because he or she has a quality or set of qualities which the other hundred do not have. John might love Frieda because she alone has a shyness which is underlined by a crooked smile and a lisp, or because her shyness is conjoined with winsomeness and a fetching way of walking like a day-old gazelle.

At this point it is important to mention possible exceptions to the claim that an emotion is based on knowledge or belief about properties. The usual candidate for being such an exception is fear or, rather, certain cases of fear which are often termed 'objectless'. These cases are not, I think, peculiar to fear but are found most often and most plausibly in connection with fear. Fear and cognate emotions such as fright are usually described as evaluating their object, at least in part, as dangerous to the person concerned. Now, if this is correct, it would not seem strange for there to be a fear which might evaluate one's very ignorance of the situation, one's lack of knowledge, one's not knowing anything about the object, as dangerous. Thus fear of the dark may not be fear of the absence of light but fear of the absence of knowledge or, to put it more exactly, fear arising because one does not know what might be out there in the dark and because one thinks that there might be something to injure or startle one. My imagination might suggest holes or pits to fall into, things to attack or startle, or more ethereal enemies.

So with certain cases of fear one could claim that we have cases in which a person is overcome with fear but there is no object to this fear and he cannot say why he is afraid. Because such a fear is not directed at an object, one will not have made any judgment explicitly or implicitly about the properties of an object. But equally, perhaps, one could say that the fear in such cases is about being totally in the dark literally or epistemologically. In consequence, one could say that what one fears is the situation of being in no position to cope because one does not know what is happening or liable to happen. From here one might be able to make out a case that such fear is based on judgments about properties of one's situation, for example that the situation is describable as one which I do not know anything about or with which I believe I am unable to cope. Alternatively what are often described as cases of objectless fear might be better described as cases in which the object is not properly formulable or expressible, as with fear of something which is subconscious or fear of such a large number of imagined ills that one cannot adequately grasp them as a single object or manageable group of objects, and so cannot possibly express adequately the object of fear even to oneself. Another possibility is that some cases of so-called objectless fears might be cases where one has a vague sense of foreboding, a vague feeling that some doom is about to befall one. Here the object is just vague rather than absent but it is still an object. But even in such cases one presumably has beliefs and makes judgments such as 'There are things out there which make me feel that I'm in danger but I cannot adequately describe them', and these beliefs and judgments are the basis of one's emotions.

Whether one is to say that there are cases of objectless emotions or merely that the object is rather strange, such as one's ignorance in a given situation, may be undecidable. It is probably just as easy and convincing to make out a case that there is some object, however unusual and inexpressible, as that there is no object at all; and that in consequence it is probably just as easy to make out a case that some cognitive judgment has been made, however vague, than that no judgment has been made.

Whatever one is to say about such cases, I do not think that they are peculiar to fear and its cognates. There are cases of both depression and happiness where the depressed or happy person is, at least, unable to say why he or she is depressed or happy. So, even if we admit that emotions can be objectless in some sense, it might be better to say that such cases are slightly blurred rather than exceptions to the general model of the emotions. We shall come across the problem again in the chapter on the objects of emotions.

What strike me as more formidable candidates as exceptions to the claim that emotions are based on knowledge or belief about properties, are cases of what I will call Pavlovian or reflex emotions and those which seem to be based on wishes rather than beliefs.

Pavlovian or reflex emotions are ones where an emotion is triggered off by certain circumstances even though the original judgments, on which the emotion was based, are no longer held. A woman might have received obscene telephone calls for many months culminating in one in which the anonymous heavy breather suddenly revealed that he knew her full name and address, and that her husband was absent that evening, and then said that he was about to come around, break into her flat and rape her. After fleeing to a neighbour for safety that evening, and then next week having had her telephone number changed to an ex-directory one, she finds that she still falls into near hysterical states of fear whenever the telephone rings. She knows that it is almost impossible that it could be the obscene caller ringing as, say, the new number only came into operation that day, but still she undergoes the intense emotional state of fear.

One might want to argue that, in such a case, and in all cases of Pavlovian emotions, the person concerned both knows that the conditions which previously caused her to be afraid no longer obtain, but yet still believes against all the evidence, adequate evidence, that they might still hold true. The person simply holds conflicting beliefs. An alternative explanation is that her fear is reflex. Her belief that she is in danger is gone, but the states of fear still occur, from conditioning, so to speak.

Another candidate for an emotion not based on beliefs, and which I think cannot be given a reinterpretation such that it is, is an emotion based on wishes, especially those based on wishes which cannot possibly be fulfilled, wishes such as those about some irreversible fact. One might have an emotion of yearning or hope that someone will not die of a brain tumour. One believes quite definitely that he will, yet one wishes against all the evidence that he will not. It is the wish not the belief that generates one's emotional feelings of hope and yearning. More peculiarly, but no less plausibly, one might have an emotion which is based on a wish that the past, the known past, be otherwise than it was. One knows that one's husband died during the war, the evidence is incontrovertible, but one still irrationally and emotionally wishes for his safe return. Such emotions might best be termed 'wishful thinking' emotions.

These properties are thought of from an evaluative viewpoint

Now I want to argue that the cognitive aspect of the emotions, the knowledge or belief about properties, is the basis for an evaluation. The initial judgments that something possesses certain properties, are transformed into a specific way of viewing the object. Generally speaking this viewpoint can alone adequately distinguish one emotion from another. Though perhaps not always; one may have to refer to the appetitive aspect of emotions to identify certain emotions. I myself am not convinced that one has to refer to the appetitive aspect to separate emotions off from one another, though one does have to in order to define some of them adequately.

So, for most emotions if not all, what emotion, if any, will well up in a person will depend on how he 'sees' the object he has apprehended or believes he has apprehended. A man is afraid because he 'sees' the object or situation as dangerous. A man is angry because he 'sees' the situation as offensive or insulting. A man is embarrassed because he 'sees' the situation as one in which he has lost face. A man is in love because he 'sees' some person as appealing.

To put it another way, we will only count this emotional state as a case of fear if the person's particular judgments, say, that there is a bomb in the corner of the room and that it is likely to go off, and so is likely to injure or kill him, are judgments which together can be said to fall under the general category or description of viewing the situation as dangerous. We will only count this as a case of embarrassment if we believe we have grounds for holding that the person in question feels that he has made a fool of himself or committed some *faux pas* or, in general, that he has lost face. In short, the most basic way of claiming that *x* is an example of emotion *y* is to discover the judgments, factual and evaluative, which form part of emotional state *x* and see whether they fall under the general description of the way of seeing the situation which we take to be peculiar to emotion *y*.

Now this 'light' in which the subject of an emotion 'sees' the object includes an evaluation such that, in the most objective of these evaluations, the subject can be said to rate the object according to some scale. An emotion such as fear, for example, seems to evaluate its object according to some more or less objective norm. A man will be afraid if he is told that a bomb has just been planted in the room and is about to go off, because he along with most people rates bombs as dangerous. And it is because an emotion such as fear is tied to a more or less objective rating or evaluation that a man who is afraid of flies can be said to be neurotic on the grounds that his fear is irrational and persistent, and at variance with the commonsense view or accepted evaluation of the object of his fear.[3] There are, of course, other grounds on which a person's fear may be termed neurotic; if, say, his belief gives rise to an emotion of such intensity that it interferes with his work or his life in general, to such an extent that it can be said to be inordinate or out of proportion.

Certain emotions seem to involve a subjective appraisal rather than an objective evaluation

With an emotion such as love, and presumably its opposite, hate, and possibly the emotion embarrassment, there does not seem to be

[3] See Lewin (1968, pp. 81ff.), Eidelberg (1968, pp. 310ff.).

any objective norm as to what is to count as an acceptable or rational evaluation, or by which one could predict what sort of properties are being picked out and evaluated. To take love, there is no principle or set of principles which tells a person whom he is likely to find appealing or 'good in his eyes' in the way that there are principles or generalisations as to what things are likely to be dangerous to humans. Who a person is drawn to seems to be very much a matter of a series of personal trials and errors and, in general, very much a matter for the individual person. It is very difficult to come to the conclusion that someone's love is neurotic because it is at variance with the commonsense view, or the view presumed rational (though it does seem possible to label love as neurotic on the grounds that it is out of proportion and so disruptive of the lover's life to an inordinate degree). There is no commonsense view about who is appealing in the matter of love. It is generally accepted that personal appeal is in the eye of the lover. It is very difficult to make good a case that the object of someone's love could not really be appealing to him or her.

So, while we can predict, up to a point, what sort of things a person will be afraid of – such things as being inside the lions' cage at the zoo, swimming in areas where there is a strong undertow – we cannot predict what sort of person somebody will fall in love with (unless of course we explicitly or implicitly know this particular person's past history in this matter). I would not want to deny, however, that when psychologists know more about the human personality and can shuffle human persons into very subtle personality types, it may be possible to derive principles, though they would be long and involved, as to what sort of persons any given type of person will find 'good in his eyes' and appealing and so tend to love. It may be possible eventually to state that extroverts with intellectual interests fall in love with introverts with manipulative skills, or some such. But, as the state of science stands, it is not possible, even with all the facts about an individual's personality and physiology (unless some statement about his personality implicitly or explicitly includes a statement about the sort of person he tends to fall in love with). This difference between love and fear is grounds for saying that love is very much more a matter of the individual person and his personal view of things (though an advance in psychology may one day make this into 'a matter of the individual personality type').

I have been stressing that the evaluative aspect of certain

emotions, such as love, does not involve an objective evaluation but what might be called a subjective appraisal. In his article 'Emotion', Pitcher draws attention to the tension holding between the position that certain emotions such as love are basically subjective in their evaluative aspect, and so cannot be criticised as being reasonable or unreasonable, and the position that these same emotions seem to include some type of evaluation nonetheless. He writes: 'This fact – that loves cannot ordinarily be criticized as reasonable or unreasonable – also appears to be embarrassing to the view of emotions being defended here; for if love, like the other emotions, involves evaluations, why should it not be criticizable in that way?' Pitcher offers his solution to this tension:

> The significant feature, for us, of these evaluations is that they are, in a manner of speaking, indefensible: for in them, something is deemed good in itself. The man in love wants, for example, to be with his beloved; and he wants this simply because he enjoys her company for its own sake – there is no reason for it, he just wants to be with her [Pitcher, 1965, p. 341].

I think Pitcher is correct in his solution of the tension, so far as he goes. It seems to be true that a man does not love a woman for reasons, not because there are no reasons where one might expect them, but because, if by 'reason' we mean a consideration which, if put to anyone, or at least almost anyone, would count for him, it is a category mistake to ask for reasons in such a case. Only private or personal reasons, that is no good reasons or real reasons, could be given for the rating or evaluative process in an emotion such as love. This being so, it might be useful to carry Pitcher's solution a little further by making a distinction between an appraisal (a non-object-ive a-rational rating) and an evaluation (an objective rational rating). Thus, armed with this distinction, it might seem less para-doxical to say that the evaluative aspect of certain emotions, such as love and hate, resembles more an exercise of unreasoning taste than of reasoned evaluation, and so should be termed an appraisal rather than an evaluation.

The evaluative aspect as central and the standard objection

It will become clear when I discuss the part played in emotional states by physiological changes, feelings and behaviour, that they do not succeed in distinguishing the different emotional states. For, as I will argue later in detail, behaviour and feelings need not be present on all occasions of an emotional state, but, even when they are present, they do not form any sufficiently consistent and distinct patterns which would enable one to distinguish different emotions by reference to such patterns. And as regards physiological changes, though it would seem that they must be present if something is to be called an emotional state, it does not seem to be the case that they differ markedly when forming part of different emotional states, and so provide no ground thereby for separating one emotional state from another. So, by a process of elimination, one is left with the cognitive, evaluative and appetitive aspects as the prime candidates (among the parts which were isolated in chapter 3 as being components or aspects of the paradigm of an emotional state) for features that may be used to distinguish different emotions. But earlier on in this chapter, I argued that cognitive judgments fail in this, for the same factual judgments can and do give rise to different emotions and the same emotion can be generated by different cognitive judgments. When I come to discuss the appetitive aspect of emotions I will suggest that, while they do seem to be of a pattern for each sort of emotion which intuitively we identify, there may be emotions or cases of emotions which don't readily give rise to any wants or desires at all, that is, to any appetitive aspect. So, then, we are finally left with the evaluative aspect as the linchpin of the different parts which make up an emotional state, and the differentiator of the different emotions. In separating off one emotion from another, then, one need make reference only to the evaluation which is claimed to be peculiar to that emotion, though in defining certain emotions, it may be the case that one has also to refer to the appetitive aspect.

Fairly obviously, the basic standard objection against this view of emotions is that there are not different evaluative aspects for each emotion. In an account of different emotions, what is identified as the evaluative aspect will often turn out to be the same for emotions which intuitively we recognise as different.

For example, it might be claimed that the evaluation, 'He is a fine pianist', can be central to an emotional state of admiration, joy or envy, so these, and perhaps all emotions, are not to be distinguished by reference to their evaluative aspect.

This is clearly a very serious objection but I think it can be answered, though with some difficulty. The difficulty arises, at least mainly, because our knowledge of the workings of particular emotions is still very rudimentary. Philosophers and psychologists are still doubtful that there can be any adequate model for emotions in general, so it is not surprising that comparatively little work has gone into trying to elucidate the nature of particular emotions, except perhaps from the behavioural aspect, an enterprise that has not been greeted with conspicuous success.

Prima facie, then, the same evaluation, 'He is a fine pianist' seems to be at the heart of both admiration for the pianist and envy of him. But is this really so? For a start, does it really explain a person's envy to say that it arises as a result of his evaluating someone else or his performance as fine? Surely envy involves much more than this as regards its evaluative aspect. For X to envy Y he must first of all rate Y or something Y does or has, such as riches or ability or something achieved, more highly than his own corresponding action or possession. In the first place, then, the evaluation which is part of envy must make clear that there is a gap in some respect between the person or thing envied and the possessions, abilities, or person of the envier, where the gap is revealed when a comparison is made. Secondly, the gap must be such that the person envying is or seems to himself to be on the inferior side of the gap. If I am a concert pianist I don't envy someone who has just played well enough to pass his first set of school-level piano exams. If I can run the 100 metres in 9.1 seconds I don't envy someone who runs it in 10.1 seconds (unless, of course, the person runs the 10.1 at an age when I could only do it in 11 seconds). On the other hand, I might admire someone who does the 100 metres in 10.1 seconds, even if I can do it in 9.1 seconds, particularly if the person who does it in 10.1 seconds did not appear likely to do it in that time for reasons of, say, age, sex or infirmity.

Thirdly, for envy to take root, the evaluation must be about something in which I am interested. If I have no interest in being rich, I won't envy anyone their wealth. On the other hand I might admire something which I am not interested in, such as someone's ability at accumulating wealth in a short time. So the evaluation which is part of envy, if fully spelt out, would make it clear that I was not dispassionate in regard to what I was rating as fine, whereas the evaluation that was part of admiration could be dispassionate. 'X envies Y' would involve X in rating person Y as better at Z than X himself who would like to be good at Z. 'X admires Y' would involve just rating Y as good at Z.

But clearly we still have not separated off *all* the cases of envy and admiration. A person could still satisfy these first three requirements and still admire a pianist, say, Ashkenazy. The one admiring might be himself a pianist (requirement 3), and realise that Ashkenazy is of concert pianist class while he himself is in a much inferior class (requirements 1 and 2), yet he still might admire Ashkenazy as a pianist. So I think at least a fourth requirement is needed. This is that the envious person evaluates his being inferior in some respect in comparison to someone else as displeasing or not to his liking, while the admiring person does not. While I might admire Ashkenazy's skill and be displeased, I could not say that I admired Ashkenazy's skill and that part of this admiration involved being displeased by the realisation that my playing of the piano was vastly inferior to his. On the other hand it would be absurd to say that I envied Ashkenazy his skill at the piano but to deny that the realization that his skill was vastly superior to mine in no way displeased me. Being displeased is part of the concept of envy but not part of the concept of admiration.

No doubt there will be other factors as well which separate off the evaluation which is part of envy from the evaluation which is part of admiration but the four I have mentioned will be sufficient to make clear that any objection of the sort that the evaluation 'He is a fine pianist' is common and central to both envying and admiring him, so that the evaluative aspects of these emotions at any rate are not distinguishable, is only superficially plausible. The objection does not hold, because its implied claim, that the evaluation 'He is a fine pianist' *fully describes* the evaluative aspects of envy, admiration or any other emotion, is incorrect, as I think I have shown in the case of envy and admiration. And there is no reason to believe that the labour of showing distinct differences in the evaluative aspects of envy and admiration could not be repeated in the case of these two emotions when compared with any other emotions.

I am not, of course, denying that the same evaluation 'He is a fine pianist' is both common to and central to both admiring and envying the pianist. I am denying that it follows from this that the evaluative aspects of these two emotions are therefore indistinguishable, for I am denying that 'he is a fine pianist' exhausts the evaluative aspects of both admiring and envying. In short, to say that the same evaluation E is common and central to emotions X, Y and Z, is not an objection to a theory which claims that there is a different evaluative aspect for emotions X, Y and Z, unless it is added that E fully describes the evaluative aspects of X, Y and Z. But I have been arguing that this addition would be false.

I should mention at this point that there are those who feel that my account above of how one might distinguish between admiring and envying a pianist is, at worst false, and at best unnecessary. Such a view would maintain that there is a very simple way of distinguishing the emotions admiration and envy, namely by referring to the appetitive aspect of these emotions. Envy is viewing someone's characteristics, abilities, or possessions as fine *and wishing* or *wanting* that it be otherwise. Admiration is viewing someone's characteristics, abilities or possessions as fine, full stop.

I would not want to deny that the above does afford one an easy way of separating off emotions. I think one can certainly do so, with certain pairs of emotions at any rate, by referring straight away to the appetitive aspect. Nor would I want to deny that such a method is the simpler and quicker in certain cases, and, if one is aesthetically minded, the more attractive.

What I do think it is important to realise is that the viability of this method in some cases must not make us think that there is no distinction between the evaluative aspects of the different emotions, or that the evaluative aspect is not central. More importantly I think that the distinction in the appetitive aspect always mirrors a distinction in the evaluative aspect. If wanting things to be otherwise is central to envy, then one would and should expect that the basis for this want will be found in the way the envious person views the world. An envious person is not just an admiring person who happens to have a totally disconnected want in him which runs counter to his admiration. An envious person is a sort of person, and his envy starts in the way he thinks of other people and their characteristics, abilities and possessions in comparison with himself. The envious person, unlike the admiring one, dislikes what he sees when he compares himself with others. This is why he wishes that things were otherwise than they are. This wish or want does not just come from nowhere.

My account, then, claims to show *why* a person desires what he desires when in the grip of an emotion or acting out of an emotion. It shows the genesis of the appetitive aspect rather than treating it as a magical apparition, but more of this in the next chapter.

So I would also go so far as to say that not to look for the distinction between emotions in the first place in the evaluative aspect, will be to fail to really understand the workings of the different emotions.

The objection, that some occurrent states of emotion do not include evaluations, is not fatal

Another possible objection is that certain occurrent emotional states do not seem to include any evaluative judgment at all, therefore an evaluative aspect is not essential to occurrent emotional states, and so the causal–evaluative model must be incorrect. Reflex emotions are a case in point: sudden reflex anger, instant embarrassment, the flare-up of jealousy, startled fear. The emotional reaction, the flushing or quivering or feeling of palpitations, and the emotional action, the sudden lashing out or running away or cowering, is immediate. There is not time for conscious evaluation because there is no time to form beliefs or gain knowledge.

Pitcher, in 'Emotion', is particularly interesting on the evaluative aspect of emotions and treats this sort of objection in the following way. He points out, correctly, that to argue for an evaluative aspect to emotions is not to suggest that every occurrent state of emotion need include a conscious evaluative judgment.

> The term 'evaluation', as I am using it, is not meant to suggest that the person must make an evaluational judgment, or even that he must have what might be called an evaluative belief. Sometimes the evaluation will be constituted by a conscious judgment or by a belief or assumption, but sometimes not ... If a person's anger is so great that he makes no conscious evaluational judgment or even has no conscious evaluational belief, then ... he acts *as if* he made such a judgment or had such a belief [Pitcher, 1965, pp. 334–5].

That is, writes Pitcher, often the evaluation will only amount to an 'evaluational mode of behaviour' or merely an inclination to such a mode of behaviour (Pitcher, 1965, p. 335).

This reply of Pitcher's I do not find satisfactory or sufficiently clear. Pitcher seems both to admit that no evaluational judgment has taken place, and to want to maintain that nonetheless something occurrently evaluative has taken place. Pitcher seems to be saying that with reflex emotions, say reflex anger, the instantaneous reaction of lashing out at the object of anger is evaluative in manner and so takes the place of any more fully-formed and conscious type of evaluation. But how can lashing out be evaluative? It is just lashing out. If we associate the lashing out with anger, it is not because we discern in it some evaluative colouring which we then associate with the evaluation characteristic of anger. It is because, for some reason, we infer that the person lashing out must have believed that he had been insulted, that is, he must have evaluated something as insulting. We infer *from* the behaviour of lashing out, plus the previous events (perhaps someone had said something which is usually taken to be insulting), plus our knowledge of the person lashing out (we might know that he is easily insulted or finds insults in anything) or the person who is the target for the lashing out (perhaps she is very bitchy and insulting most of the time), plus, probably, knowledge or beliefs about other factors, *to* an evaluation. We do not discover or observe evaluative aspects in the lashing out; we infer from the lashing out and other factors that the subject of the lashing out must have evaluated the situation in a certain way.

But the objection still stands. Where is the evaluation in such cases of reflex anger? Am I not being more obscure than Pitcher? He at least purported to discover the evaluation lurking in the behaviour. I seem to leave it mysteriously in the background.

I think the evaluation is to be found in the background but not in any mysterious way. The answer lies in the nature of dispositions and in recalling that I claimed that evaluations should generally be given a dispositional analysis in the context of emotions. If what I have said so far about dispositions is correct, then to be disposed to be angry when confronted by insults entails that we have lying dormant in us some structural or categorical base – some psychological or physiological factor – which can and will be triggered by certain events. If, say, the insult is direct and obvious, a slur on our character or a naked taunt that strikes home on some sensitive point, then the triggering can be instantaneous and the reaction sudden and strong. We do not have time to form a conscious evaluative judgment, not because there is not enough time to make it – for I imagine they can be instantaneous – but because we do not need time. It is quite likely to be part of our outlook, one of our natural dispositions, to be upset by slurs and taunts. Or else it is part of this person's outlook and so an embedded disposition to be upset by slurs and taunts of this kind or coming from such a person or when made in such circumstances. To some slurs and taunts, some of us react as a reflex, immediately, naturally. The evaluation once formed, long ago maybe, and reinforced, is now firmly embedded. The remark about my character does not need to be consciously pondered on so as to provoke action. The ponderings are long over, the decisions about action taken long ago. Now, when the slur or taunt comes, the behaviour follows automatically; it is a reaction. For we are *disposed* to act so.

Alston, when sketching his 'comprehensive view' of emotions in his article 'Emotion and Feeling', also confronts the problem that those who make evaluation central to emotion have difficulty in making sense of reflex emotions or objectless emotions where the evaluative aspect seems to be missing. His solution to the problem is the following:

> We may find a way out by noting that the cases of emotion without typical feelings and without conscious evaluations of objects are not clear cases. They are not the cases a person would give if he set out to explain to someone what an emotion is. One would not evince lack of understanding of the concept if he should raise a doubt as to whether these cases are cases of anger, fear, or whatever. This suggests the hypothesis that these applications of the term are derivative from its application to more full-blooded cases in which all these factors are present. It may be that the concept of emotion is like many other concepts, such as religion, poetry, and science, in that we cannot explicate it without making a distinction between central (paradigm) cases and cases which deviate from the paradigm in lacking some central feature but do not deviate sufficiently to completely inhibit the application of the term. Thus the full range of cases exhibits what Wittgenstein called 'family resemblances'. There is a list of typical features, such that some are present in all cases, no one feature is present in all cases, and only the paradigm cases exhibit all the features [Alston, 1967a, p. 486].

But this solution ends up being a capitulation. For if one explains, say, reflex emotions as 'cases which deviate from the paradigm in lacking some central feature but do not deviate sufficiently to completely inhibit the application of the term', then one is caught with one's philosophical trousers not merely down but off and incapable of recovery. If emotion is defined as an evaluation which causes abnormal physiological changes, how can one claim that, if, with some candidate for being an emotional state, there is no evaluation present but only abnormal physiological changes, then this abnormal physiological state by itself can still merit the term 'emotional state'? 'Indigestion' might be defined as a certain causal conjunction, in the way 'emotion' is on the causal–evaluative theory. 'Indigestion' might be defined, oversimply, as 'stomach upset caused by eating food'. We would not be tempted to call x a case of indigestion if it was a stomach upset but in no way to be associated with the attempt to digest food. How then can Alston plausibly claim that an abnormal physiological state, not associated with an evaluation, could still merit the title 'emotion'?

Moreover, it is questionable to say that a physiological state caused by an evaluation is the paradigm, but a physiological state by itself is to be associated with this former paradigm as a deviation from it. Why is the former the paradigm and the latter the deviation? If evaluation is central to emotion, such that cases including evaluation are central cases, then why consider cases without evaluation cases of emotion at all? *A fortiori* if evaluation is part of the very concept of emotion how can cases without evaluations in any sense fall *under* the concept?

But to return to the difficulty about deciding which case is the paradigm, how does one decide which of two competing cases is the central one without being arbitrary? Is it *statistically*? If so, Alston would have to present evidence that reflex emotions – the supposed less central cases – occur less often than non-reflex ones. Does one decide in favour of the *most complex* case? But why consider the most complex the most central? It could be that it is deviant in having accretions rather than the simpler case being deviant in being truncated. Is it that certain cases are *more obvious*? If the ones that include evaluations are the more obvious cases of emotion, then we are back to the original problem, why call cases of physiological upset without evaluation causing it less obvious cases rather than not cases of emotion at all?

So I find neither Pitcher's nor Alston's solutions tenable. If x is to be claimed as an emotional state then it must include an evaluation. If the dispositional nature of evaluations themselves is properly understood I see no real difficulty in coping with reflex emotions. An evaluation can be active but not conscious. That I am afraid of

Alsatians is true now though I am writing at my desk. If an Alsatian suddenly appeared I might be plunged instantaneously, reflexly, into a state of fear. Some time ago I formed the view that Alsatians are very dangerous. This evaluation has a structural or categorical basis, a physiological or psychological factor, which lies dormant in me such that it can still be said of me that I believe Alsatians to be very dangerous though I am not thinking of Alsatians at this moment. This factor can be activated instantaneously as a reflex to make me physiologically upset and cause appropriate behaviour as well, most likely, but not to cause any conscious mental acts or episodes which could be labelled as 'evaluating'.

So I see no reason to fudge or capitulate when faced with the objection that some occurrent emotional states do not include *occurrent* evaluations.

The backward-looking/forward-looking and approval/disapproval distinctions between emotions

While there will be occasion to discuss the backward-looking/forward-looking distinction[4] between emotions in some of the later chapters, it seems best to introduce the distinction in this chapter as it is based on the evaluative aspect of emotions. The distinction is one between emotions whose evaluation is of some present or future object or situation, real or imagined, that is forward-looking emotions, and emotions whose central evaluation is of something in the past, immediate or distant, real or imagined, that is backward-looking ones. An example of a forward-looking emotion is fear. Its evaluation, 'that is dangerous', anticipates some possible injury or harm in the future. An example of a backward-looking emotion is grief. Its evaluation, 'that is a grave loss or misfortune', reflects on some injury, harm or loss that has already occurred.

But in fact the distinction is not as neat and tidy as the above might lead one to believe, for there are instances of what are characteristically backward-looking emotions that are forward-looking. Grief, for example, can be about the future. One can anticipate a loss or misfortune and grieve about it. A mother who weeps when her son is condemned to death is at least partly grieving over the future loss of her son.

Though this is less clear, there do seem to be reasons for

[4] See Gordon (1969, Vol. LXVI, pp. 409ff.), Kenny (1963, pp. 72ff.).

supposing that characteristically forward-looking emotions might sometimes be backward-looking. Fright, which usually arises as the result of some present occurrence, may at times occur as a result of reflection on some past event which still frightens one, though one might argue that this is a case of a past occurrence relived and made present so that the fright is about a present event rather than a case of fright about a past occurrence. Love would normally be thought to be about present objects though it does seem that one might still love someone knowing that they are dead and while not believing in any form of afterlife. And in this example it seems implausible to claim that the person concerned is just reliving a past love made present or that one is loving a person made present in one's thoughts or imagination.

Nevertheless there is some reason to preserve a distinction to be found in the fact that emotions like fear, love and embarrassment are most often, and so characteristically, forward-looking, while grief and despondency and anger are characteristically backward-looking. This distinction will also be found useful, as we shall see in later chapters, as providing reasons for deviations on the part of particular emotions from the paradigm model of the emotions, and for explaining why we think of some emotions as less useful than others.

Another distinction between emotions which is basically a distinction in the evaluative aspect of different emotions is the approval–disapproval distinction.[5] Emotions such as love, joy and admiration seem to include an evaluation of their object which can be classed as a pro-evaluation or approval. Emotions such as hate, contempt and revulsion clearly include an evaluation of their object which is disapproving. And I think that this distinction is fairly tight. It is hard to think of an emotion whose evaluation does not fall into either the approval or disapproval category, and somehow includes an evaluation of the object as indifferent. One might think here that boredom, given that one could be said to have an emotion of boredom, might be an example, but one who is bored by something presumably has a negative attitude towards that thing and, in that wide sense, disapproves of it. If I am bored by a programme on television, it seems fair to say that I don't think much of the pro-

---

[5] Arnold and Gasson (1968, p. 206) have a version of this distinction, called positive and negative emotions. However they do not adequately identify this distinction as an evaluative one.

gramme. Ennui, again given that one could be said to be emotionally in a state of ennui, might be a stronger counter-example, but this may be so only because ennui does not seem to include an evaluation at all but to be a state of being without anything to interest one at all. One is not so much rating something as uninteresting as having nothing to interest one. It is a sort of boredom which does not entail being bored by anything but entails having nothing around to interest one either positively or negatively. Perhaps the reason why the approval–disapproval distinction between emotions seems tighter than most distinctions between emotions is that all emotions seem to include an evaluation, and an operative evaluation has to be either positive or negative. If it isn't, it disappears, or at least does not move us. An evaluation that never moves us will be one which does not give rise to an emotion and so will not be found among any list of emotions.

Finally, C. E. Cassin draws attention to a distinction which is sometimes drawn between emotions such as shame, envy, guilt and remorse which, it is claimed, presuppose moral values, and emotions such as fear, anger, love, despair and hatred which do not (Cassin, 1968, pp. 569–70). Cassin rightly suggests that the claim that the items on the first list of emotions always presuppose moral values, and the items on the second list non-moral values, is incorrect, though he does not take the matter much further. What is wrong with the distinction is clear enough. The values presupposed by the emotions on the first list must be at least stretched to include broader social but non-moral values and, at other times, squeezed to include narrower more intimate values. Shame might result from failing an examination, from a breach of good manners, from 'muffing' a toast, from failing to live up to someone's expectations. Guilt might be over regrettable non-moral shortcomings such as boasting or obtuseness. Similarly with the other emotions on the first list. On the other side, the supposed non-moral emotions can presuppose moral values. Love might be based on an attraction for the moral goodness of the beloved (presumably love of God and the saints is), hatred might be based on a belief about someone's wickedness, despair might be over one's sins and anger over someone else's. So all in all there is not much to be gained by pursuing that distinction any further.

5

The appetitive aspect of the emotions

The second most important aspect of the emotions is probably the appetitive aspect because, when present, and most emotions though not all seem to include this aspect, it will mirror and lead on from the evaluative aspect. For example, the fearful man's evaluation, 'this is dangerous', will lead on to a want or desire to avoid the danger or be rid of it. On the other hand the evaluation, 'that was a grave loss or misfortune', as forming part of sadness or grief, might not lead on to any desires. At any rate it is this aspect of emotions, the appetitive aspect, and why and when it is present in emotions, which I want to discuss here.

So, in detail, in this chapter I will argue:

(1) That some emotions contain an appetitive aspect;
(2) That the appetitive aspect is distinct from the evaluative but connected to it in two ways;
(3) That distinctions between emotions based on the evaluative aspect are reflected in the appetitive aspect;
(4) That there are distinctions between emotions directly related to the appetitive aspect.

That some emotions contain an appetitive aspect

That the concepts of some emotions entail the concepts of certain definite types of desires is suggested by the fact that some emotions are among those things that are put forward not merely as a motive in the sense of cause of an action but also as a motive in the sense of explanation, not merely for an action but for a particular sort of action. A soldier might explain to the military court why he did not go on patrol into enemy territory by saying that he was afraid. In such a case fear would be an adequate (though, for other reasons, perhaps not acceptable) explanation for his action, because it is understood that fear makes people want to avoid or be rid of danger by fleeing or avoiding going near the danger. Again, a son might explain to his father his extravagance in spending the whole of his monthly allowance on clothes for his girl friend by saying that he loved her. In such a case love would be an adequate (though, again, perhaps unacceptable) explanation of the extravagance, for it is known that love not merely issues forth into benevolent actions but is prone to acts of extravagant altruism.

Another reason for believing that the concepts of certain emotions include reference to desires is entailed by the fact that we believe that behaviour can reveal the presence of such emotions. It is precisely because intuitively we associate the emotion love with a certain tendency to centre one's activities around a single person, with acts of altruism, with a certain type of possessiveness, that we posit certain wants as part of the concept of love, say the desire to be in the presence of the beloved in preference to that of others, and to care for and please the beloved. To take another example, running away is a possible clue to the presence of fear because we believe that fear is one of the things that can cause us to run away, because in turn we explicitly or implicitly accept that fear gives rise to the desire to avoid some apprehended or presumed danger. But this connection between emotions and behaviour will be explored in some detail in a later chapter.

Finally there is a suggestion in the very positing of an evaluative core to the emotions that emotions will very often include appetitive aspects. This connection I will now endeavour to unravel.

The appetitive aspect is distinct from the evaluative aspect yet connected to it

It is most important to get rid of a basic objection that the appetitive aspect is not really distinct from the evaluative one, and so is not worth special treatment. For it might be argued that the evaluative aspect of the emotions is so tied up with the appetitive that there is no real distinction between the two, that is, that the evaluative aspect entails the appetitive aspect.

I would not want to deny that the evaluative aspect of the emotions leads on to and in that sense might be said to overlap the appetitive aspect. Indeed I will later stress this point as being one of the explanations of why behaviour which derives from the wants and desires of emotions can be said to be typical or appropriate to particular sorts of emotions. On the other hand I think that one can make out a case that the evaluative and appetitive aspects are logically separate. One reason for thinking this is that one seems to need a bridge of some sort to get from 'emotion x evaluates object o in manner m' to 'emotion x gives rise to want w in regard to o'. and a bridge implies a gap to be bridged. From 'evaluating the object as dangerous' to 'wanting to avoid or be rid of the dangerous object' one must appeal to some such psychological generalisation as 'one seeks to avoid what is dangerous'. This principle is not a logical tautology, for it does make sense to say that Fred evaluates o as dangerous but he does not want to be rid of o, for there are some who court danger or who feel that, while it might not be something to be positively courted, it is not something that one should shrink from or avoid.

Yet I would want to argue that a person who did not want to avoid or be rid of danger was a paradigm of the fearless person rather than of the fearful, and that in consequence one must see fear as present in just those cases when the evaluation that something was dangerous does lead on to the desire to avoid or be rid of the danger. In short this is a claim that there is a conceptual tie-up, though not a logical one, between 'X is dangerous' and 'a want to avoid or be rid of X', and that this tie-up forms part of the very concept of fear. For I do not think that a person is really in a state of fear till he, not merely believes he is in danger, but wishes ardently that he were not, that is, has a desire to avoid or be rid of the danger. (Though, as I have mentioned in the previous chapter, I think that a full clarification of the evaluative aspect of fear would be sufficient to separate it off from other emotions.) Cases of fear are just those cases of viewing something as dangerous which, given that we are rational, guide our wants in a certain direction and so, usually, our behaviour. On the other hand there are emotions, and I think grief is one of them, which do not seem to have any wants as part of their concept. The evaluation which is central to grief might be described as 'that was a grave loss or misfortune' with the implication that it is in some sense a loss or misfortune to the person making the evaluation. One would not want to deny that he was genuinely grieving, or that he was in any way irrational, if he also informed us that he had no particular wants in consequence of his evaluation. This is an indication that wants are not part of the concept of grief.

In the next section I will suggest a reason why such a dichotomy exists between emotions which have desires as part of their concept and those that do not.

I have suggested that, besides a causal connection, there is a rational connection between the evaluative and appetitive aspects of certain emotions. By a rational connection I mean that one can make out a case that 'our ordinary rational man' would find good reason for the desires associated with an emotion in the very evaluation he makes as part of that emotion. So it would be eminently rational for a man who evaluates something as dangerous to consider that this is good reason for him to want to avoid or be rid of this danger. Such an evaluation would count with him as both a sufficient reason and a cogent reason for such a want. Because our ordinary man does move rationally from the evaluative aspect of fear to its appetitive aspect, the ensuing principle 'one seeks to avoid what is dangerous' may be held to be a reasonably grounded psychological generalization. It is not a truism because there are genuinely fearless people but such people are in a minority, perhaps a very small minority.

I think, too, that the cases of emotions where there is a rational connection between the evaluative aspect and the appetitive aspect might well be co-extensive with those where wants form part of the concept of emotions, for we would not give a special 'part of the concept' label to cases of wants which were not predictable and constant, and, if this predictability is not because of a logical entailment, then it is a fair surmise, with people at any rate, that it will be because of a rational connection.

So, while it seems true that with certain emotions there is a rational tie-up between evaluations and desires, such that desires form part of the concepts of such emotions, it is equally clear that there are certain emotions where there is no such tie-up. This is another good reason for distinguishing the appetitive aspect of emotions from the evaluative aspect, and studying the connections between them.

That distinctions between the emotions based on the evaluative aspect are reflected in the appetitive aspect.

There is good reason to refer again to the backward-looking/forward-looking distinction between emotions in this chapter, for it seems to provide us with some reason why the concepts of certain emotions include wants but the concepts of other emotions do not.

We would expect to find that forward-looking emotions or the characteristic cases of forward-looking emotions include wants as part of their concept, for one would expect an evaluation about some present or future situation to lead us to do something in regard to the situation, or at least to formulate desires about the continuation or outcome of the situation. We have displayed this with fear. But grief directed to the past, say to the death of one's daughter, does not naturally lead one to want to do anything, for one cannot alter the past. One might have a general want, or rather *wish*, that things had been otherwise than they were. This wish may be futile but it is not illogical or impossible. However, that such a wish is futile is not sufficient reason to argue that it is not characteristic of grief and so not part of its concept. Such wishing is not irrational. Indeed, being aware of some grave loss or misfortune, as one is with grief, is good reason to wish that things were otherwise. So it could be that grief characteristically gives rise to such (admittedly futile) wishing. It may be that wishing plays the role in regard to backward-looking emotions which wanting does in regard to forward-looking ones. But at this point it might be objected that grief that one's daughter died last week does in fact lead naturally to desires to do things, such as to give her a decent burial, and comfort her father and brothers and sisters. But the impetus for these desires is not the evaluation, 'my daughter's death is a grave loss and misfortune to me', which is central to my grief, but the judgments 'giving someone dear to one a decent burial is right and proper and expected' and 'her father and brothers and sisters need comforting and I'm best able to do it', or similar ones which can be readily connected to the desires.

Ultimately, I think that the reason why we would say that grief does not have any desires as part of its concept is that it makes perfectly good sense for us to say '*X* grieves for *Y*' and '*X* has no desires deriving from his grief for *Y*'. There just are cases in which people grieve over something, and no desires, or behaviour stemming from them, are thereby generated. Grief seems to be mainly a reactive emotion rather than an active motivating one. It is the registering and reacting to one's loss; it is not a being-stirred-up-to-do-something emotion.

There are, of course, other distinctions between emotions related to the evaluative aspect which are in turn reflected in the appetitive aspect, such as the approval–disapproval distinction. Emotions, such as love, joy and admiration, which are approval emotions, because they evaluate their objects as good or pleasant or worthwhile in some respect, will give rise to desires to seek out the object. Opposed to these are disapproval emotions such as hate, disappointment, contempt and revulsion, which in general rate their objects negatively, and so give rise to desires to avoid the object. Some emotions, though categorisable as approval or disapproval emotions, may not give rise to desires at all. Grief, as we have seen, does not give rise to any characteristic desires, yet it is clearly a disapproval emotion for it evaluates its object as being a loss and misfortune. The reason for this is exterior to the approval–disapproval distinction and derives from its being a purely reactive, backward-looking emotion.

Distinctions between the emotions directly related to the appetitive aspect

Emotions could be divided in a way which is more directly related to the appetitive aspect. One way would be to see them as socially useful or socially useless. Emotions such as love and sympathy could be seen as bringing people together harmoniously because they give rise to desires to be with people and to help them, and so frequently to sociable and altruistic behaviour. On the other hand emotions such as hate, envy, jealousy and anger could be seen as socially divisive or anti-social as they give rise to desires to avoid others or even to wishes that they come to some misfortune, which in turn is at least more likely than not to lead to malicious and anti-social behaviour.

Again emotions could be divided into personally useful and useless emotions. Thus an emotion such as fear can be seen as giving rise to desires which are useful in protecting the fearful person from danger. An emotion such as envy may be seen as giving rise to desires which are personally useless because its characteristic wants are that someone's good fortune, which is seen as better than the envious person's, not last or be reversed. Most often the upshot of such desires will be either a disruption of the life of one or other, or both. Thus we speak of jealousy, envy and hate as eating away at the subject of these emotions, as well as being socially divisive. They occupy one's attentions and stop one doing something more positive and useful with one's time.

One could probably make a number of other distinctions between emotions related to their appetitive aspect. What is clear is that a great deal of what is typical and characteristic of the various emotions will be traceable to this aspect. Indeed, as we shall see in chapter 9, the various different forms of the typical and the characteristic in emotional behaviour will be a function of the strength and intimacy of the connection between the appetitive side of emotions and the resulting behaviour.

6

The objects of emotions

In this chapter I want to investigate the connection between an emotion and its object. As we shall see, what this connection amounts to will depend very much on what sense of the highly ambiguous term 'object' is being employed. So, in detail I want to argue that:

(1) Emotions have a formal object;
(2) Emotions have a particular object;
(3) Particular objects can be either material or intentional;
(4) Particular objects can be either illusory or non-illusory;
(5) The formal object sets limits on the possible particular objects of emotions.

The formal object of emotions

Let us start by once again considering the case of fear. It seems that, generally speaking,[1] one can make no sense of a fear that is not conceptually related to some danger or presumed danger for the reason that one says that a person is in a fearful state rather than some other state only if he admits to believing that he is in danger. It is no good saying 'I'm afraid' and then adding 'But I don't think I'm in danger' if one wants to be taken seriously. Yet one can say, logically, and seriously, 'I'm afraid but I don't know of what.' But, as I suggested earlier, even in such latter cases of so-called objectless emotions, we might still claim that there is a content to the fear. Generally speaking, then, there is a content to all fear, which could be generalised as 'the dangerous'. It is this generalised content to all fears that is called the formal object of fear. Although, as will emerge in the ensuing discussion, the term 'formal object' can be highly misleading and is somewhat of a misnomer.

[1] Though there are, of course, the cases of Pavlovian fear and the cases of fear based on conflicting beliefs, which I discussed in chapter 4.

An emotional state, then, is labelled as 'fear' rather than 'love' or 'grief' because the feelings, physiological changes and desires – and the ensuing behaviour if any – which form the state are believed to be the result of an evaluation that something is dangerous rather than that it is appealing (or good in the eyes of me, the lover), which would be the evaluation typical of love, or that it is a grave loss or misfortune, which would be the evaluation typical of grief. The categories 'the dangerous', 'the appealing' (or 'the good in my eyes') and 'the grave loss or misfortune' are what is called the formal object of fear, love and grief respectively. O. H. Green has suggested that 'the object or circumstances taken in the way which is appropriate to a given emotion might be called the *formal object* of that emotion' (Green, 1970, p. 553). Kenny (1963, pp.189 ff.) has called the formal object the 'appropriate' object, and explained that 'to assign a formal object to an action is to place restrictions on what may occur as the direct object of a verb describing the action.' This is where this notion is usually left but, for reasons which will emerge, I think that the matter can be put more precisely and informatively.

For a start, it is most important to realise that the formal object of an emotion seems to be the *evaluative* category under which the appraisal or evaluation of a particular object, material or intentional (these terms will be explained later), falls on a particular occasion. Indeed the fact that the particular evaluation or appraisal falls under the general evaluative category associated with an emotion as part of its definition or concept is our ultimate licence for saying that this emotional state is of such and such an emotion. That is when some sort of sifting of evidence or guesswork has revealed that the evaluative elements of these particular states can all be said to be of the same evaluative type, we say that they are all states of the same emotion. And the description of the *type* of the evaluation or appraisal is the kernel of the concept of the emotion in question. Thus an emotional state will be called 'fear' if its object is evaluated as dangerous, because the formal object, the general evaluative category appropriate to fear, is 'the dangerous'. Again, an emotional state would be called 'shame' if it could be categorised or pigeon-holed as an emotional reaction caused by the evaluation of oneself as guilty of some regrettable shortcoming, for 'guilt for some regrettable shortcoming' is the formal object of shame.

Now the formal object of an emotion is part of the concept of that emotion and in that sense is non-contingently related to it. No description of the concept of fear is correct unless it includes the word 'danger' or some synonym for it.

It might be objected, and by implication be held to impugn the whole notion of a formal object, that 'the dangerous' does not really capture the formal object of fear because one can evaluate something as dangerous and be, say, excited rather than afraid.

This objection does not take account of the fact that *all* cases of fear will be found to include the fearful person's evaluating the object of his fear as dangerous, while *only some* cases of excitement will be concerned with danger. No one denies that some people are excited by danger. A racing driver might evaluate driving in the Indianapolis 500 as a dangerous enterprise yet strive to take part. If this evaluation and the desire to experience the danger produce an emotion, then it is likely to be excitement. But not only dangerous situations are exciting. A person might be excited at the prospect of being taken to dinner at a posh restaurant or at the news that he has won the Pools.

But this objection does serve to make it clear that 'the dangerous' is at best only a very rough generalisation of the evaluative category peculiar to fear and to no other emotion. Fully to separate the evaluative aspects of fear and excitement one would have to go into more detail. At the least one would have to spell out the evaluation of the object of fear as not merely 'dangerous' but 'disagreeably so' as well, for the person who is excited, even if by danger, cannot claim to find the danger disagreeable. And this difference in the evaluative aspects of fear and excitement must be correct, otherwise how could one explain that a fearful person typically shuns the danger, but an excited person typically does not, when the danger is the object of his excitement.

Just as in chapter 4 we saw that, while the evaluative judgment 'He is a fine pianist' may be part of the evaluations giving rise both to admiration and to envy, it cannot be an adequate account of the evaluative aspects of both emotions, so now we can see that the judgment 'That is dangerous' may be part of the evaluative aspects of cases of fear and excitement, but cannot be an adequate account of both. So to refer to the formal object of an emotion is misleading, because in the first place it is not an object at all but a generalised evaluative category, and in the second place because it is only inadequately generalised as a rule. The formal objects in common use in philosophy and psychology are at best only very rough and ready accounts of the basic characteristics common to the particular evaluations in individual occurrences of an emotion. Strictly speaking the formal object of fear, being a generalisation of the evaluative aspects common to all cases of fear, should include mention not merely of 'the dangerous' but also, at least, that this is seen as 'disagreeably so'. An adequate generalisation should mention *all* the characteristics which are common to the things which are being drawn up into a type or class by the generalisation. 'The dangerous' clearly does not do this in the case of fear, and we have seen that other commonly used formal objects, those for admiration, envy and excitement, fail in a similar way.

On the other hand there is some use for the term when properly understood. Ideally, stating the formal object involves giving an adequate account of the general category under which the object (given that there is one) is evaluated in any case of a particular emotion. And this gives one a quick reference point for defining and distinguishing emotions, and, in general, for understanding the working of any emotion, for it is the evaluative aspect which is central to each emotion.

I suggest that it might be a failure to take account of the notion of a formal object, misleading though it might be, that has led J. R. S. Wilson into arguing 'that the notion of a non-contingent relation [between an emotion and its object] rests upon a confusion' (Wilson, 1972, p. 177). He argues rather that the connection between an emotion and its object is causal. Because Wilson has more or less discarded talk about formal objects (though I think he in fact makes use of a similar concept, as we shall see), he does not appear to consider that what his opponents may mean by a non-contingent relation between emotion and object is the non-contingent relation between the concept of an emotion and its *formal* object. For this latter view is compatible with Wilson's view that there is a contingent causal connection between an emotion and its object, for by 'object' here I think Wilson is referring to particular (material) object.

While, as we shall see, a material object, being a particular spatiotemporal item can be the cause of an emotional state, a formal object can not. It seems to be a category mistake to say that the general evaluative category, under which certain particular spatio-temporal objects come to be appraised or evaluated, caused my emotional state. A formal object (which, strictly speaking, should always be written as formal 'object'), being an evaluative category, is a generalisation, a type description, not an instantiation of that description or a token. So it is not spatio-temporal nor particular, two requirements for something being a cause. A formal object, being a type or category, is in a different sphere of discourse from particular items and causal talk. On the other hand, evaluative categories, being concepts, can have a non-contingent conceptual connection with the *concepts* of emotions, and so there is a sense in which there is a non-contingent relation between emotion and object; indeed, as we have seen, the formal objects of emotions are part of the *defining* concepts of particular emotions.

Like Green and Kenny, Wilson himself seems to have made use of a loose version of the notion of formal object, except that he has not used the phrase 'formal object'. Wilson writes:

> If I describe an emotion in terms of the *kind* of item anything which was its object would have to be, I am not thereby referring to its object, any more than in describing a template in terms of the kind of thing it would fit round, I am referring to any particular thing it would fit round [Wilson, 1972, p. 98].

I think that Wilson's template is also a *loose* version of the notion of formal object. It is loose because it does not make mention of the fact that an essential aspect of this template is that it is evaluative. The kind of object which an object of fear has to be is a dangerous one, and 'dangerous' is an evaluative category, though this one happens to be more objectively grounded than most. The evaluative nature of the formal object will be seen more clearly with an emotion like love whose object has to be 'appealing' in a certain sense. There is no denying here that 'appealing' does not readily serve as a description enabling anyone to pick out anything. If I ask someone to go into the next room and pick out what is appealing, it will depend entirely on whether he picks out what is appealing to him or to me, or appealing under this aspect or that, as to what he brings back. The template which is at the heart of the concept of particular emotions is an evaluative one, not a purely descriptive one, though, as we have seen, the evaluation has a cognitive base and sometimes the two are connected closely.

Perhaps all these difficulties, largely a matter of being misled by the term 'formal object', might be avoided in the future if the term 'general evaluative category' or 'evaluative template' is substituted for it, or mentioned alongside it.

The particular object of emotions

I have been arguing about the nature of the formal 'object' of an emotion. Now it is time to introduce the notion of a particular object. The particular object of an emotion is always some particular item – such as a thing, a person or animal, an event, or the content of one's own beliefs or imaginings, to name a few possibilities – which is the target or focus of an actual emotional state.

Now the claim that emotions have a formal object might be thought to imply that an emotion must also possess a particular object, for it might be argued that there must be a connection between the notion of an evaluative component of an emotion and the claim that any actual emotional state of that emotion must be focussed upon a particular object. For, if an emotion must have a formal object, and if a formal object is a general evaluative category under which falls each particular evaluation that is part of actual states of that emotion, then it may seem as if particular emotional evaluations must be evaluations of something particular, that is of particular objects. For it does seem to be a very odd claim to say that this emotional state of fear, for example, includes an evaluation of the situation but is not an evaluation of any particular item. How can one evaluate without evaluating anything particular? An evaluation must have a focus or target which is rated or evaluated.

At this point we are confronted once again with cases where emotional states appear not to be focussed on any particular object. Our examples of such objectless emotions were fear and depression of certain sorts, and perhaps happiness on certain occasions as well. For there do seem to be well attested cases of people being afraid or depressed but also being unable to pick out anything, real or illusory, as the particular object of the fear or depression. That is, there are cases of emotional states which appear to have no focus or target of any sort and so certainly nothing which could be called a particular object or target. They are, so to speak, emotions aimed out at the world but ones that do not come to rest in any one spot or on any one thing.

These seemingly diverse and opposed positions, that emotions have formal objects which implies that particular emotional states must include evaluations of particular objects, and that on the other hand there do seem to be cases of objectless emotions, can be reconciled. In the first place the notion of a formal object or general evaluative category of an emotion would only imply that a particular evaluation be part of any emotional state of that emotion, not that the particular evaluation has a particular object, if by the term 'particular' one means single clearly describable item. So, secondly, we must admit that there is still a basic lack of clarity about the meaning of the term 'particular' in the phrase 'particular object' in this context. The term 'particular' in the phrase 'particular object' does not imply that a single or simple item be focussed on or that the item be capable of being described in any definite way. The term merely implies that the emotional state is about something rather than nothing, though this something might be vague, inexpressible, imponderable and the content of a false belief. On the other hand, it might on occasion be something which can be picked out and described quite clearly and succinctly. Thirdly, if the particular object is a material one, this will imply, as we shall see, that the something is spatio-temporal in the broad sense, that it occurs in the world, that it is a token not a type.

So, as I have suggested previously, objectless emotions are only objectless in that they do not have a particular object which can be *expressed*, if at all, clearly and succinctly, or *localised*. For example, objectless fear or depression might be focussed on something like one's consciously or subconsciously realised ignorance or inability to cope with the situation; that is, the object is complex and difficult to describe: one's inability to cope with the situation or, perhaps, one's inability to cope with life itself. A particular object is not merely just not nothing, it is something which can be focussed on sufficiently for one to evaluate it as, say, dangerous or futile. To that extent it is something that the subject of the emotional state has picked out, consciously or subconsciously.

Finally it is worth noting that not all emotions can have objectless instances. Certain emotions, such as love and hate, are always directed at a particular object in a rather circumscribed sense, namely at individuals, whether they be humans, animals, or, though this will be discussed, perhaps plants and inanimate objects. Love and hate do not seem to be able to get going unless focussed on something quite definite, locatable and expressible. It seems more than just odd in the sense of eccentric to say 'I'm in love but with whom or what I don't know' or 'I hate something but I'm unable to say who or what it is.' One might speak of being full of love or hate yet not being so about anything in particular. But here one is surely speaking dispositionally, implying that at the moment one feels able (or even prone) to love practically anyone one comes across or that one is in such a dark mood as to feel hate for anyone who crosses one's path.

So the particular object of emotions is something which is particular only in the sense that it can be focussed on by the evaluation at the centre of some particular emotional state. And when it is a material object, it is a spatio-temporal item in a broad sense, a token not a type. Pitcher gives his version of the claim that emotions have a particular object in the following way:

> Note that I thus use the expressions 'having an object' and 'being directed towards an object' very broadly: when I say that an emotion is directed towards an object I do not necessarily mean that there is some individual thing, person, or animal towards which it is directed. If a person is standing on a swaying bridge and is afraid of falling into the gorge, there is no individual *thing*, in the sense of physical object, person, animal, etc., that is the object of his fear. Still, there is a reference to something beyond the person himself, or beyond his present state, or at least beyond the emotion itself [Pitcher, 1965, pp. 326–7].

What one may need to modify in Pitcher's account of the particular object which every emotional state must include is his suggestion that it be a reference to 'something beyond the person himself, or beyond his present state'. This is surely untrue. As we shall see in the last section of this chapter, shame is a reflex emotion, which is focussed on the person himself having the emotion. And embarrassment is an emotion which refers to one's present state not beyond it. As we shall see in the very next section, Pitcher has probably been misled by the overtones of solidity and otherness conveyed by the word 'object'.

Material and intentional objects

Most philosophers who make a distinction between material and intentional objects embark on a long discussion of the nature of intentionality, carefully distinguishing this term from the term 'intensionality', and by reference to substantival expressions in certain grammatical positions in a sentence and the application or reference of these expressions, derive a very obscure account of the notion of an intentional object. This distinction is then made to bear the burden of several levels of significance; namely about the existential status of objects, about whether the subject of a psychological or intentional state or activity has correct beliefs about this object or not, and how the psychological or intentional state or activity is affected depending on whether the subject's beliefs are correct or not. I want to try and obviate the immense difficulties of building all these levels into the one distinction by simply reducing the material/ intentional object distinction to one about the existential status of the object. The other two levels will be built into a separate distinction, the non-illusory/illusory object distinction, which will be discussed in the next section.

So the distinction which I am aiming at by a material/intentional object distinction in the context of emotions is one between actually existing things, or 'material objects', though these are not necessarily composed of matter in the physicist's sense, and things which turn out not actually to exist. And for my purposes at any rate, I think that this distinction can be best made by concentrating on the notion of material object, which is easier to define, and then simply defining intentional objects as all the remaining types of particular objects of psychological states or activities. I shall define the distinction so that it is exhaustive of all types of particular object and no other types remain. I will also limit my discussion of this distinction to the context of emotions, for it is on the nature of emotion that I am trying to shed light.

First let us take an example of this simplified distinction at work. If I fear that the bomb in the package over there will go off at any moment, and if the package really contains a bomb which is primed and about to go off, then my fear has a material object. What I focus on and evaluate is an accurately described, real bomb which is about to go off. The particular object of my fear really exists in the world. If on the other hand the bomb turns out to be a pair of old boots wrapped in newspaper, then the object of my fear, 'the bomb', is an intentional object in some way manufactured by my mind. For what in fact I have focussed on and evaluated is a pair of old boots in newspaper, misdescribed by me as a bomb. And again, it should be remembered that a material object need not be material in the way a bomb is, for an electric charge, a field of force, a person's attitude, an utterance . . . can all be material objects. The sense of 'material' that is being used is closer to the sense of 'materialised' meaning 'turned out to be the case in the world'.

Though I will discuss the non-illusory/illusory object distinction in the next section, it is important to note at the outset that the intentional-object/material-object distinction does not run parallel with the non-illusory/illusory object distinction. Not all intentional objects are illusory. Take the following example. If I love my dear departed grandmother, the particular object of my grief, my granny, is an intentional object, because she no longer exists. It is an intentional object, because it does not pass the test for a material object, namely that the description under which the object is focussed upon and evaluated is instantiated in the world. 'Does there exist something in the world which answers the description "my grandmother"?' 'No'. Then the object is an intentional one. But this does not mean that the object of my love, my grandmother, is illusory, for I do know that she is dead. The particular object of my love is not other than I supposed it to be, at least in respect of its status as a material or intentional object.

But I shall get back to the non-illusory/illusory object distinction in a moment. First I want to sharpen the material-object/intentional-object distinction a little more. This might be done in the following way:

> Where p is a proposition and A is a term or description, one could sort sentences, which ascribe intentional psychological states or acts, M, to a person, into two basic types:
>
> (a) Fred M's that p. e.g. 'Fred believes that it is raining;
> (b) Fred M's A. e.g. 'Fred loves his grandmother'.

If, for the sake of simplicity, we now restrict attention to (b), as this is generally the form of sentences ascribing emotions to people, then a (b) sentence will ascribe a *material* object to Fred's psychological state or act, such as an emotion, if and only if:

> (c) $(\exists x)$ (Fred M's x and x is A)
> where the 'is' is best taken to mean 'is the actually existing referent of'.

Thus, if we take our three previous examples:

> (i) 'I am afraid of the bomb' when there is a bomb;

(ii) 'I am afraid of the bomb', when there is no bomb;

(iii) 'I love my grandmother' but she is dead;

then, using our test, (c) above, it will follow that, (i) ascribes a material object to my fear, because there is an actually existing bomb and it is what I fear and is also the referent of my description of what I fear, 'the bomb'; (ii), on the other hand, ascribes an intentional object to my fear because there is no actually existing thing which is both what I fear and is the referent of my description of what I fear, 'the bomb'; (iii) ascribes an intentional object to my love because there is no actually existing thing which is both what I love and is the referent of my description of what I love, 'my grandmother'.

Non-illusory/illusory object distinction

While the material-object/intentional-object distinction has its use, as a way of sorting out the existential status of objects, traditionally this distinction has been made to carry much more weight than this, being used also to sort out difficulties about having correct beliefs about the object as well as difficulties about psychological states or activities based upon correct or incorrect beliefs about the objects of such states or activities. I believe that one is more likely to sort out these latter difficulties if one removes the burden of sorting them out to a separate distinction. In the past, what I will call the non-illusory/illusory distinction has been conflated with, and made to form part of the material/intentional object distinction. I want to distinguish them.

Now the illusory/non-illusory object distinction is, in the first place, partly an epistemological one. The distinction is partly between having correct beliefs about the objects of one's psychological states or activities, including beliefs about their existential status, or not. But the distinction is also partly to do with the grounding of these psychological states or activities upon those beliefs. So it has two levels. I might love my grandmother even though she is dead. If I know she is dead, yet still love her, then the object of my love is non-illusory. On the other hand I might love my grandmother, believing she is alive, when in fact she is dead. Now, if my love for my grandmother is conditional upon her being alive, such that my love for her would cease if I knew she was dead, then the object of my love is illusory. If, however, my love for my grandmother is not conditional on her being alive, and would not cease if I found out that she was dead, then the object of my love is not illusory.

I retain this distinction among those to do with the object of emotions because the upshot of this interplay between beliefs about the object and the ensuing psychological attitude to the object is illusion or non-illusion *about the object*. Just as mirages are strictly speaking failures of recognition, they are also in an important sense illusory objects.

But let me try and sharpen up this distinction in the following way.

> Where M is a psychological or intentional activity or state, and A is a term or description, and P is a set which includes the existential status and properties of A, then employing again our (b) sentence of the form, 'Fred M's A', we can say that A is a *non-illusory* object if and only if
>
> (d) 'A has status and properties P, F believes that A has P, and P is the basis of F's M.'

This will become clearer when, making use of our test (d), we see how it works with the following examples, where the 'believing that ...' clauses give the ground for the M activities or states (in these examples, Fred's love):

> (i) 'Fred loves Marcia' believing she is alive, when she is not;
> (ii) 'Fred loves Marcia' believing her to be a woman, when she is not;
> (iii) 'Fred loves Marcia' believing she is kind, and she is;
> (iv) 'Fred loves Desdemona' believing that she actually exists, when she is only a fictional entity.

(i) ascribes an illusory object to Fred's love because Marcia does not have the existential status of actually existing which Fred believes she has and which his love is conditional upon; (ii) ascribes an illusory object to Fred's love, because Marcia has not the property of being a woman, which Fred believes she has and which his love is conditional upon; (iii) ascribes a non-illusory object to Fred's love because Marcia has the property of being kind which Fred believes she has and which his love is conditional upon; (iv) ascribes an illusory object to Fred's love because Desdemona has not the existential status of actually existing, which Fred believes she has and which his love is conditional upon.

There are, of course, almost infinite possibilities to the ways in which one can be mistaken about the object of one's emotion such that this affects one's emotion (or other psychological activity or state). Only one of these ways will be to imagine the object to be a material or actually existing one when it is not. That is why in the previous section I hived off that distinction from this one. The important distinction for the understanding of the emotions is really the illusory/non-illusory object distinction for this sheds light upon the way our supposed factual beliefs about the object of our emotion can affect the stability of our emotion when these beliefs, which form the ground for the emotion, turn out to be mistaken. If our emotions have non-illusory objects it means that they are based upon correct beliefs about the object; if not, that they are based upon incorrect beliefs about the object. This might be made more tangible by a consideration of the term 'infatuation'. One sense of the term 'infatuation' is, I think, that one's love is based upon mistaken beliefs about the object. Everyone else realises that she is cruel, selfish and vain. I think she is kind, altruistic and modest, and base my love of her upon this. My love will be real but since its object is illusory – given that all the others are right about her and I am wrong – my love will probably not last, as I will find out the truth one day. This is why we also consider 'infatuation' to be a sort of failure term; it refers to a love that cannot last because it is so badly grounded. Hence, 'infatuation' is also a pejorative term. We speak of someone's love as infatuation because we not merely think that it won't last but because we think it is shallow, that is, badly grounded.

Wilson has suggested (Wilson, 1972, pp. 97ff.) that it might be better to discard any distinction at all between the different objects of emotions, and instead to talk only about the grounding or foundation of emotions. Thus emotions which are badly grounded in beliefs will be malfounded, and ones which are not so will be well-founded or properly grounded. But to make a malfounded/well-founded distinction between emotions, one has eventually to spell out the difference by reference to mistaken beliefs about the nature or status of *objects*, such as misdescriptions, misidentifications, mislocations, misevaluations, and such like, which generate illusory objects or views of objects. So a wellfounded/malfounded emotions distinction is not distinct from the non-illusory/illusory object distinction, or not wholly so, for it incorporates it. It makes use of the non-illusory/illusory object distinction by explaining that mal-founded emotions are just those ones which have illusory objects, and wellfounded ones and those which do not. One could, of course, make the distinction between wellfounded and malfounded emotions without mentioning the terms 'illusory' and 'non-illusory' but I cannot see that one could do so without explicitly or implicitly making use of the concepts. And if one has to make use of the concepts, why not refer to them explicitly and in as clear a way as possible? The wellfounded/malfounded distinction is not in competition with the illusory/non-illusory one but it can be argued that the former needs the latter.

Although I have argued that the objects of emotions may be either non-illusory or illusory, the emotions are not illusory. Jim's love for Frieda may be based on a misdescription of her which in turn gives rise to a misevaluation of her, such that his view of Frieda is false and illusory, but this is no ground for thinking that the emotion of love which Jim has toward Frieda as a result of his beliefs and evaluations about her is illusory. The emotion is real, as it actually took place, but it is malfounded because it is based on mistaken beliefs or evaluations. We might want to label it as super-ficial but we cannot say it is not genuine.

The limits imposed on the particular objects of emotions

Fear is one of the most catholic of emotions. Practically anything seems to be an object of fear, at least for someone, though we do brand some fears as neurotic and so as phobias. But the objects of phobias are illusory objects and so give rise to malfounded fears. They are objects which *should* not be feared rather than ones which cannot be feared. In discussing the limits set by the formal object or general evaluative category associated with a particular sort of emotion, I am concerned with finding out what *cannot* be feared or loved or hated, or *cannot* be the object of shame or embarrassment.

Anthony Quinton writes that

> to love someone, in the personal way in which this means more than simply to like them very much, as one might a house or a car, is to identify oneself with the interests of the object of love. So only those beings that literally have interests, in other words persons in the restricted sense, can be loved [Quinton, 1973, p. 105].

If Quinton is right, we must look to the core part of the emotion love, its formal object or general evaluative category, for a reason why this might or might not be so. Love, as I have previously suggested, seems to evaluate its object as 'the appealing' or 'the good in my, the lover's, eyes', but this is clearly not sufficient. Pure physical appeal for a person tends to generate sexual attraction rather than the attraction deriving from love, though physical attraction might be part of the attraction due to love, and sexual attraction might on occasion be a powerful ally of love. I suspect that Quinton is right in implying that a genuine lover must evaluate the person of the beloved, not just the surface physical attributes, and that the person includes reference to, besides personality traits, interests. So for 'appealing' one should substitute something like 'appealing in a personal sense'.

But in granting this I do not think that we limit love to humans. Animals will have some sort of personality and clearly have interests of a basic variety, such as interests in survival and not being cruelly treated. However, we have only to consider how odd it would be to claim to love a plant to realise that personal involvement is needed for the claim to be in love. With an individual plant this seems impossible because plants cannot communicate or express themselves to us in such a way that *individual* personalities and individual interests could emerge. Thus the feeling of oddness, and linguistic oddness when such claims are expressed, is a sign that certain objects, such as plants and inanimate things, fall outside the limits imposed on the possible objects of love by its formal object.

Embarrassment seems even more circumscribed than love. I don't think one could be embarrassed by what one does in the presence of a dog (though some people might be embarrassed by what a dog does!) much less by a plant or inanimate thing, because that sort of embarrassment seems to involve interpersonal interplay of a very sophisticated order. Embarrassment at one's own actions involves awareness or belief about someone else's view of one. We are embarrassed when we think we have lost face or made a fool of ourselves or committed a *faux pas*, that is, when we think we have done something that makes others think less of us. Because of this reflexive parameter to embarrassment, there can be no emotion of self-embarrassment, though there can be an emotion of self-love. We can evaluate ourselves as appealing to ourselves in a way which includes our personality and have a strong desire to forward our own interests. We cannot evaluate ourselves as having made a fool of ourselves in front of ourselves, or evaluate ourselves as having lost face in front of ourselves. You cannot make a fool of yourself in solitary confinement. Embarrassment at ourselves, and I think at what someone else does, is to do with our public persona and its supposed debasement.

To take a final example, the general evaluative category or template of shame might be described as a person believing that he is guilty of some regrettable shortcoming. In contrast to embarrassment, shame can be isolated. The person in solitary confinement, the person alone, can feel shame. On the other hand one's shame might be and, perhaps, most often is affected by what others think of what one has done. Though shame can be generated by feeling guilty about something we have done, shame is often generated by others making us feel guilty about what we have done. We might be shamed by others by being caught *in flagrante delicto*. Or, if we respect them, and realise that our action offends their ideals or standards, but not our own, we might feel shame only if they find out about our action. Shame seems to be set going by a realization that one has failed to do what is right by failing to live up to some set of ideals or standards, personal or shared. The object of shame, then, is acts offending against standards, chiefly our own acts but not always. One can feel ashamed of actions which are ours by proxy. One can feel shame or be ashamed of what others, associated with us, such as relatives, friends and colleagues, have done. We cannot be ashamed of what Nixon has done unless we are related to him or worked in his administration or endorsed him in some way. So the object of shame is actions in some respect owned by us, which have offended against some standards or ideals acknowledged by us or those we love or respect.

So the general evaluative category or template peculiar to each emotion, its formal object, not merely gives a particular flavour to the wants, desires and behaviour stemming from that emotion, it limits the emotion to a particular set of objects. To see this from the other direction, one could say that the emotions are specialised reactions limited to our view of certain portions of the world or to certain segments of our performance in the world.

7

Physiological changes and the emotions

In this chapter I want to attempt to analyse a particularly neglected area in the philosophy of the emotions, the relations between physiological changes and emotions. I should remark that it is philosophers, not psychologists, who tend to neglect this aspect of the emotions. As I suggested in the introductory chapters, in philosophy the Cartesian view of the emotions has generally held the stage, and in recent years philosophers have concentrated almost exclusively on emotions as if they were purely internal mental events. Thus they have concentrated on puzzles to do with the cognitive and evaluative aspects of the emotions and their relation to the objects of emotions, often, as we have seen, in a way that did not adequately distinguish the evaluative strand from the purely cognitive. Excepting their denial that emotions are feelings, philosophers have had very little to say about the 'bodily motions' part of emotions, particularly in recent times, even though, somewhat ironically, it is this very aspect of emotions which distinguishes them from being just beliefs and desires of certain sorts.

So in this and the next chapter I will concentrate on these bodily aspects, the physiological changes and feelings. In detail, I will attempt in this chapter to clarify the physiological aspect by

(1) Trying to elucidate what exactly is to be understood by the term 'physiological change' in the context of an emotion;

(2) Showing that particular physiological changes are not part of the concept of any particular emotion and are only linked causally to the cognitive–evaluative–appetitive part of an occurrent emotional state;

(3) Showing, however, that the notion of a physiological change is part of the concept of an emotional state as such;

(4) And, finally, by drawing out some consequences of this analysis regarding the connection between physiological changes and feelings, and physiological changes and the observability of emotions.

The term 'physiological change' in the context of an emotion

First a brief explanation of my use of the term 'physiological change' rather than the more usual phrases 'physiological disturbance' or 'bodily upset'.[1] I am chary of using terms such as 'disturbance' or 'upset' as they may lead one into the dual error of thinking that all physiological changes associated with emotion are of an alarming or disturbing nature and that all bodily changes associated with emotion are experienced by the subject of them. When, in discussing quotations from other philosophers, I do use such terms as 'physiological disturbance' and 'bodily upset', I wish them to be neutral as regards such suggestions.

What exactly is meant by the phrase 'physiological changes'? I think that Goshen, in his article 'A Systematic Classification of the Phenomenology of Emotions', gives a useful catalogue of the sort of thing which this phrase refers to:

> The physiological phenomena which occur during the actual period of time in which the individual is experiencing an emotion (e.g. fear) include: increased pulse rate, increased respiratory rate, increased muscle tone, pupillary dilation and peripheral vascular changes such as flushing, sweating or pallor. The gastrointestinal tract might also exhibit increased levels of motility. The individual subjectively experiences certain sensations including muscular tension, tightness of the throat, dryness of the mouth and increased levels of alertness. The overall impression, psychologically, is that of an adrenergic response [Goshen, 1967, p. 488].

There are two points to notice here. In the first place, Goshen seems to mention only the unusual physiological changes which could be called disturbances or upsets. He should also have made mention of the physiological changes such as a *decreased* pulse rate and *decreased* respiratory rate, for there seems to be no good reason for believing that these do not also occur in emotional states, when, for example, a person is very happy and feeling unusually calm. Again, ennui,

[1] See for example, Alston (1967a, pp. 481–2).

may involve a decreased pulse and respiratory rate, and muscular relaxation. It may prove to be the case that the majority of the changes linked with emotions show an increase of physiological activity rather than a decrease. Indeed, intuitively, this would seem to be the case. But since this is a purely empirical matter, and since there is no reliable evidence to this effect, it must be left open.[2]

Then, as a second point, Goshen seems to hint at but not carry through an important distinction when listing the physiological changes associated with emotion. The distinction is that between physiological changes which we are subjectively aware of and necessarily so, those which we are necessarily not aware of, and finally those of which we may or may not be aware depending on the circumstances. The subject must always be aware of tightness of the throat, dryness of the mouth, and perhaps, an increased level of alertness if these are feelings, for you cannot have unfelt feelings, that is feelings of which one is unaware. On the other hand it may be possible to define all these terms without reference to feelings. There seem to be no items in Goshen's list of which we are necessarily unaware. The only possible candidates for this category seem to be pupillary dilation and pallor; with the stipulation that there is no mirror about! But the very fact that such a stipulation must be introduced means that they are not really candidates for items of which we are necessarily (logically or empirically) unaware. So, the other items listed by Goshen appear to fall reasonably clearly into the third category, namely the physiological changes which we may or may not be aware of depending on the circumstances. We can feel increased pulse rate, increased respiratory rate, flushing, sweating, muscular tension, and, probably, increased muscle tone and an increased level of motility in the gastrointestinal tract, and we can observe our pupillary dilation and pallor in a mirror; but it is also the case that all these changes can occur without our being aware of them, for example when asleep, unconscious, or drugged, or simply when our attention is wholly occupied by what is going on around us, or (in the case of pupillary dilation and pallor) we have no mirror about.

It is important to note that, in this chapter, I am only concerned

---

[2] There seems in fact to be reasonably well tested evidence about relaxing emotions. The activation of the parasympathetic nervous system seems to be the core of the physiological changes part of some emotional states. See G. Dumas (1948b), esp. pp. 116–18; and Izard (1972, Ch. 1).

with the physiological changes of which the subject may or may not be aware depending on the circumstances. I am only interested in the category of bodily changes which *can* exist without the subject of the changes being aware of them. The other category of bodily changes, from which some items on Goshen's list are drawn, includes bodily sensations, and the discussion of these I will defer to the next chapter. However, towards the end of this chapter, I will briefly discuss whether there is any connection between physiological changes and the bodily feelings which occur more or less simultaneously.

A final preliminary remark. It is important to stress that the word 'unusual' is to be understood whenever the phrase 'physiological change' is mentioned in connection with the emotions. Some physiological changes are always going on in our body but the ones which are linked with emotions are both noticeable and unusual. We do not link emotions with such things as a pulse rate, a respiratory rate and a skin colour but with an *increased* pulse rate or a *decreased* respiratory rate or an *unusual* colouring such as occurs with blushing.

However in that sense of 'unusual' the physiological changes resulting from feeling very cold or tired or from just having finished a 100 metre sprint are also unusual. How then do the physiological changes associated with emotion differ from these? They differ in two ways. In the first place they differ in terms of their causal ancestry. The physiological changes associated with feeling cold, such as shivering and going blue, result from a person's being too long in a very cold temperature and physiologists can trace the causal connections. The physiological changes associated with being emotional are those which result from a person's evaluation of his situation and neurophysiologists and experimental psychologists are beginning to trace out the causal links. A person can be very cold and embarrassed at the same time yet it is possible to separate off at least some of the physiological changes associated with feeling cold from those associated with being afraid by tracing the causal connections involved in each state. Even those untutored in physiology can work out that when a naked man who is a member of the Icebergs' Club and has just emerged from his midwinter dip in the icy river blushes, and his blushing coincides with the appearance of his boss's wife on the river bank, the blushing should not be put down to the cold but to embarrassment.

Secondly the physiological changes associated with emotions differ in kind from those associated with feeling cold, tired or over-exercised at least to the extent that they form a recognisable set which differs from the sets associated with these other physiological conditions, though there may be overlap between the sets. Physiologically there is a definite limit to the physiological changes which evaluative attitudes can give rise to and so these physiological changes form a recognisable set. No emotion, for example, can make us go blue or freeze our joints in the way that low temperatures can, and no amount of exposure to low temperatures can make us blush. As we have seen, neurophysiologists and experimental psychologists tell us that by and large the physiological changes associated with emotion are those which can be triggered off by activity in the limbic system of the brain, which in turn causes activity in the hypothalamus, and so by and large are those changes associated with discharges or other divergences from the normal equilibrium state of the autonomic (sympathetic and parasympathetic) nervous systems.

Particular physiological changes and the cognitive–evaluative–appetitive part of an occurrent emotional state

It is not an uncommon view among psychologists and philosophers that there is a characteristic core-pattern of physiological changes unique to each particular emotion and that, unless there were such a core-pattern, we would never recognise emotions in others.[3] A more radical view along these lines (which was held, as we have seen, by J. B. Watson) would be to say that the word 'fear' or the word 'love' is the label of a distinctive core-pattern of physiological changes such that in recognising a particular physiological pattern in another we are recognising the particular emotion he or she is undergoing.

As these views concern an empirical matter, it is important to refer to the experimental evidence concerning them. Schachter and Singer, in their article 'Cognitive, Social, and Physiological Determinants of Emotional State', give a short survey of the experimental evidence both in favour of and against the above views and conclude that, while the matter is empirically still 'an open question'[4] (Schachter and Singer, 1962, pp. 379–80) 'the numerous

[3] For example, Arnold (1960, Vol. 1, and p. 179).   [4] See also Schachter (1970).

studies on physiological differentiators of emotional states have, viewed en masse, yielded quite inconclusive results. Most, though not all, of these studies have indicated no differences among the various emotional states' (Schachter and Singer, 1962, p. 397).[5] Goshen takes a more definite standpoint about the conclusion to be drawn from the experiments. He writes that 'When the different types of emotion (e.g. fear *versus* anger) are examined minutely in respect of physiological changes only, there does not appear to be any significant difference, so that physiological distinctions between differing emotions are only quantitative, and not qualitative' (Goshen, 1967, pp. 488–9).

While the experimental evidence so far available seems to give little or no comfort to the view that there is a pattern of physiological changes peculiar to each emotion, Goshen's conclusion does seem rather sweeping. For, while there is a reasonable presumption in favour of there being a core-pattern of physiological changes common to many emotions (occurrent emotional states), and while there is no solid evidence that there is any pattern of changes peculiar to each emotion, there are physiological changes which seem to be found more often in one group of emotions than in others. Perhaps this is what Goshen means by there being 'quantitative differences' only among the various emotions, though this phrase does not really capture the point I am making. To take an example, weeping (the activation of the tear ducts) seems to occur more often with occurrent states of grief, fear and elation than with, say, the occurrent states of disgust, hate or envy.

In a brief comment in his article 'Emotion and Feeling', Alston gives us a more philosophical reason for not equating bodily upsets (as he calls physiological changes) with emotion. He argues that if emotions were considered to be bodily upsets then we would seem to be landed with the unacceptable conclusion that love, fear, jealousy and other emotions are just the same sort of thing as stomach upsets and startled reactions.[6] We could no longer give reasons for saying that queasiness is not an emotion or that love is not just a bodily upset. One could continue along Alston's line of

---

[5] This was also the result of the later attempts to distinguish at least some emotions, in particular fear and anger, by reference to the excretion of adrenaline and noradrenaline. See Marianne Frankenhaeuser (1975, esp. pp. 218–22).

[6] Alston (1967a, p. 485): regarding this argument, I would like to suggest that one sense of 'startled reaction' (reacting with alarm at something apprehended and evaluated) is more akin to an emotion than to a stomach upset.

thought by saying that if we made such an equation then there would be no point in having a term 'emotion' because there would be no difference between this term and the term 'bodily upset'. But this type of argument cannot be conclusive about such an empirical matter for it just may be the case that through ignorance we have in our language two terms, 'emotion' and 'bodily upset', for one and the same thing.

The matter seems to have dried up more or less at that point. In recent years, whenever a philosopher has considered the relation between physiological changes and emotions, a rare enough event, he seems to have assumed that the evidence from experiments is that there is no relation at all between physiological changes and emotion. I want to make out a case that, while there is no conceptual link between the notion of any particular physiological change or any pattern of physiological changes and the concept of any particular emotion, there is a causal connection between the cognitive–evaluative–appetitive part of an emotional state and the concomitant physiological changes.

Schachter and Singer point out in their article that subjects excited by an injection of adrenaline (epinephrine), given in such a way that the patients did not realise that they were being injected with a drug, did not report having emotions till they were put in a context of euphoria or anger (Schachter and Singer, 1962, pp. 395–6) In other words, though undergoing strong physiological changes, notably an increased pulse rate and respiratory rate which gives a sensation of having palpitations, they did not consider themselves to be in an emotional state till they were provided with suitable 'cognitions'. That is, they did not consider themselves to be in an emotional state until they were placed in a situation in which they were more or less led into making the evaluation or appraisal peculiar to some emotion. Schachter and Singer point out that in 1924, Marañon had also found that he could not produce a genuine emotional reaction by injecting adrenaline into subjects till he provided them with 'appropriate cognition'.[7]

Considering these experiments, one is led into postulating that a person labels his own sensations of physiological changes with the name of a particular emotion, if and only if he connects their occurrence with a specific type of evaluation (or appraisal) of the

[7] From 'Contribution à l'étude de l'action émotive de l'adrénaline', *Revue Française d'Endocrinologie*, No. 2, 1924, pp. 301–25. See also Munn (1961, p. 325).

situation, which in turn is associated with the concept of a particular emotion. A person will speak of his sensations of physiological changes, even though, unknown to him, they are chemically induced, as somehow connected with the emotional state of, say, love, if he believes that these physiological changes are somehow connected with the appraisal of the situation as one in which he believes he loves someone.

What the experiments which I have so far referred to do not tell us is whether the subjects *only* connect their physiological changes with their evaluation (or appraisal) of the situation if they *believe* that the evaluation somehow caused the physiological changes. This will be so irrespective of whether this belief in fact be true or not. However, some other experiments conducted by Schachter and Singer suggest that the subject of the physiological changes must believe that the evaluation of the situation, which is peculiar to some emotion, generated his physiological changes if that subject is to report having undergone some emotion (i.e. emotional state). When Schachter and Singer told certain of their subjects that the injection which they had just been given was of adrenaline, and also told them about the physiological changes and bodily sensations which would be produced by the adrenaline, then these subjects proved 'relatively immune' to attempts to manipulate them into thinking that they were undergoing an emotional reaction. That is, they proved 'relatively immune' to attempts to manipulate them into thinking that their physiological changes were part of an occurrent emotional state (Schachter and Singer, 1962, pp. 395–6.) It seems that they were immune because they knew that their evaluation of the context was not the cause of their physiological changes and bodily sensations. For the only difference between this set of experiments and the former ones was that, in this set, the subjects were told the exact *cause* of their physiological changes and the accompanying bodily sensations or feelings, namely the adrenaline.

These experiments seem to point to a conclusion that is parallel to Ryle's contention in Chapter IV of *The Concept of Mind*, that it is by applying a causal hypothesis that I identify feelings as being of a certain emotion (Ryle, 1949, p. 105). Though Ryle would not agree with this gloss, Schachter and Singer's experiments suggest that I say the feelings are of, say, love if I believe that the feelings are caused by my belief that I am now in love with someone. It seems that in like manner a person labels his physiological changes as emotional ones if he believes that they are caused by the evaluation (or appraisal) of the situation in a way that is peculiar to some emotion.

Bruce will link his own blushing with the emotion love only if he believes that his blushing is a result of his now seeing Moira with whom he believes he is very much in love. Someone else seeing Bruce blushing may identify the blushing as being from embarrassment because this person believes rightly or wrongly that yesterday Bruce accused Moira of being dishonest and vowed never to see her again so that, in consequence, he is embarrassed at being caught in the same room with her. What is clear is that, irrespective of the correctness of either identification, the identification is always attempted by means of a causal hypothesis of a certain sort. That is, by trying to work out what situation, or rather what view (evaluation or appraisal) of the situation, is causing the particular physiological changes in question.

The notion of a physiological change and the concept of an emotional state

Another aspect of Schachter and Singer's experiments suggests that there is a conceptual link between the notion or concept of a physiological change as such and the concept of an emotional state as such. They pointed out that a number of subjects, inhibited by drugs from having any *noticeable* physiological changes, were placed in paradigm emotional contexts yet, having apprehended and evaluated (or appraised) the situation adequately, they did not report that they were undergoing an emotion (Schachter and Singer, 1962, p. 382). This experiment suggests that a belief that some unusual physiological changes are taking place is necessary if a person is to have grounds for claiming that he is in an emotional state; without this belief one cannot attribute an emotional state to someone (oneself or another).[8]

Of course, it may be the case that a person is undergoing physiological changes as a result of an evaluation peculiar to some emotion and yet doesn't know it, because he is somehow distracted or inhibited from knowing this. In such a case he would be undergoing an emotional state but not have grounds for asserting this. And this fact, that he could not assert that he was in an emotional state in such

[8] For further psychological work on this point, see Goldstein, Fink and Mettee (1972).

a case, would be further grounds for the claim that to believe one is in an emotional state, one must first believe that one is undergoing physiological changes caused by an evaluation (or appraisal) peculiar to some emotion. And, in turn, this would be further grounds for holding that there is a conceptual link between the notion of an emotional state and the notion of a physiological change.

If this is so, then Kenny may be far too sweeping when he writes in *Action, Emotion and Will* that 'There is a conceptual connection also between a feeling and its object, whereas the physiological processes studied by psychologists lack intensionality. Bodily changes may be the vehicle of an emotion, but they are not themselves emotion' (Kenny, 1963, p. 38). I suggest that Kenny, in his proper anxiety to make it clear that 'the somatic phenomena characteristic of particular emotions occurred also in connection with quite different emotions' (Kenny, 1963, p. 39) that is, that there is no pattern of physiological changes peculiar to each emotion, may have put his position too strongly. He seems in the quoted passage to be saying, or to leave himself open to be interpreted as saying, that bodily changes are not part of the concept of emotion itself, that is, of emotion in its primary occurrent sense of emotional state. Whereas what he should be saying is that no particular physiological or bodily changes are part of the concept of any particular emotion.

Leaving aside the experiments which seem to show that physiological changes are an essential part of the concept of emotion in its sense of occurrent emotional state, there is another good reason (though not compelling argument) for holding this. In our ordinary locutions, we associate the notion of 'an emotional state' with unusual bodily activity such as extreme agitation or unusual bodily states such as an unusual colouring of the face. If I inform you that I have lost your book, your reaction may be to work yourself up so that you go red in the face, speak far faster and more loudly than normal, tremble and appear taut around the face. If so, it would not be out of place to say 'There's no need to get emotional about it. I'll buy you another copy.'

To sum up, then, in this section I have argued in various ways that it seems inconceivable to be in an emotional state and not to have undergone unusual bodily changes of some sort. To be *in* love (that is, to love emotionally, in a very strong sense), for example, but never to be in any unusually agitated or excited physiological state, or never to be in any unusually calm or serene physiological state seems inconceivable. This is true only of the phrase '*in* love', as contrasted with the word 'love'. For the early stages of love, the 'in love' stage, are deemed to differ from the later stages precisely by being a period of strong occurrent emotional states, particularly as regards the bodily reaction and, if any, behaviour aspect.

So it is essential to a claim to be in love that a physiological change, which is in one sense a divergence from the normal physiological metabolism and which is discoverable at least by a careful observer, has taken place at some time in the presence of the person or as a result of one's attitudes towards and appraisal of that person. Just as it is absurd to make a dispositional claim to be in love but never to have had any feelings for the person concerned, so it is conceptually absurd to make a dispositional claim to be in love but never to have been in an extraordinary physiological condition. For such a claim is parasitic on the claim to be or at some time to have been in an emotional state, and this point is ultimately a point about the dispositional–occurrent distinction and about the concept of an emotional state, not about the concept of love as such.

I do not want to give the impression that the above arguments only apply to the 'in love' state or stage, for I would argue that the arguments should apply to any stage of any emotion. It is just that the point is easier to grasp when put in the context of the stronger, clearly emotional stage of love.

There is further, though weak, supporting evidence for the view I am urging in the fact that one of the ways in which we assess the intensity of an emotion is from the intensity of the various physiological factors associated with the occurrence of that emotion (that is, of that emotional state). If Jim and Sam are angry with one another so that Jim is red in the face, shaking and shouting, while Sam is pursing his lips, narrowing his eyes and speaking in an even but steely voice, an onlooker has some reasons for saying that Jim is more angry than Sam. Obviously, they cannot be compelling reasons, for it may be merely that Sam is dissembling or else better able to control himself.

Again, we so associate emotional states with unusual physiological changes, and we so associate marked physiological changes with paralysis of good judgement, that 'under emotional stress' is allowed as a plea of mitigation in the law courts of some countries. The murder which is committed as a crime of passion is not considered as criminal as the *sang-froid* murder because we associate emotions with hot blood and with physiological changes which often amount to a disturbance and clouding of sober good reason, cool calculation and balanced decision. I do not want to deny, of course, that part of the explanation of 'crime of passion' as a plea will also be tied up with the fact that, with certain emotions, such as jealousy, it may be very difficult to refrain from activity. Certain emotions have a very strong appetitive aspect, and so tend to issue in action, and the stronger the emotion the more ungovernable is the urge to act.

Some consequences

Since we have seen that both feelings (bodily feelings as different from, say, feelings of elation which have more the character of a fully developed emotion) and physiological changes are associated with emotional states, it is time to ask whether the feelings associated with, say, love are the sensations caused by the physiological changes associated with the emotion.[9] As a question of cause and effect, like all such empirical matters, it can only be decided finally by experiment. However, since it is argued that the paradigm bodily feelings such as twinges, throbs and tickles, have at least proximate physiological causes, this is good reason for thinking the physiological changes which are associated with an emotion on some particular occasion will be the ones that cause the bodily feelings which are associated with that emotion on the same occasion. In simpler terms, since we associate, say, a throb, with some proximate physiological cause such as the heart beat and consequent pulse rate, then, if we associate the bodily feeling, throbbing, with love on some particular occasion, and the physiological change, increased pulse rate, with love on the same occasion, it is most likely that the throb is caused by this physiological change, the increased pulse rate, rather than by any other. This will be so because it is this physiological change which is most noticeable, and perhaps the only one noticeable, or indeed discoverable, and so has the best credentials for being associated with the unusual feeling, the throbbing.

This link between some physiological changes and feelings generates a new distinction for us between the physiological changes associated with emotion: between those which are introspectible and those which are not. For only those physiological changes which

[9] For psychological work on this point see Brady (1970, esp. p. 70).

we can introspect will count as feelings, though by this I do not wish to imply that such physiological changes are only discoverable by introspection. A physiological change, such as an increased heart-beat and blood flow, may be felt and so introspected – for attending to the feeling will be attention to the felt physiological change – but it may also be discovered by feeling one's pulse and listening to one's heart beat. Feeling one's pulse is not introspection in the sense explained, though feeling one's pulse race is, because it amounts to an inner private awareness. It should also be clear that not all physiological changes associated with emotion can be paired off with a corresponding feeling. Only the introspectible ones will. We can discover that our pupils are dilated – by looking into a mirror – but not feel them dilating or feel that they are dilated.

But if it is the case that the bodily feelings associated with emotions are causally linked with at least some of the bodily changes associated with emotions (with particular emotional states), then this will be further good reason for asserting that it is unlikely that there are any *particular* physiological changes which are to be linked conceptually with any *particular* emotion. For, as there seem to be no particular bodily feelings (feelings in the sense of Ryle's throbs, twinges and tickles) which can be linked conceptually to particular emotions,[10] and since there is an alleged causal link between a particular bodily feeling and a particular physiological change, so there will be no particular physiological changes, at least of the introspectible kind, which can be linked conceptually to particular emotions.

It is worth noting however that, all the same, we do consider physiological changes to be an important indicator that *some* emotion (no particular emotion perhaps, but some group of emotions) is present. If we can form a causal hypothesis of sufficient strength to enable us to say that such and such a physiological change in such and such a person is the result of that person's present view of the situation, that is, if we can identify the physiological change in question as being of such and such an emotion, then we can look upon the physiological change as a reflex indicator of the presence of that emotion. It can also serve as a check on the genuineness of that emotion (for we cannot manipulate or engineer our

[10] For a fully argued version of this claim, the reader should consult Ryle (1949, Ch IV, pp. 83ff.), and Kenny (1963, Ch III, pp. 52ff.).

physiological changes in normal circumstances). Being reflex, such an indicator will be more trustworthy than a non-reflex one such as a verbal one and may well be evidence for or against the truth of such verbal avowals. If we know that Bruce has been 'keen on' Moira for some time and if we now see Bruce blush when she enters the room, we will quite likely believe that this is a sign that Bruce is still in love with her, in preference to believing Bruce's later non-chalant avowal that he no longer cares for her at all and had indeed forgotten all about her.

It is because the physiological changes caused by the emotions show on a person's face and body, and because these are the only observable item that is tied conceptually to the notion of an emotional state that, contrary to the views of some philosophers,[11] we can be said to observe another's emotions.[12] Though, as we have seen, particular physiological changes are not to be conceptually identified with particular emotions, physiological changes should be considered as part of occurrent emotions in general.

So far it may seem that I am saying that, if one can see anything which is causally linked to the core part of emotions (of occurrent emotional states), namely to the cognitive–evaluative–appetitive part, then one is seeing the emotion. But this would not be true, for in some cases it would be like saying that if one sees the vapour trail of a jet-plane then one is seeing the jet-plane. My case is different. I am saying that if one sees the body-work of such and such a jet-plane then one is seeing that jet-plane. I have argued that the core part of an occurrent emotional state is only causally linked to any particular feelings or particular physiological changes, which form the other part of such an emotional state. I have also argued that this position is not incompatible with holding that there is a conceptual link between the claim that there is an occurrence of a particular emotional state, and the claim that some sort of physiological changes, generally associated with a discharge of the sympathetic or parasympathetic nervous system, must therefore be present. This will not be true of any claim about behaviour or feelings, for one can be in an emotional state and not engaging in any behaviour, or be in an emotional state and not be aware of it. This claim about the conceptual link between emotional states and

---

[11] For example, Aune (1963, p. 198).
[12] Perkins (1965) puts forward literary examples which show that we speak of seeing emotions but not why we do so.

physiological changes entitles us to say that, when we see particular physiological changes which have been causally linked to a particular emotion, then we are seeing an occurrence of that particular emotion. That is, when we see particular physiological changes which have been causally linked to the evaluative component peculiar to some emotion, then we are seeing part of the occurrent emotional state of that particular emotion. Our reasons for identifying the occurrence as of that particular emotion, however, will be considerations other than the presence of the physiological changes, namely the evaluative component or some clues to it.

If it is true that behaviour is not linked conceptually to the notion or concept of an emotional state, then I cannot say that to observe emotional behaviour is to observe the emotion; it only amounts to observing the manifestation of an emotion. Observing behaviour causally linked to a particular emotional occurrence, but whose concept is not linked conceptually to the notion of that particular emotion or to the notion of an emotional state as such, is then logically on a par with observing the vapour trail causally linked to a particular jet-plane. And in such a case one is entitled only to say 'I see that he is in the grip of such and such an emotion' and not 'I see such and such emotion', just as when one sees only a vapour trail one is entitled to say 'I see that a jet-plane has flown across the sky' and not 'I see a jet plane'. But I shall devote a later chapter to investigating the exact connection between emotions and behaviour.[13]

[13] For further reading concerning experimental data about the physiological aspects of emotions, the reader is referred to p. 15, nn. 6 and 7.

8

Emotions and feelings

There is a considerable literature which sets out the reasons why we should not equate feelings with emotions.[1] I have set out some of these reasons when discussing the feeling theory in chapter 1, but little work has gone into assessing the part that feelings do play in emotions. It is this latter task that I wish to engage in here.

So in this chapter,

(1) I draw out the implications as regards the link between feelings and emotions of a brief passage in Ryle's *The Concept of Mind*;

(2) I discuss whether certain feelings can be said to be associated invariably with certain emotions or not;

(3) I discuss whether our feeling terms are as neutral as has been supposed;

(4) I discuss some competing theories of how in fact we link feelings with emotions and the part feelings play in identifying emotions;

(5) I try to stress in a positive way the part that feelings play in occurrent emotional states.

Ryle and the link between feelings and emotions

Feelings do not come labelled as to what they are feelings of or as to what they are caused by. One labels them as feelings *of* something only by working out a cause or a content. So in the first place I am going to argue that one labels a feeling as *of some emotion* only after causally correlating it with the core or defining aspect of that emotion, namely the evaluations and desires peculiar to that emotion. On the other hand it must be remembered that one can

[1] For example: Ryle (1949, Ch. iv, Sections 2 and 5, and 1951), Kenny (1963, Ch. iii), Pitcher (1965), Alston (1967a), Bedford (1956–57).

describe a feeling, say as a 'twinge', *before* working out whether the feeling is part of an emotional state, such as love or fear, or caused by some physiological malfunctioning, such as indigestion. For 'twinge' may be the correct descriptive term for the content of some feelings experienced.

Ryle puts the first of these points in his usual pungent style in Chapter IV of *The Concept of Mind*. He writes: 'But the point here being made is that whether we are attaching a sensation to a physiological condition or attaching a feeling to an emotional condition, we are applying a causal hypothesis. Pains do not arrive already hall-marked "rheumatic", nor do throbs arrive already hall-marked "compassionate"' (Ryle, 1949, p. 105). And Ryle makes clear on the same page that by 'causal hypothesis' he means 'rule-of-thumb experimental process, reinforced, normally, by lessons taught by others'. He argues that, just as we come to realise that a pain is a caused-by-needle pain by locating the pain in the finger in which the needle is and by finding that the pain is alleviated by removing the needle from the finger and by sucking the finger, so in like manner we come to realise that a certain dull pain is one of indigestion by finding that it is correlated with nausea and loss of appetite and is relieved by medicine and hot-water bottles, that is, that it is correlated with the ordinary man's recognition of the presence of indigestion. (And this correlation is presumably noted on more than one occasion.) It is in much the same way, Ryle insists, that we label feelings as emotional ones. A throb is said to be one of compassion, Ryle would presumably say (he does not actually work out the emotion example for us), if we find that this throb is constantly correlated with a realisation that someone is suffering and the wish that he were not, and is constantly correlated with the finding that the throb goes away when the person's suffering is alleviated.

Ryle might also have mentioned that sometimes we might recognise the pin as the cause of the pain because we saw the pin *go into* the finger and simultaneously felt pain (and noted such a correlation on more than one occasion). In much the same way we might come to recognise that someone's suffering caused our throbbing feeling, and so come to label it as one of compassion, if we noticed that the beginning of the throbbing coincided with our being aware of someone's suffering (and noted this correlation on more than one occasion).

I think that Ryle is right, and that it is correct to say, though Ryle would not put it in this way, that we do label feelings as emotional ones by linking them to certain evaluations, and to the desires usually consequent on these which, when coupled with physiological changes, mark the presence of an occurrent state of a particular emotion, and I think that it is correct to assert that such a linking should be called a causal one. A compelling piece of evidence for the view that the link between feelings and the emotions they are feelings of is a causal one, is the set of experiments previously mentioned, carried out by Schachter and Singer in America (Schachter and Singer, 1962).[2]

Schachter and Singer induced strong feelings (of palpitations) into various subjects with injections of adrenaline and found that the subjects would say that they were experiencing feelings of fear, feelings of euphoria, just feelings, or drug-induced feelings, according as to whether they were put in a context of fear, a context such as usually causes euphoria, a more or less neutral context, and a context (not necessarily neutral) in which the subjects were told the source of the feelings which they were experiencing (i.e. they were told that they had been injected with adrenaline). In the cases in which the feelings, unknown to their possessor, were caused by adrenaline yet labelled as of fear or·of euphoria, we have a case of someone linking the feelings with a certain emotional evaluation of the situation without the evaluation being in fact the cause of the feeling. Ryle would presumably say, and I think correctly, that in such cases the subject is still applying a causal hypothesis but doing so in a mistaken way; and that he is doing this is borne out by the fact that, in certain of the Schachter and Singer experiments, the ones when the subject knows that his feelings are caused by the drug adrenaline, he has no desire to attribute them to emotions even if the situation is an emotional one.

It might be argued that Schachter and Singer cannot really decide whether, in cases where the subjects are not told that they are being injected with adrenaline, it is the adrenaline that is causing all the feelings the subject has or whether the apprehension and evaluation (or appraisal) of the situation by the subject as being a situation of, say, danger, is causing some feelings as well.[3] But, in a sense, this is irrelevant to the philosophical issue; for, whether the feelings are

[2] Again also see Schachter (1970).
[3] See Plutchik and Ax (1967) and Ax (1971).

caused in fact by the drug wholly or partly or not at all, or by the beliefs and evaluations of the situation wholly or partly or not at all, and whether the subject of the feelings correctly labels them as to what they are feelings of or whether they should be called feelings of anything or not, what is certain is that they always attempt to label their feelings by reference to the *cause* of their feelings. So, as regards feelings in the context of emotions, correctly or incorrectly, we label feelings as emotional ones just so long as we *believe* that the feelings are *caused* by our evaluation of the situation as being a situation appropriate to such and such an emotion.

Are certain feelings invariably associated with certain emotions?

It is interesting to note that the name of any feeling such as a 'throb' or 'twinge' is connected to an emotion by saying 'a throb *of*. . .' or 'a twinge *of*. . .' where the phrase has to be filled in with an emotion word but in such a way that it is clear that the phrase can be filled in on other occasions by terms other than emotion ones, such as words for diseases or wounds. The implication is that feelings such as throbs and twinges are not invariably associated with emotions and much less with particular emotions. (A little later on in this chapter I will cast some doubt on the neutrality of such terms as 'throb' and 'twinge'.)

One's intuitions are that there is no one special feeling that we can invariably connect with any particular emotion and with that emotion alone. There does not seem to be, for example, any special 'lovey' feeling that infallibly heralds the presence of the emotion love.[4] If there were, then one would have grounds for saying that one was in love without knowing or believing that there is any person whom one loves, or having any other grounds for believing that one was in love. But in fact it seems impossible to assert that one is in the grip of such and such an emotion just by introspecting the quality or type of one's present feeling. Indeed our introspections tell us a very different story. On Monday night an occurrent state of love might result in my having palpitations (for my beloved has returned after a long absence); on Tuesday afternoon I might feel dizzy with love (because the continued presence of my beloved for

---

[4] Georg Simmel (1957, p. 19) is one who seems to hold the contrary. Hegel (1942, p. 261) also seems to hold this view.

the last twenty hours has over-excited me); on Wednesday morning I might feel unusually relaxed because of love (the security of the continued presence of my beloved may have caused it). And it would seem that, according to introspection again, one can have palpitations because of an occurrent state of fear or guilt, or feel dizzy with anger or embarrassment, or feel unusually relaxed because of happiness or grief. Further, one might have palpitations because of a heart condition, feel dizzy because of too much wine, and feel relaxed because of a drug.

In the experiments that I have already referred to, Schachter and Singer maintained that these experiments support the view that there are no invariable physiological patterns by which to differentiate emotional states and it seems that they include feelings as part of the physiology of emotional states. (For example, they speak of the subject *being aware* of 'palpitations, tremor, [and] face flushing', that is, of *feelings* of palpitations, tremor and flushing; and regard the question 'How would he [the subject] label his present feelings?' as one of the questions to be answered by their experiments. [Schachter and Singer, 1962, p. 381].)

But there are difficulties with this view. In the first place, Schachter and Singer, by injecting adrenaline into their subjects, induced in them as far as feelings were concerned only 'palpitations, tremor, and sometimes a feeling of flushing, and accelerated breathing (Schachter and Singer, p. 382). A subject was limited to these feelings because adrenaline only affects the sympathetic nervous system and so only gives rise to those feelings caused by the physiological changes which he describes in the following way: 'systolic blood pressure increases markedly, heart rate increases somewhat, cutaneous blood flow decreases, while muscle and cerebral blood flow increase, blood sugar and lactic acid concentration increase, and respiration rate increases slightly' (Schachter and Singer, p. 382). So, while it might be true that all or most occurrent emotional states include the feelings and physiological changes attendant on 'a discharge of the sympathetic nervous system' (Schachter and Singer, p. 382) it is patently untrue to say that the *only* feelings and physiological changes found in emotional states are those derived from the discharge of the sympathetic nervous system. A clear case of a physiological change and consequent feeling, which is connected with at least one emotion but is *not* one of those feelings and physiological changes in Schachter and Singer's list of those derived from the discharge of the sympathetic nervous system, is *the prickling in the eyes from weeping* in so far as it occurs as part of an occurrent state of grief. The activation of the tear ducts is surely a genuine physiological change and must in consequence give rise on occasion to feelings (for it is not a physiological change such as, say, hormonal secretions of which, because of the way we are made neurophysiologically, we are not directly aware).

More importantly, the weeping is clearly not a physiological change that we think of as occurring typically as part of the occurrent states of *all* emotions. Though one does, on occasion, weep with, say, joy or out of fear as well as with grief, it is rare to weep with envy or hate or disgust. So weeping can give rise to a feeling or feelings which are not usually part of the occurrent states of many emotions. So, while the feelings and physiological changes induced by an injection of adrenaline may be a good enough imitation of the feelings and physiological changes usually associated with occurrent emotional states to help induce in subjects a belief that they were undergoing emotional states, this fact does not prove that such feelings and physiological changes are the *only* ones associated with occurrent emotional states. In fact some emotions typically include feelings and physiological changes (such as the feelings associated with the activation of the tear ducts) not associated with a discharge of the sympathetic nervous system; and perhaps all emotions involve such feelings and changes at times.

But even this revision of Schachter and Singer would not re-instate the view that there is a pattern of feelings and physiological changes associated invariably with any particular emotion. It would only imply that there are some feelings and physiological changes which are part of the occurrent states of some emotions quite often, of others not very often, and of others very rarely. And this seems to be the correct picture. For example, the feelings associated with weeping may occur rarely in occurrent states of anger or envy or disgust, less rarely in the occurrent states of emotions such as shame or fear or elation, and quite often in the occurrent states of emotions such as grief or remorse.

Feeling terms and their neutrality

Now I want to add to this picture by taking a completely different tack. I want to discuss whether our common terms for feelings are as evaluatively neutral and so as purely descriptive as they are generally supposed to be. Ryle has said in *The Concept of Mind* that 'pains do not arrive already hall-marked "rheumatic", nor do throbs arrive already hall-marked "compassionate"' (Ryle, 1949, p. 105). While it may be true to say that feelings do not come labelled as to what they are of, I want to argue that our labels for feelings often reveal what we think of the feelings, and so often reveal hints as to what sort of thing (such as what sort of emotion) feelings so labelled are likely to be of.

I suggest, then, that one reason why we might describe our feelings as, say, downcast and forlorn, is that we already know or have assumed or guessed that the context is one of, say, grief or remorse. Words such as 'downcast' and 'forlorn' are not as neutral as they might have seemed at first sight. To describe a feeling as 'downcast' already intimates that the feeling is burdensome or attached to some burdensome situation and so is unwelcome. The adjective 'euphoric' suggests the opposite; the feeling to which it is attached is not a burdensome, undesirable or unwelcome feeling. Given that such a term as 'downcast' is already 'loaded' in the way described, it is no wonder that it will sound contradictory to speak of a downcast feeling of joy.

In much the same way, I suggest that Ryle's basic descriptive labels for feelings, labels such as 'throbs', 'pangs' and 'twinges' (Ryle, 1949, pp. 83–4) are not quite the neutral terms they might appear to be. We do not speak of twinges of happiness or twinges of love, or of twinges after drinking a wine which we liked and found agreeable. 'Twinge' carries with it a connotation of unpleasantness, no matter what context it is used in. It is 'reaction-loaded'. It comes already hall-marked with what we think of the feeling it labels. It is a pejorative term. *The Concise Oxford Dictionary* defines 'twinge' as 'sharp darting pain' and so, via the meaning of 'pain', has built into it the notion of being unpleasant and undesired.

Further, a feeling which is described in 'reaction-loaded' terms will often *ipso facto* be causally 'loaded' to some extent. If a feeling is described as a 'pang' or 'twinge', it will usually mean that the field of possible causes is instantly narrowed. For we can usually infer correctly that the person with the feeling believes that it is not caused by an event which he welcomes or finds agreeable. A feeling described as a 'pang' or 'twinge' is usually precluded from having been caused by joy or from being the result of an act of kindness.

Often it will be of use to describe feelings in this 'loaded' manner. A doctor, for instance, may find it useful to discover whether his patient regards his feeling as disagreeable or not, whether it is a pain or not.

One can make out a case that feelings need not always be labelled in this 'loaded' manner. Better or more neutral labels may be more physiologically exact ones, more purely descriptive ones, ones such as palpitations, dizziness, tense, relaxed, hot, cold, steady and shaky. Terms such as 'palpitations', 'dizziness', and so on, do not come 'loaded' with a reference as to what we think of the feelings they label, and so do not come with built-in hints as to what might have, in our opinion, caused the feelings, or as to what context these feelings usually occur in.

All this may seem to be a digression. But, in fact, it leads to the important philosophical point which will help us to fill in the general picture of the relation between feelings and emotions. This point is that, from the fact that we speak of having twinges of remorse but not of joy or love, we cannot conclude that the feelings which are part of an occurrent state of remorse are different from the feelings which are part of some occurrent state of joy or love. It might be the case that the feeling which, in the context of remorse, we call a 'twinge', is the same feeling which, in the context of joy or love, we call a 'flutter'.

Some competing theories about feelings and emotions

Perhaps one could sum up the general picture of the relationship between feelings and the emotions in the following way. The feelings which are drug-induced, the feelings which are part of an occurrent state of love, and the feelings which are part of an occurrent state of embarrassment, may well be the same; and the empirical evidence available seems to indicate that, sometimes at least, this is the case. Even if the feelings are not qualitatively the same, there are good reasons for asserting that what makes us associate the label 'drug-induced', rather than 'love' or 'embarrassment', with them on one occasion is not some introspective belief that this feeling is peculiar to some particular emotion, but a belief or realisation that some thing or some evaluation (or appraisal) of the situation is the cause of the feelings.[5] To label our feelings as *of* something is to give a causal explanation of them by means of a causal hypothesis.

I think that this simple model of the relation between feelings and emotions will help one steer carefully through the vague and potentially misleading comments such as Mary Warnock's that 'I think that it is true to say that everything which I shall call an emotion could also be called a feeling.'[6] This could be taken to mean that there is a single feeling peculiar to each emotion or even that there is a single peculiar feeling which each emotion word is the name of; both positions as we have seen are mistaken. It is not misleading if it is taken to mean that feelings are part of the occurrent state of any emotion (this will be argued more fully towards the end of this chapter), or that, given our present terms for feelings, many of them are such that they come with a built-in implication or hint that some emotion or some sort of emotion caused the feelings they label.

In his book, *Action, Emotion and Will*, Kenny makes a statement to the effect that we identify feelings as emotional ones by means of motivated behaviour or symptoms. He writes:

> For it is not just an unfortunate accident of idiom that we use the same words, such as 'love', 'anger', and 'fear', in the description of feelings as we do in the attribution of motives. The two uses of an emotion-word are two exercises of a single concept; for it is through their connection with motivated behaviour that feelings are identified as feelings of a particular emotion [Kenny, 1963, p. 38].

He expands a little on this later on:

> It would be nearer the truth to say that, on the contrary, a feeling is a feeling of a certain emotion only if it occurs in the context of an action fulfilling a certain motive-pattern. But this is not quite true, partly because feelings are linked more directly to the symptoms of an emotion than to motivated action. Trembling, blushing, psychogalvanic reflexes, and cardiac disturbances are symptoms of fear and shame; attempts to avert a danger or conceal a past crime are typical actions motivated by fear and shame [Kenny, 1963, p. 98].

[5] As Dilman (1963, Vol. 5, p. 197) says when writing of Sartre's theory of the emotions, 'In saying what emotion a person feels we make claims about his awareness of the world at the time'.

[6] Warnock (1957, p. 43) in a symposium with A. C. Ewing.

I do not think that it is correct to say that we always or even mostly identify feelings as emotional ones by relating them to motivated behaviour or to physiological symptoms such as trembling, blushing, psychogalvanic reflexes and cardiac disturbances. In the first place we can identify and do identify a feeling as an emotional one even when there is no observable motivated behaviour going on. And in the second place, as I have already argued (in chapter 7), physiological changes such as trembling, blushing, psychogalvanic reflexes and cardiac disturbances, are no more to be attached to fear and shame as symptoms than to be attached to love or hate or anger as symptoms or to be considered symptoms of a heart condition, drugs or electric shock.

As I consider that this second point has already been dealt with, I will only argue for the first.

Let me begin with an example. I am sitting down, drinking tea in the cafeteria, when in walks Joan. I experience certain feelings. I might identify these feelings as ones of love, even though I am sitting down quietly drinking tea in a cafeteria, that is, even though I am not engaging in any sort of behaviour except drinking tea (which cannot be said to be typical of any emotion), because I know that I am in love with Joan and have noticed that she has just entered the room. It is my appraisal of the context (my realising that Joan is present and my believing that I love her), which makes me identify my feelings as ones of love.

Leaving aside the uneasiness one always gets when there is a suggestion that a word is attributed differently in a second or third person context than in a first person context, one might try to sustain Kenny's position by asking 'Is Kenny's alleged method of identifying feelings as emotional ones the only one possible in the third person context?', or 'Can we only identify another's feelings as, say, those of love by referring exclusively to motivated behaviour?'. I am afraid that the answer is again 'No', though, it is true, the matter is slightly different when considered from the point of view of an observer.

Let us take the same example. Someone observing me drinking my tea in the cafeteria, given that he infers that I am experiencing some feelings as a result of seeing me agitated, that is, as a result of seeing me trembling or blushing or the like, cannot yet identify my feelings as ones of love. As before, behaviour cannot enter into the matter of identification as no behaviour except that of drinking tea is going on. The trembling and blushing, which may well be noticeable to an observer, are (as I have argued elsewhere) symptoms but not of any particular emotion. They are only signs or symptoms that I am agitated and so probably feeling something or other; they are a hint to an observer that probably I am experiencing some feeling, but they tell the observer nothing more than this. It seems true that it is necessary for the observer to know or guess that I view the situation in the way appropriate to love. If the observer already knows, because I previously told him, or strongly believes on good evidence gathered previously as to my view of Joan, or simply guesses that I am in love with Joan and knows or believes or guesses that I have seen Joan enter the cafeteria, then he can correctly identify my feelings as ones of love.

Another case that is difficult for the Kenny thesis is that of a situation in which we can identify the feelings as emotional but in which, while it includes behaviour motivated by an emotion, the behaviour in question is at best ambiguous as to what its motive is. Take the case of Jim killing his grandmother. Killing a grandmother is not behaviour which can be said to be typical of any particular emotion. If one were not told anything else about the case, one might hazard a guess that Jim's behaviour was motivated by greed or hate, or sadistic pleasure. But one can work out that Jim's killing his grandmother was from a motive of love, and so that any feelings resulting from the relevant evaluative attitude are ones of love, if one knows that Jim is or was extremely fond of his grandmother and that Jim knew that she was afflicted with painful terminal cancer; that is, one can say that Jim killed his grandmother out of love and that his feelings were of love in such a case only if one has first decided, on the basis of working out Jim's beliefs, evaluations and consequent wants as regards the situation, that Jim loved his grandmother.

Of course, one need not always have to make these evaluations and desires explicit in order to identify feelings as being ones of such and such an emotion. It is true that in some situations one can identify feelings by linking them to typical behaviour, but this immediate identification by means of typical behaviour seems to be restricted to emotions, such as fear, which exhibit reasonably typical patterns of motivated behaviour. A man who is running away from something (which is indicated by his repeatedly looking behind or over his shoulder), clearly agitated by this, and warning others against remaining in the area, is probably afraid. Unfortunately some emotions do not seem to be of this type. There does not seem to be a standard pattern of behaviour that we typically associate with, say, remorse or hate. Love seems to fall somewhere in between these two extremes.

More importantly, one step further back, behaviour itself can be related to an emotion in such a way as to be said to be usually motivated by that emotion, only if over the years people have come to know that the subject of such behaviour has appraised the situation in such a manner as to warrant the attribution of a particular emotion to such a subject. In brief, for behaviour to be called 'typical' of such and such an emotion, then a correlation between the relevant behaviour, and the evaluations and desires central to the concept of the emotion in question, must at some time have been set up.

The part feelings play in occurrent emotional states

Since the primary task of philosophers such as Ryle, Alston, Kenny and Bedford, in the context of feelings and emotions, seems to be to show that emotions are *not* feelings in the sense that emotion words are *not* the names of particular feelings, I will now try to stress the part that is played by feelings in emotions and particularly to stress that an emotion does usually include feelings in its occurrent states.

Alston in his article, 'Emotion and Feeling', writes that:

It is noteworthy that typical uses of the general term 'emotion' have to do with emotional states rather than attitudes or other general dispositions or liabilities. One is not termed an 'emotional person' because of having a lot of admiration, contempt, or gratitude toward other people, but rather because of frequently getting into states of anger, indignation, grief, or joy and expressing them freely [Alston, 1967a, pp. 479–80].

Ewing makes a similar point when he writes in his paper, 'The Justification of Emotions', that:

Now I do not wish ... to make the discussion of emotion a discussion of feelings, but the element of feeling is surely central to the ordinary use of the word. This is shown by the simple fact that it is clearly wrong to speak of a man as 'in an emotional state' unless you are prepared to imply that he has strong feelings of some sort at the time, or at least just before or after. The definition of 'emotion' given in *The Concise Oxford Dictionary* is 'agitation of mind, feeling, excited mental state'. I suppose Prof. Ryle would say that it refers only to excited action, but I should have thought that, if we saw somebody acting in an 'emotional' way but were not satisfied that he had felt anything, or thought he felt very little, we should not say that he was in an emotional state but only that he acted as if he were. Nor would one describe the fainter feelings as emotions.[7]

Alston is stressing that we speak of people in relation to a particular emotion mainly because we have at some time or other observed them to be actually in a particular emotional state. Ewing is stressing the fact that this entails that the people in question must have had feelings.

These philosophers are correct in emphasising that the primary sense of the term 'emotion' is its occurrent sense, and that the primary indicator of the presence of an occurrent state to the subject of such a state is the presence of feelings. As I have argued in an earlier chapter, the other use the term 'emotion', the dispositional, is parasitic on the occurrence of emotion states, that is, feelings, physiological changes and behaviour which signal the activation of the evaluative attitudes peculiar to particular emotions.

All this is seen very clearly in the case of the emotion of love. We use feelings very much as an indicator of the presence or absence of (emotional states of) love and, I think, rightly so. We say such things as 'Don't you love me any more?' when the other person has not 'shown feeling' (that is, has not been emotional and so has not led observers to believe that he or she was experiencing feelings), in a situation when this could be expected. Again, we might argue from 'I don't feel anything for you any more' to 'I don't love you any more' and, I think, again rightly so; for if, as I have argued, the dispositional use of 'love' is dependent on emotional episodes or occurrences still being a possibility, then it follows that 'I love you' is dependent on the speaker having had physiological changes and, usually, the consequent feelings for the other in the past and, in general, retaining a liability to become emotional (including having

[7] Ewing (1957, p. 59.)

feelings) about them in suitable circumstances in the future. If the speaker, for, say, the last three years, has never shown any sign of emotion (of having the emotional reactions of unusual physiological changes and the feelings consequent on them, though it is possible to have the former but not the latter) towards the other in circumstances in which it could be said to be reasonably expected, then the speaker can no longer have grounds for saying 'I love you'. One cannot very easily claim to love someone in the emotional sense and expect the claim to be believed, and at the same time claim never to have had for that person any feelings which can be causally linked to the evaluation and desire aspects of love. The connection between emotion and feelings is as strong as that.

9
Emotions and behaviour

In this chapter I want to investigate the nature of the links between emotions and the behaviour[1] stemming from them. I propose to do this by discussing the following topics:

(1) The behaviour typical of an emotion, which is typical in a much looser sense than an equivalent claim about behaviour being typical of an appetite;

(2) The view that behaviour typical of an emotion is linked conceptually to that emotion;

(3) The failure of the view in (2): none of the ways in which behaviour is typical of an emotion implies such a conceptual link;

(4) The factors, of which there are a number, that militate against being able to specify with any degree of exactitude what behaviour will flow from any particular occurrence of an emotion;

(5) The link between emotions and behaviour, which is causal and based on the appetitive aspect of emotions;

(6) The link between emotions and behaviour, which besides being causal, is also rational;

(7) The conclusion that behaviour does have some part to play as an indicator of the presence of emotions.

Emotional behaviour is typical in a looser sense than behaviour typical of an appetite

In *Action, Emotion and Will*, Kenny writes that 'there is, again, no

---

[1] It should be noted that in this chapter I limit the term 'behaviour' to purposive behaviour. For an account of the relation between emotional expression or involuntary behaviour, such as facial expressions, I refer the reader to Gray (1971, Ch. 3).

particular form of behaviour which is characteristic of an emotion in the way in which eating is characteristic of hunger' (p. 48). This observation can readily be seen to be borne out.

Eating is characteristic of hunger because it is the only thing that satisfies hunger. But there is no particular 'form of behaviour' which satisfies an emotion and so can in that way become so closely associated with it as to be said to be characteristic of it. Now, although it may be thought that fear includes a fairly simple and straightforward desire that some danger be avoided, and that some desire for safety be satisfied, when examined closely, this avoidance is not a straightforward piece of behaviour in the way that eating is. One can avoid danger by running away (if the danger is, say, a bomb which is about to go off), by killing something (if, say, the danger is from a wild animal), or by not going somewhere (if the danger lies in being too close to a cliff's edge), and so on. In fact the whole notion of the emotions 'being satisfied' seems odd; partly because their appetitive aspect does not seem to be a demand that some very particular item be supplied in a very particular way, which, when supplied, will appease some craving or dissolve some tension; and partly because, anyway, they do not always aim at a satisfaction in the sense of appeasement. While with emotions such as anger the concept of appeasement may seem to fit, with emotions such as joy and love it seems completely inappropriate.

An emotion is not merely a bodily event, and so cannot be a simple bodily craving that must be silenced or relieved. A man is hungry if his body is in a certain condition, no matter what he believes, and this condition gives rise to the simple and definite want that this condition be changed. Thus hunger leads to a fairly clearly defined form of typical behaviour. A man is undergoing an occurrent emotional state only if, among other things, he *believes* certain things about some thing, person or state of affairs and *evaluates* these things in a certain way. The beliefs and evaluations in turn generate quite a large number of *desires*, such as, with fear, the desire to avoid or be rid of the danger, or, with love, the desire to be with the beloved, to please her, to cherish her and protect her, and to have her return the love. All of these desires, associated with a single emotion, must mean that an emotion cannot lead to a very clearly defined form of typical behaviour. For most of these desires can be manifested in a great variety of ways. One can fulfil the desire to please someone by sending them a present, by obeying their commands, and by doing a myriad of things. So, it can be argued with some justification that, if more or less any item from a large spectrum of behaviour can be reasonably expected in any situation of love, then the whole notion of 'typical behaviour' must be very much loosened if it is to be applied to an emotion such as love.[2]

The view that behaviour is linked conceptually to an emotion

O. H. Green seems to feel that, not only do we link behaviour to emotions as typical expressions of them, but that we have grounds for saying that the link between emotions and such typical behaviour is conceptual. He seems to hold that emotional behaviour comes already branded with a particular emotion word. He holds that, if we are to recognise emotions in others, definite sorts of behaviour must be conceptually connected with certain emotions so as to form part of their definition, rather than be merely causally connected in various ways. Green writes in 'The Expression of Emotion' (*Mind*, Vol. 79, 1970), that 'it is necessary that emotion-terms are defined by reference to a person's behaviour in certain circumstances' and that the 'behaviour which is described in defining emotion-terms must be typical' and that behaviour which is typical is, generally speaking, 'behaviour which is at least subject to a person's control or modification' (p. 552).[3] I am taking it that what is part of the definition of *x* is necessarily part of the concept of *x*; though not *vice versa*, so that Green's view is that some behaviour typical of some emotion is part of the very concept of that emotion. Let us examine this view.

Does the way in which behaviour is typical of an emotion imply a conceptual link?

One sense of 'typical' is that in which smoke is said to be typical of fire. This sense of 'typical' seems best to be explained by saying that from our knowledge of how fires 'work', and from our experience of a number of fires, we can say that smoke is *a natural concomitant* of most types of fires. The word 'natural' is used here because smoke

---

[2] In connection with this view, see Frijda (1970, esp. pp. 249–50).
[3] On the other hand it should be noted that in a later article, Green (1972, pp. 25–6) does concede that 'no sort of purposive behavior is characteristic of some emotions. Grief, despair, sorrow, and depressive emotions generally are examples'.

is related to certain types of fires as the natural physico-chemical resultant or manifestation of the burning of certain materials.

By analogy, in the emotional context, tears are the typical resultant, in the sense of natural resultant, of grief or sadness, for crying seems to be part of the physiological reaction which goes to constitute the occurrent emotional state of grief or sadness. Embracing might be said likewise to be typical, in this sense of natural, of love in that it is a manifestation that results or wells up naturally from some appetitive aspect of some sorts of love, from some such desire as that of being physically close to the beloved which, in turn, is derivable from one of the general desires associated with love, namely to be with the beloved and to share his or her life.

Yet, because the relation of smoke to fire, and of actually embracing (as distinct from the more general want from which it stems) to love, does not hold in all cases of fire and love, there can be no *conceptual* tie-up between fire and its natural manifestation and between love and its natural manifestation. Just as there are smokeless fires, so there are loves, such as that between a teacher and his pupil, and that between an abbot and his monks, in which embracing is considered inappropriate; and even genuine cases of erotic love or maternal and paternal love in which circumstances inhibit embracing.

Another sense of typical is the merely statistical sense of *commonly or frequently found as a concomitant of*. Thus an acrid smell might be said to be typical of fire in so far as it is a concomitant of most types of fire. But not all fires have such a smell, and so it cannot be part of the concept of fire as such. For the burning of pine logs, sandalwood and incense (and, no doubt, a number of other substances) gives rise to a sweet smell. Muttering endearments may be said to be an expression which is statistically common and hence typical of certain types of love, such as adult homosexual and heterosexual love, and maternal love, but not of other types such as fraternal adult and filial love.

A third sense of 'typical' in this context would be that in which avoiding coming into contact with the flames is considered to be a typical reaction to fire. This sense of typical is that of *appropriate or sensible or rational response* to fire. It is a voluntary conscious response though it may be based on previous reflex reactions to having been burnt by flames. By analogy, refusing to go up the Eiffel Tower would be the appropriate, sensible or rational response for someone with a fear of heights.

But because one can imagine cases of people acting rationally but not avoiding fires (people committing suicide, motor cyclists who leap through flames in circuses, fire-eaters), and of people with a fear of heights acting rationally but climbing up to high places (to save someone, to escape something), then we must say that there exists no conceptual tie between what this sort of behaviour is typical of and the behaviour itself.

One rational or appropriate reaction (avoiding a fire in order not to be burnt, avoiding high places because of one's fear of them) may be considered more typical than another reaction which is also rational or appropriate (not avoiding fire in order to perform a trick for gain, not avoiding heights in order to win a considerable bet), because the former is not merely the statistically more usual of these appropriate reactions but the better grounded of the two. It is not merely appropriate and predictably so, it is the more rational, all things considered. So behaviour which is not merely appropriate or sensible in the circumstances but *the most appropriate* in the circumstances, amounts to a further separate sense of typical behaviour.

A fifth sense of typical would be that of *conventional behaviour*, which neither naturally flows from the desires or attitudes or other aspects of an emotion, nor is a rational reaction or response to an emotional situation. There does not exist a ready example in the context of fires, though one could imagine it being a convention in a society that, whenever a fire was lit or broke out, one threw a piece of one's clothing into it because of a superstition, no longer believed but mechanically followed, that if one did so then one would never be consumed by fire. We may take love as the example. Instances of love behaviour which are typical yet neither particularly rational (though not necessarily irrational) nor natural, nor even statistically very common (at least nowadays), would be strong though culture-bound conventions such as the sending of Valentines, the wearing of engagement rings (when this is taken to symbolise not merely a promise of marriage but a relationship of love as well – this convention *is* still quite common), and 'saying it with flowers'. This sense of typical behaviour does not even begin to make a claim to be conceptually tied to whatever it is typical of. Behaviour becomes conventional in a variety of ways, for example, through habit, the breakdown of the belief which made it a rational response, a partly historical and partly aesthetic liking for the behaviour itself, all three, or through something else again. The very difficulty in describing clearly the way behaviour becomes conventionally associated with something, points to the fact that it is neither a natural nor rational response to anything, and has little or no logical connection with what it symbolises by convention.

Conventional behaviour will only be linked typically or characteristically to what it is behaviour of, if a sufficient proportion of people adopt it. The conventional behaviour of people in love in the town of Onitsha in Nigeria, or the love-behaviour of the Blackfoot Indians of Calgary in Canada, will not be typical of love as such if they do not occur outside Onitsha or outside the Blackfoot Tribe. Then, something only qualifies as a convention in the above sense if a significantly large number of people do it. If only I, or one or two others, parted their hair in the middle whenever they fell in love, this would not qualify as conventional behaviour. It would only qualify as 'a personal eccentricity', a term which by definition implies minority behaviour. Eccentricity ceases to be eccentric when a sufficient number of people adopt it.

Difficulties in specifying emotional behaviour

I think then that I have given grounds for rejecting Green's view of the relation between emotions and behaviour as typical and thereby conceptual. But there is a less implausible view of the link between emotion and behaviour. This view, which I have already hinted at when discussing Kenny's views, is that the concepts of certain emotions, though not all, include certain reasonably specific *desires*, though not to do behaviouristically specific things. In the case of love, one of these specific desires is that the love be returned. Now, it is hard to pin down what sort of actions would follow from wanting one's love returned. Kindness, flattery, attentiveness towards the object of love . . . or all three, or none of these? Kindness flattery, and attentiveness could all be said to be appropriate to wanting one's love returned, because they could all be said to stimulate or be likely to stimulate affection. But, on the other hand, so could a hundred other actions or pieces of behaviour, such as gallantry, generosity, boasting, and in some circumstances feigned indifference and self-sufficiency. It does not seem possible to delineate with any specificity what actions would follow from a desire such as that one's love be returned. The concepts of love and some other emotions almost certainly entail more than one want or desire and in consequence will almost certainly not entail just one type of behaviour (supposing that such wide-ranging wants, considered singly, could entail any definite behaviour). On the other hand, grief and despair do not seem to contain any very clearly specifiable desires at all as part of their concepts; and, in this sense, they are less active emotions than love or fear. What behaviour does occur in the context of such emotions would have to be attributed to desires that arise out of the personality of the person having the emotion rather than from the emotion.

Then there is another factor which partly explains why it is hard to predict what sort of behaviour will result even from emotions which have specifiable want or appetitive aspects. Behaviour motivated by, say, fear will vary according to the *object* of fear. As Kenny himself says in another place, 'The behaviour which is actuated by fear of getting fat is not the same as that which is actuated by fear of getting thin' (Kenny, 1963, p. 99). The same is true of love. Love of a soldier for his comrade-in-arms may typically take the form of sharing his food packages from home with him, encouraging and protecting him during the stress of battle, and generally being in his company more than in the company of the other soldiers. The love of a pupil for a teacher may take the form of verbally defending the teacher against any criticism, being on his best behaviour in the teacher's class, laughing at all the teacher's witticisms both weak and strong, and doing his homework for that teacher with exceptional care. So, without knowing a great deal about the object of the emotion in question, one cannot get very far in predicting what sort of behaviour will result from that emotion. And even knowing the kind of object, in the case of an emotion such as love, will not get us very far. One must know a great deal about *the subject* of the love as well. Upon hearing that Ferguson loves O'Reilly, one cannot even begin to predict what Ferguson will do in O'Reilly's presence without knowing a great deal more about both Ferguson and O'Reilly, such as their age, sex, status and temperament.

The link between emotions and behaviour is a causal one based on the appetitive aspect of emotions

I have argued earlier on in this book that feelings and physiological changes are said to be of or associated with particular emotions as a result of a causal hypothesis linking the feelings and physiological changes with the emotion. Here I want to argue that behaviour as well is associated with an emotion only in so far as it is believed that the behaviour is caused, indirectly, by the beliefs and evaluations (or appraisals) of the emotions in question, and, proximately or directly, by the desires which make up the appetitive elements of such emotions. There may be, as I have already hinted, emotions such as grief or despair which are exceptions to the above model. For it may turn out that, for example, grief is to be defined merely as the emotional reaction to an evaluation of a certain kind; and that the filling out of the 'emotional reaction' aspect does not include a reference to any behaviour as being even usually present. But I suggest that my discussion of the connection between emotions and typical behaviour does suggest that such emotions are the exception and not the general pattern.

Behaviour needs to be interpreted or to have at one time been interpreted for us; it does not come already interpreted. We have to connect the behaviour to an emotion and we seem to do this on the basis of a causal hypothesis. We say that putting one's hands at the back of someone's head and then running one's hands up and down the neck is fondling and caressing, rather than an easing of the crick in that person's neck, because we have first identified the situation as one of love. This identification may be made in various ways. But what is necessary is that we have some sort of clues or information which may allow us to guess or realise that the person, who is manipulating the neck of the other person, loves, merely pities, or is compassionate towards him or her, or is merely over-joyed about something. In the first place, the clues may be ones as to the state of mind (beliefs, evaluations, appraisals, and wants . . .) of the person manipulating the other person's neck. If we had no previous information as to such a person's state of mind, and if the one whose neck was being manipulated and the one who was doing the manipulating did not display any behaviour which we might in any sense call typical of the object or subject of some emotion, then we probably could not guess what emotion, if any, was causing the manipulating. The above situation would be further complicated if both the persons concerned, say, had their back to us, such that we could not see their expressions.

Of course, actual situations are normally full of clues as to what exactly the behaviour going on is caused by; we hear snatches of conversation, we see facial expressions, we see behaviour which may be said to be typical in one or some of the senses of that term which I have already discussed. And in a great number of situations we are knowledgeable observers. We already know about or have some information about the beliefs, evaluations, and desires of the persons whose behaviour we are watching. We don't have to look for further clues.

So while, as I have argued, no particular behaviour is part of the concept of love, and if the behaviour described above is not a mere conventionally-adopted sign of love, then to interpret this behaviour as being *love* behaviour, one must be able (ultimately at least) to deduce, correctly or incorrectly, that the behaviour in question is done *out of love*. That is, one must deduce that the behaviour is *caused by* love, that is, caused by that part of the emotion love which connects up with behaviour, namely desire.

Graham Greene puts some of the things I have been trying to say, about the connection between emotions and behaviour being less than conceptual and basically causal, in a rather interesting way in his novel *The End of the Affair*. The protagonist, Bendrix, is recalling his past:

> I would have liked to have left that past time alone, for as I write of 1939 I feel all my hatred returning. Hatred seems to operate the same glands as love: it even produces the same actions. If we had not been taught how to interpret the story of the Passion, would we have been able to say from their actions alone whether it was the jealous Judas or the cowardly Peter who loved Christ?

The link between emotions and behaviour, besides being causal, is also rational

On the other hand, as became clear when I was discussing the various senses in which behaviour could be said to be typical of emotions, the connection between emotions and behaviour is usually stronger than a mere contingent causal connection, though not as strong as a conceptual link. The connection between emotion and behaviour can be natural, conventional or rational, but especially rational. The appetitive aspect of emotion usually does not just happen to lead to just any sort of behaviour, it leads to behaviour which can be seen as a rational concomitant of the set of desires peculiar to the emotion in question. And if this rational extension of the desire into behaviour becomes almost reflex or instinctual, at least when referring to particular cultures or to specific races, the connection can be called natural as well. For a person in love to embrace the beloved is not merely a rational extension of the lover's wanting to be near the beloved and share his or her life, and in that sense possess him or her, it is so much part of the upbringing of people in most Western societies that it can be seen as natural. As we have seen, there are causal connections between emotions and their behaviour which seem to have little or no rational basis, at least net any longer, and should be seen as conventional only. The sending of Valentines by lovers at a particular time of the year is an example of this. But it should be clear that, even with conventional behaviour, there is usually some vestige of a rational connection left. To send Valentines is, or used to be recognised as, recalling the ardent and unquenchable love of St Valentine and so can be seen, quite reasonably, as the sending of something which is a symbol of one's ardent and unquenchable love.

Since we are talking of purposive behaviour, it will be clear that reason, reasoning about purposes or means to fulfilling desires, must have some part in the behaviour which stems from emotions. The emotional person, who acts on his emotions, will explicitly or unwittingly be acting so as to implement in as rational a manner as possible the desires which arise as a result of his emotions. To be afraid is to have, among other things, a desire to avoid or be rid of the real or supposed danger. If the danger is thought to be from a bomb in the corner of the room, then the rational man will try to run out of the room. Or a very brave and rational man will try to remove the bomb from the room and put it in some wide open space and then make sure he and everyone else nearby is out of the vicinity. The running away and the removing of the dangerous object are both rationally appropriate to a person's fear of a bomb as well as causally connected to the desires that arise as a result of fear of a bomb.

I suspect that those who would want to say that behaviour is part of the very concepts of emotions have come to hold this view, at least in part, by *rightly* wanting to resist holding for a *mere* causal connection between emotions and behaviour, but by *wrongly* concluding that the only alternative is to hold for a conceptual connection. There is a third alternative, I believe, which I have described as a causal connection directed or channelled into fairly specific forms, and clearly appropriate forms of behaviour, by reason. So this third alternative can be described as a causal connection governed by reason such that the result is an appropriate causal connection; but this of course does not make it into a conceptual connection.

Behaviour as an indicator of emotions

In this chapter I have been mainly concerned to argue against any tight conceptual connection between emotions and behaviour. Now in conclusion I feel that I should redress the balance a little by stressing the part that behaviour does play in emotional occurrences.

Behaviour, particularly if we include utterances under this term (see chapter 10), will usually be the starting point for attributing some emotion to someone. Asking for a first person emotion-statement will, I suppose, always be the pre-eminent method of finding out if someone is in an emotional state. But since people can and do tell lies, and can be and often are mistaken about their own emotions, we will always want to check these avowals by reference to other indicators, and I think that it is correct to say, as Bedford has, that: 'I do not believe that we either do, or should, take any notice of anyone's protestations that, for instance, he loves his wife, if his conduct offers no evidence whatever that he does.'[4] But this could be misunderstood. It cannot mean, as we have seen, that behaviour is conceptually related to the concept of any particular emotion or even to the notion of an emotional state in general in the way that physiological disturbances are, for I can think of someone being emotional but not engaging in any sort of conduct; he may, for example, be sitting there looking and feeling embarrassed but not be doing anything. So I think that what Bedford means is the following. I don't think that we would *believe* that, say, someone loves his wife, if he has *never* acted in a way that exhibits that love, particularly if it is known that he did not so act on occasions on which rationally he would be expected to show his love for his wife by his conduct. *A fortiori* we would not believe that someone has a certain emotion if he has often acted in a way that is rationally

---

[4] In 'Emotions' Bedford (1956–57); reprinted in *Essays in Philosophical Psychology* (1967, p. 85).

incompatible with that emotion. The reason for arguing thus, or part of the reason, is that we do look upon behaviour as an 'external' or public indicator of 'inner' or private states, the beliefs, evaluations, and in particular the wants involved in emotions. If no behaviour that could be interpreted as stemming from, say, love is ever present in a putative love relationship, and the person is rational, then there is good reason to believe that the desires which make up part of the very concept of love, and which usually lead to appropriate actions or behaviour, are not present.[5]

Finally Bedford is not, or should not be, arguing that essential evidence for saying that X loves Y is that X has shown typical love behaviour motivated by love on some one particular occasion; for to say this would be to adopt the view of O. H. Green, to which I have already put compelling objections.

---

[5] This point about behaviour being the usual and most reliable indicator of emotions will be less true in the purely aesthetic context, such as that of watching a film. For, as Wilson (1972, p. 83) has put it, 'it may be a distinguishing feature of aesthetic emotions, as opposed to real life ones, that they are dissociated from behaviour'.

10

Emotion statements

This chapter is a brief survey of the ways in which emotion statements are used, for some of these ways have either gone unrecog-
nised or have been overemphasised to the exclusion of others. It is
really an addendum to the previous chapter, as at least one sort of
emotion statement could be said to amount to emotional behaviour.

Bedford has argued that emotion statements do not describe but
interpret behaviour (Bedford, 1956–57, p. 288). Cassin, while
accepting that this is a plausible view of third person statements
about emotions, considers that it is not very plausible in the context
of first-person emotion statements (Cassin, 1968, pp. 564–5).
O. H. Green seems to hold the view that statements such as 'I am
angry' are always reports (Green, 1970, Section iii, pp. 562–5). I
think that none of these philosophers has told the whole story.
Rather, I shall make out the case that,

    (1) Statements of emotions may report emotions;
    (2) They may interpret them;
    (3) They may express them in such a way as to become part of
       the emotional behaviour itself;
    (4) Finally, there are uses which are parasitic on the interpretative.

The first person statement as report, interpretation and expression

The statement 'I love you', referring to emotional love can, first of
all, tell you, or report, that I am now undergoing, or have undergone
in the past, and am likely to undergo in the future, the emotion love
in regard to you. It can be distinguished from a case of an interpretation of behaviour, because no behaviour may now be going on or
ever have gone on in your presence. I may be just telling you about
the emotion which, in the past, I have experienced in regard to you
even though I may have managed tc suppress or disguise it in your

presence. I may be presenting you with the first inkling of the emotion I feel for you.

'I love you' can also be an interpretation of the emotional state which I am in and which you notice I am in. You might have asked me 'Are you all right? Is there something upsetting you?' and I might have replied, interpreting for you my agitation, 'I love you'. The statement is offered by me as explanatory or interpretative of the behaviour you remarked on. A report relates what is the case; an interpretation explains the significance of what is the case. An interpretation is a second layer over and above relating the facts. In the present context being given an interpretation enables someone to place behaviour under an appropriate emotion label.

If the statement 'I love you' is said in a slightly hushed tone of voice and with a trembling lip and a softening of the facial expression, and if at the same time as saying it I put my arms around your neck and nuzzle your ear, then the statement 'I love you' is on a par with the putting of the arms around your neck and the nuzzling, indeed it is part of the performance if you like. In such circumstances these gestures, given that I was sincere, would be neither reports nor interpretations but expressions of my love for you. If the statement 'I love you' is on a par with them, as it seems to be, then it too should be called an expression of love.[1] Unless the use of 'I love you' in such a context is an expression of love, it may well be superfluous as what it reports is likely to be known and, if my behaviour was sufficiently typical of someone in love, it would not be needed as an interpretation.

Green argues that utterances such as 'I love you' said in a loving tone of voice or 'I am very angry' said in an angry tone of voice, do not pass his four tests for being an expression of an emotion. Of these he says 'a person's behaviour, verbal or non-verbal, is an expression of emotion when and only when it (1) provides evidence for saying that the person presently has the emotion expressed, (2) occurs in the appropriate circumstances, (3) is subject to the person's control or modification, and (4) is sincere,' (Green, 1970, p. 551). Now, he claims that the utterance 'I am very angry' in a tone of anger fails tests (1) and (4). As regards test (1), he holds that the utterance does not provide evidence that the utterer really is angry,

---

[1] Alston (1965a, p. 29), writes, 'We do not say that someone is *expressing* a feeling unless his performance is relatively spontaneous, unless the verbal utterance issues directly from the feeling, and takes on a coloration therefrom.'

rather than something else, in the way that uttering 'Alas' really does reveal the emotion the utterer is undergoing. Leaving aside the fact that my dictionary explains 'Alas' as an expression of 'grief, pity or concern', and so not distinctive or revelatory or characteristic of any particular emotion, I fail to see that 'I am very angry' said in an angry tone is not revelatory of anger. It is hardly an utterance to be associated with any other emotion, and it seems more revealing of anger than his example, 'Alas', is of any particular emotion.

At this point he asserts that 'the person expresses his emotion not in making the statement as such but in the way he made it' (Green, 1970, p. 565), that is he distinguishes what is said from the way it is said, allowing that the latter but not the former might be an expression of emotion. But how can one separate off the tone of voice from the linguistic content of a speech act in such a case? I might utter the words 'I am very angry' in an emphatic or vehement tone of voice and Green would be prepared to admit that, because of the vehemence, this might count as an expression of the emotion anger, for to be vehement is to express the vehement nature of one's anger. But vehemence cannot occur alone. It is surely adverbial. It modifies actions including speech acts. It is to do something with great or even violent emphasis. But the emphasis is tied up with the doing, it colours the doing and is given direction or point by the doing, for other emotions can be expressed by emphatic words, for example hate. Just as the tone colours the words, so the words colour in the tone. Certainly we decide that the speech act is not a report or not simply one by registering the strong tone, and, most probably, seeing the tone as continuous with a flushing of the countenance and gesticulations, but the vehemence could not exist without its host speech act, and it would not express anything definite without its host speech act. The vehemence is a vehement speech act.

Green's claim, that 'I am very angry' said in an angry tone of voice fails his test (4), is also difficult to make sense of. Green rightly claims that 'the person who makes a statement about emotion is only required *per accidens* to have the emotion in question' in order to be sincere, but to sincerely express emotion one *must* have the emotion in question (Green, 1970, p. 565). But to use this as a basis for claiming that 'I am very angry' said in an angry tone of voice cannot be an expression of emotion, seems to me to beg the question. To be sincere when I say 'I am very angry' in an angry tone of voice,

I must be angry, and the 'must' there seems to have the same force as that in the claim that, to be sincere, you must be genuinely grief stricken, or full of pity or concern, if you utter the word 'Alas'. For Green to suggest that the 'must' is weaker in the first case, is to beg the question as to whether the utterance is just a report or an expression like 'Alas'. For it is true that reports can be sincere though mistaken, such that I can say sincerely 'You are angry' when you are not.

So we have not found good reasons for supposing that first person utterances such as 'I love you' said in a loving tone of voice, and 'I am very angry' said in an angry tone of voice, cannot be expressions of emotion in certain circumstances.

The uses of emotion statements parasitic on the interpretative use

Now, I think that the interpretative use of an emotion statement can carry a number of uses as parasitic upon it. It is because one interprets behaviour for a purpose, for example to denounce it (particularly in the context of emotions such as jealousy or hate or anger), or to excuse it (particularly with emotions that are generally approved of), that the interpretative use of an emotion statement carries other parasitic uses. Let us take as an example, the use to excuse. If I administer a hefty dose of morphine to my mother-in-law which kills her quite quickly and then I am arraigned before a court of law and accused of murder, in defence, by way of excuse or exculpation and in general of a rebuttal of the charge, I might say simply 'I loved her'. I might then go on to explain that I administered the lethal dose in order to relieve my mother-in-law from the excruciating pains of an incurable cancer. While my statement is a report of the love I had for her, certainly, and also an interpretation of my behaviour, in the context it also takes on the dimension of an excuse and exculpation. I doubt whether there could be a non-parasitic use of 'I love you' or 'I loved you' as an excuse because the context of an excuse is when one's behaviour has already been given another more malicious or damaging interpretation.

Second and third person statements as reports and interpretations

Third person statements about love such as 'He loves her' may be either an interpretation of his behaviour or, when no behaviour is or was in evidence, a report on him. Since it can be an interpretation of behaviour it is clear that it can also have the senses which we have seen are parasitic on the interpretative sense. I don't think that there could be an expressive use of a third-person emotion statement because expressions of emotions will only be made by the one having the emotion and not by the one commenting on the one having it.

Second-person love statements seem only to be of three kinds; reports, interpretations and the uses parasitic on the interpretative use. Second-person love statements as expressions of emotion seem impossible for the same reason that the third-person ones were, namely that only the person undergoing the emotion can express it. There is no problem about using the statement 'You love her' as a report of an emotion if one remembers that it is possible for a person to have an emotion, to be in the grip of an emotion, but not realise it and so be in a position to be told that he is in the grip of the emotion. One can be very angry and not realise it, say, because one is engaged intently in denouncing one's opponent in debate. After the debate is over, my team-mate might say to me 'You got very angry with Ferguson' and I might say in astonishment at this revelation 'Heavens, did I? I didn't mean to. I must apologise to him.' Likewise, one can be in the grip of the emotion love and not realise it, say, because one is engaged at the same time in defending the object of one's love against a charge of dishonesty. Jim's championing Mary against the charge of dishonesty may be carried out with such passion and fervour and bias that it is clear to everyone but himself that he is in love with Mary. After the heated defence of Mary is over, a friend who had been present the whole time might whisper to him 'I think you're in love with Mary'. Because the person in the emotional state was unaware that he was in it, the statement 'You were angry' or 'You love so and so' is a report. It cannot in the context be an interpretation for the person spoken to, because he was unaware of the relevant behaviour, such as the agitations or gesticulations or facial expressions or bias, on which an interpretation might have been based. One can only be said to be giving an interpretation of behaviour when the one to whom the interpretation is given either already knows about the behaviour that is being interpreted for him or else is told about the behaviour in the process of being given the interpretation. In the above examples the person addressed with the statements 'You were angry' and 'You love so and so' was both ignorant of the behaviour which was the evidence for the statements and was not told about the behaviour when informed of the emotional states which he had been in the grip of.

It might be clearer if I put it this way. To tell X he was angry cannot be a process of explaining or interpreting to X his own behaviour if X is unaware of his own behaviour, it must be a simple report, just as to tell X it is about to snow cannot be interpreting for him the weather signs in the sky if X is blind. There is a difference between a report to someone which results from interpreting something and the process of interpreting that something to him.

The interpretative use of the second-person love statement is also reasonably clear if one bears in mind that you can be in an emotional state and realise it but not know its significance, that is, not be able to identify it correctly. You might say to me 'I feel both excited and shy about going to Mary's party. I don't know why. Perhaps it's because I haven't been to a party for a long time'. I might reply 'You are in love with Mary' and then go on to support with evidence my interpretation of your present emotional state. There are probably other cases when an interpretative use of the second person emotion statement is in order. For example, I might be able to interpret Ferguson's behaviour to him, telling him that it points to his being in love, not because he doesn't know this but because he does not want to admit it and so be held responsible in certain ways.

Since there is an interpretative use of second-person love statements, there will also be the uses parasitic on the interpretative use, though these would appear to be rare. Though not a common occurrence, one can perhaps imagine having to interpret the behaviour of a very guilt-ridden or confused person in such a way as to stop him blaming himself, that is, in such a way as to enable him to excuse his behaviour to himself. One might have to say 'Look, you didn't do it out of selfishness or nastiness, *I* can see that. You did it because you love her. So, you mustn't blame yourself'. In a more elliptical conversation, one can imagine the simple statement 'You love her' doing the same job.

I I

Emotions and motives

In this chapter I want to investigate what sort of explanation is being given when someone says 'He did x out of such and such emotion' or 'Such and such emotion was his motive for doing x'. I will argue for the following:

(1) The term 'motive' should not be limited to contexts where we expect the motivation not to fall within the standard range;

(2) The motive which is said to be behind an actual action is to be construed as a cause;

(3) The motive which is said to be behind an actual action is to be construed as entailing a *desire* which is a cause;

(4) However, not all actions which can be said to be done out of some motive can be said to be actions which the agent wanted to do;

(5) Emotions as motives which are said to be behind actual actions are to be construed as involving desires as causes;

(6) Emotions and motives can be reasons but not intentions or aims;

(7) Motives are not always to be construed as desires which are causes but as desires which could have been, are or could become causes;

(8) In conclusion, construing motive explanations in terms of desires makes better sense of the connection between motives and behaviour than do alternative accounts.

The use of 'motive'

Alston and Peters use the term 'motive' *only* when it is suspected that the motivation for an action 'does not fall within the "standard" range'.[1] My reason for not doing the same is that I think there are

[1] Alston (1967b, p. 401). Peters (1960, p. 29) holds a similar view about the use of the term 'motive'.

cases in which one can ask for a motive for an action without suspecting that the motivation falls outside the standard range. If I, more or less completely ignorant about the stock market, ask someone who 'plays the market' the following question, 'What was your motive in selling those BP shares so soon after you bought them?', the circumstances are such that I am seeking information only and have no informed idea as to what is the standard range of motivations in such cases. In fact it is often reasonable to look for a motive even when it is thought that the motivation *does* fall within the standard range. The policeman might want to make sure that his presumption about the suspect's motive, based on his knowledge of the standard range of motives in such cases, is correct. Or a father might think it morally instructive to get his son to admit that his motive in taking the cake reserved for his sister was the standard, but morally reprehensible, one of selfishness and in consequence to get his son to feel shame.

I suspect that Alston and Peters should be saying that, though strictly speaking one can always legitimately ask for a motive when it is suspected that there is one, it seems overly formal or stilted to ask for one when the answer is obvious or superfluous. But to say this is to say no more than that one should not ask someone to spell out what is obvious. One *could* ask, when sitting at table with someone, what was his motive in putting the fork with food on it into his mouth. If we *do* not ask such a question, it is because the answer is obvious, not because it would be logically inappropriate to use the word 'motive' in such a context.

If one wants to make a distinction between motives and motivation, I suspect that a clearer and more useful one would be that which is set up by defining 'motive' as 'the deliberate cause or candidate for such a cause of a human action' and 'motivation' as 'all other sorts of causes of uncoerced human behaviour' (causes such as drives or reflexes, conscious or unconscious). My reasons for such a distinction will become clearer later on in this chapter.

The motive

In the first place I want to argue that a motive is often, though not always, introduced as some sort of cause. If the Inspector says to the Sergeant 'What caused Jones to commit such a horrible crime? He seemed such a gentle chap', it is just as sensible for the Sergeant to reply 'Greed', or 'Hate', as to reply 'Drugs' or 'Alcohol'. In other words it is not uncommon for motives for actions to be given in answer to a demand for the cause of the action.

It also seems to be the case that any motive explanation for an action can be given a causal interpretation, though it may well bear other interpretations as well. Assertions such as 'Jones' motive for the assault of the teller and robbery of the bank was greed' or 'Ferguson's motive for moving the Bill for the Abolition of Estate Duty was personal gain' can always bear the interpretations 'Greed caused Jones to rob the bank and brutally assault the teller' or 'The desire for personal gain caused Ferguson to move the Bill for the Abolition of Estate Duty'.

More importantly, the statement 'Jones' motive for the bank robbery was greed' can be retranslated into 'Greed caused Jones to rob the bank' without any addition of meaning, and in affirming the former statement one is automatically committed to affirming the latter one. For there would be an inbuilt contradiction in making a statement such as 'Though his motive for robbing the bank was greed, greed did not cause Jones to rob the bank.' However, it might be logically legitimate to say 'Though his motive for robbing the bank was greed, it was drink that caused him actually to rob the bank.' This can be given an interpretation which amounts to saying that the proximate cause or immediate cause of his action of robbing the bank was drink, while the remote cause which the immediate cause or catalyst was responsible for bringing into operation was greed. It would be logically contradictory to say 'Though his motive for robbing the bank was greed, greed played *no part* in causing him to rob the bank.' While we may allow that the motive for an action was not the *whole* cause for some action, if we claim to have found the motive for the action then it means that we believe we have found at least part of the cause of that action.[2]

But it is equally clear that such motive statements must be statements about a particular type of cause, for not all causal statements are motive statements. For a start, rather obviously, it is only legitimate to ask for, or speak of, motives where persons are concerned. An electron, a tree or a fish don't have motives. Then, requests for *the* motives of actions must not be made merely in the context of persons but in the context of persons as causes or agents

---

[2] Peters (1960, pp. 39–42) is one who seems to deny that to find a motive for some actual action is to find at least its partial cause.

for some action. 'What is Jones' motive for his hunger strike in prison?' is a logically legitimate statement while 'What is the motive for Jones' hunger?' is not, for in the former case it is presumed that Jones himself is the cause of his hunger while in the latter case it is not.

Finally, not all cases of a person causing something allow for a motive statement to be legitimately made about that action. For, while it is legitimate to say 'Jones caused the accident by falling asleep at the wheel', it is not legitimate to go on from this and ask 'What was Jones' motive for the accident?' Citing *the* motive for an action is only legitimate where the agent of the action is deemed to have *deliberately* caused the action in question. It would be legitimate to ask for Jones' motive in causing the accident if it were thought that he did so by forcing the other car off the road.

This point will be seen more clearly if we imagine someone saying 'His motive for the assault was greed but he didn't commit the assault on purpose'. We would say that such a statement is contradictory, for part of the meaning of 'he had some motive for the action' seems to be 'he deliberately did that action'. To do something for a motive is to do something on purpose or deliberately, though the reverse is not necessarily true. One might agree to do something, and in that sense do it deliberately, yet not want to do it or have the desire to do it as a motive.

The motive which is a cause as entailing a desire

In what sense then is a motive a cause, given a context where the action to be explained is done on purpose? I shall use examples to show that a motive is often a cause, given a context where the action to be explained is one that is believed to have been done by a person, *because he wanted or desired to.*[3] That is, a motive is often proffered as the cause or a putative cause whenever an action is to be explained by a desire, and this action is believed to have been done on purpose in so far as the person desired or wanted to do it.[4]

Though some of the resulting translations may seem grammatically odd, my basic contention that motives which are acted upon

---

[3] See Grice (1967, pp. 13–15) who argues for the formula 'no motive without a desire'.
[4] For a fuller discussion of wants as causes, see Goldberg (1965, pp. 71–2), Donnellan (1967, Vol. 7, pp. 85ff.)., Alston (1967c), Pears (1968), Schild (1971, No. 55, pp. 687ff.), Lyons (1973c, Nos. 63–4, pp. 591–4) (a reply to Schild above).

are to be construed as involving desires as causes seems to be borne out by the fact that we find that all explanations in terms of desires can, without change of meaning, be translated into explanations in terms of motives, and *vice versa*. 'He hit her because he wanted to hurt her', 'He played poker into the early hours of the morning because he wanted to win enough money to buy a sports car' and 'He lay down because he wanted to regain his strength for the final assault tomorrow' can all be translated without loss of meaning into 'His motive for hitting her was to hurt her', 'To win enough money to buy a sports car was his motive for playing poker into the early hours of the morning', and (though this is odd-sounding, probably because in the context to ask for or proffer a motive would seem superfluous) 'His motive for lying down was to regain his strength for the final assault tomorrow.' And the examples 'His motive for running away was fear', 'His motive for staying home was to deceive his neighbours' and 'His motive for seeking that particular position was self-aggrandisement' can all be retranslated without loss of meaning into statements of desire: 'He ran away because he wanted to avoid the danger', 'He stayed home because he wanted to deceive his neighbours' and 'He sought that particular position because he wanted to enhance his personal prestige'.

I do not want for a moment to deny that this task of retranslation becomes difficult in some cases. In the following motive statements it is not easy to see what desires lie hidden. 'His motive for staying at home was laziness' and 'The motive for his crime was jealousy.' The reason for this difficulty is, in the case of jealousy, our ignorance of its workings, and, in the case of laziness, the fact that there is an ambiguity in this concept. To take laziness first, do we translate 'His motive for staying at home was laziness' as 'He stayed home because he didn't want to work' or 'He stayed home because he wanted to loaf.' In other words, do we explicate the meaning of 'laziness' in terms of indolence (or a reluctance to work) or in terms of loafing (or a positive liking for doing nothing in particular)? With jealousy, in the case of a sentence such as 'His motive in setting fire to his neighbour's house was jealousy', do we translate it as 'He set fire to his neighbour's house because he wanted to hurt his neighbour', or 'He set fire to his neighbour's house because he wanted to destroy his neighbour's chief source of pleasure', or neither? I think that the correct answer is neither, for these two translations seem to leave out two essential ingredients of jealousy, envy and resentment. One cannot be said to be jealous of X but not to envy X or resent his possession of some asset or supposed asset or his good fortune or supposed good fortune. So I think that a better, though probably still partial, translation of the sentence 'His motive in setting fire to his neighbour's house was jealousy' would be 'He set fire to his neighbour's house because he envied or resented the fact that his neighbour, in possessing the house, possessed some asset or supposed asset, good fortune or supposed good fortune.' Then to complete the translation I would have to define envy as entailing some desire or desires.

Again, the examples which I gave involving fear and aggrandisement may also be disputed. It may be claimed that fear involves a desire to avoid the danger rather than, say, a desire to run away or to be rid of the danger. Or it may be claimed that self-aggrandisement is to be defined in terms of a desire to enhance one's personal prestige, rather than a desire to increase one's power or wealth.

The important point is that fear, self-aggrandisement, laziness and jealousy can only figure as motives for actions that have been performed in so far as they are thought to include wants. In consequence, it is part of the philosopher's job to uncover the desires which are included in their concepts. If laziness, for example, were not defined in terms of some desire or other but was defined as a state of physical lassitude brought on by overwork, drugs, or indeed anything other than a desire, then it would no more make sense to say 'His motive for staying at home was laziness' than it would to say 'His motive for staying at home was the effect of overwork' or 'His motive for staying at home was drugs'. It seems that we put forward something as a motive to explain some action that has taken place only in so far as implicitly or explicitly we believe that what is proffered as a motive entails a want to do or not to do something. If we are convinced that something has actually functioned as a motive yet we find difficulty in expressing it in terms of some desire, then this must be merely a technical difficulty – a difficulty caused by our ignorance of the workings of the thing in question.

But to say all this does not, I think, rule out unconscious or subconscious motives. If one can have unconscious or subconscious purposes, aims, or desires which can causally influence behaviour, and it is generally held that one can; and if, as I have been arguing, motives are just desires which can and often do turn out to be actual causes of behaviour, then one can have unconscious or subconscious motives. And if all wants, conscious or unconscious, are deliberate in so far as they are purposive, then it cannot be objected that there are no unconscious motives on the grounds that there cannot be deliberate 'items' in the unconscious or subconscious. Besides, I think that one commits oneself to holding out for unconscious and subconscious motives, if one commits oneself to the thesis that one can have an emotion (that is, be in an occurrent emotional state) and not realise it. I would want to espouse this latter thesis. If such an unrealised and so subconscious emotion can cause some of my behaviour through its appetitive aspect, and if emotions can be motives in so far as they have an appetitive aspect which can causally influence behaviour, then my emotional behaviour can be the result of subconscious motives.

Not all actions done from a motive are actions the agent wanted to do

It is important to note that it is not a contradiction to say 'His motive for the assault was greed but he didn't want to assault her'; and to say 'His motive in running the police car off the road was hate but he didn't want to run the police car off the road' is not to say something logically odd. For one can perfectly well do things for some motive without wanting to do them. If, for example, I assault someone out of greed I might not have *wanted* to assault them. It may be the case that my greed could not be satisfied any other way than by robbing them and, since they resisted, by assaulting them as well. To put it more generally: though it seems that all motives which are acted on do include a desire, not all the actions which result from acting on the desire can be said to be wanted. One might feel that certain unwanted actions (such as the assault and robbery in the above case) must be accomplished in order to do or gain what one does want (in the above case, the gaining of money). That one desires x does not entail that one necessarily desires all or any particular means to obtaining x.

Emotions as motives involve desires

I think that we have now arrived at the point where we can see reasonably clearly what sort of explanation we are giving when we put forward *an emotion*, such as love or fear or jealousy, as the motive for some action. Besides, it is interesting to note, as R. S.

Peters has pointed out, 'there is a well-established tradition about the use of the word "motive" which links it with emotion, which is made explicit by the Oxford English Dictionary'.[5]

Because some emotions entail desires (that is because some emotions have an appetitive aspect), such emotions can function as active motives behind actions. In so far as an emotion entails some desires, it can function as the cause or instigator of an action, for to want something sincerely entails that one will try to get that something when the appropriate circumstances arise.

To cite an emotion such as love as the motive for some action is to cite the appetitive aspect of that emotion as the cause of that action, that is, as either the proximate or remote cause. To say that Jim killed his mother-in-law, who was suffering excruciating pain from terminal cancer of the lung and spine, out of love, is to say that Jim killed his mother-in-law because of one of the desires that make up the appetitive aspect of love. This in turn means that Jim's killing his mother-in-law must stem from a desire to please her (if, for example, she had actually begged him to administer an overdose of morphine) for it could not easily be interpreted as stemming from a want to care for and cherish her (for it does not seem very plausible to suggest that he believed he would be caring for and cherishing her by stopping the pain through death, for cherishing and caring imply keeping the object of such attentions alive. Though his action would show *that* he cared, meaning that he was greatly concerned.) And the other main desire which seems to be discernible in the appetitive aspect of love, to be in the person's company in preference to the company of others, is obviously not applicable in such a case!

As has been implicit in some of the examples of motive statements that I have used, emotions aren't the only things that can function as the motives behind actions, because they aren't the only source of operative desires. The desires for food or drink or sleep or shelter or peace and quiet, and so on, can also function as the motives for actions: the desire for food can be the motive for an escaped convict's breaking into a shop; the desire for sleep may be my next-door neighbour's motive in moving out of such a noisy neighbourhood.

[5] Peters (1960, p. 48). Peters (1960, p. 37) quotes the relevant OED passage: 'It [the OED] defines 'motive' as 'That which "moves" or induces a person to act in a certain way; a desire, fear, or other emotion".'

Emotions and motives as reasons but not intentions or aims

Emotions as motives can also function as reasons for actions. In the
first place, it seems that motives can function as reasons where the
word 'reason' is understood to mean 'explanation', for motives can
serve as the explanation of some action either by placing that action
within a larger pattern of endeavour or merely by explaining its
genesis, in terms of some particular desire or desires.

For example, when the little boy answers his mother's question
'Why did you hit Johnny?' by saying 'Because he took my marbles'
or by saying 'Because he hit my cat', the little boy is hoping to
explain his action of hitting Johnny. He tries to do this by placing
it in the wider context or pattern of being a punishment visited on
Johnny for some mischief, and hoping that in such a context the
action will be acceptable to his mother.

However, he might have replied by saying 'Because I was afraid'.
In such a case the little boy is explaining the genesis of his action by
saying that the emotion fear gave rise to his action and by hoping
that actions done out of fear are less liable to blame than other
actions. If the little boy had been a sophisticated adult he might have
been able to substantiate and bolster this causal explanation by
explaining that fear gives rise to a desire to avoid or be rid of the
object of fear and that hitting Johnny is one possible way of making
Johnny, the object of his fear, go away.

So emotions can be both motives for and reasons for an action.
An emotion entails as part of its concept certain wants: these can be
offered as either the identified *cause* of an action (that is as one sense
of 'motive'), or as either a *causal explanation* of the action or an
explanation of the action in *terms of some wider endeavour or purpose*
(that is as one of two different senses of 'reason'). I think that it is
true to say that the motive behind an actual action can always be a
reason for the action it gives rise to because one sort of reason is a
causal explanation.[6]

It has often been said that motives cannot be causes because
motives are reasons and reasons are not causes. This is rather
ironical, since it is partly in so far as motives are causes that
motives can be reasons, in the sense of causal explanations. To say
that if X is a reason for Y then X cannot be a cause of Y, does not

[6] For a fuller discussion of this area, see Davidson (1963).

recognise the simple truth that something can fulfil two different functions so long as these functions do not entail contradictory aims. In its role as cause, a motive is part of an actual causal chain; in its role as reason a motive is what is referred to in reply to an explicit or implicit request for an explanation.

However, it is true to say that not all reasons are to be described as causes, and it should be noted that a motive can function as a reason in such a sense. This sense of 'reason' is something like 'sufficient condition for causing'. Thus Hercule Poirot can say that 'Everyone in this room had a motive for murdering the dead man'. Here by 'motive' he cannot mean that everyone in that room is the cause of the murder (or at least it would be a most unlikely hypothesis to put forward). He seems rather to mean that everyone in the room is a putative or possible cause or, from another angle, has a desire or the like which would be sufficient to cause the possessor to murder the man now dead.

However, I do not think that it is true to say that, in so far as motives are wants, they are intentions (where an 'intention' means an 'intending to do something'). I think that it is correct to say that wanting to do x does not entail intending to do x. I can want to punch someone on the nose but, for reasons of prudence, have no intention of doing so. Intention, besides being forward-looking (being cited most often before an action has been performed), as many have pointed out, seems to have some sort of *'imprimatur'* or commitment attached to it. A desire, it seems, can become an intention only if one sees no objection, prudential or otherwise, to mobilising it when favourable circumstances occur.

Does having a motive for doing x entail having x as an aim? I don't think that it does, even if by 'aim' one does not mean 'intention' (as in the sentence 'I aim to force my way in, no matter what he says'). If by 'aim' one means 'purpose' or 'goal', then having a motive for doing x does not entail wanting to do x and so does not entail having x as an aim, goal or purpose. This view was implicit in the earlier discussion of the case where someone assaulted and robbed a person out of greed and so had a motive for assaulting and robbing but yet did not want to assault and rob him. He might have felt that he was forced against his wishes to assault and rob the person in question.

Further, while it would seem odd to speak of emotions or motives in general as aims, emotions or motives can give rise to aims. An emotion such as love does not seem able to function as the goal of an action. It is not the sort of thing that one can set out to achieve through action, but an emotion such as love gives rise to aims or goals. An emotion, as a motive for some action may, though as we have seen it need not, have given rise to the aim which the action set out to achieve. If I kill my mother-in-law with an overdose of morphine out of love for her, then, besides saying that love caused my action, I might be saying that love provided the goal or aim of the action, which was to alleviate her suffering. Indeed, because emotions entail wants and wants entail aims or goals to be achieved, emotions often give rise to action, that is, endeavours to achieve certain goals or aims. So, in general, motives cannot themselves be said to be aims or goals but only to give rise to or include aims or goals.

Motives are not always desires which are causes but are desires which could have been, are or could become causes

The Poirot example above can also be used to bring out the positive side of what I have briefly referred to by saying that 'by motive he (Poirot) cannot mean that everyone in the room is the cause of the murder'. I mean the positive side of the thesis that motives are not always to be construed as desires which are causes, because only the motives for actual actions are to be thus construed.

In the Poirot example, only the murderer's desire was in fact a cause. Yet the others can be said still to have had a motive for the murder; that is, the others in the room had desires or could be presumed likely to have desires which, given different circumstances, or other causal factors, could have caused the death. Unless this were so we would not have a reason for saying that they had a motive for this murder. They must have 'resident' in them (at least as the structural basis of a disposition) something which can be construed as at least able to and, given certain circumstances, liable to have led them to commit a similar act of murder. For, in general what leads a rational person into action is a *desire* to do that action or to achieve some goal through that action or to gain something which for contingent reasons can only be obtained through that action.

So, then, my general thesis is not that motives as such are causal desires (though the motive behind an action is to be construed as such), but that motives are desires (which are dispositions) which, given certain circumstances could have been causes of the action in question, even if in a round about way. Only some motives turn out in fact to have been 'activated' or, so to speak, made operational and issue in actions. They might be overruled by some stronger wants or by prudential considerations, or they might become too etiolated to generate behaviour, or just wither away completely.

When, before he has solved the case, Poirot says that all the people in the room have a motive for the murder, he means that he has not yet been able to trace back the causal connections to show which person's desire was the operative one – that is, which person's desire was *the* (occurent or activated) motive which actually caused the death directly or indirectly. Positively, he means that in theory it could be shown that each person in the room had a desire which, given suitable circumstances, could have led rationally to the act of murder in question, a desire which could have been the cause, though that is not to say they all wanted to commit the murder.

Motive explanations in terms of desires make better sense of the connection between motives and behaviour than do alternative accounts

Let me first briefly discuss some well-known views of motives in the context of emotions as motives.

I find Ryle's account of motives (and, following him, Wilkins' account of emotions as motives) less than satisfactory (Ryle, 1949, Ch. IV; Wilkins, 1971, p. 140). The reason for this is that Ryle construes *all* motives in terms of dispositions, and a particularly law-like version of them at that. He has said that 'the imputation of a motive for a particular action is not a causal inference to an unwitnessed event but the subsumption of an episode proposition under a law-like proposition' (Ryle, 1949, p. 90) for 'to say that he did something from that motive is to say that this action, done in its particular circumstances, was just the sort of thing that that was an inclination to do. It is to say "he *would* do that"' (Ryle, pp. 92–3). Now, this has odd consequences when attributing emotions as motives for action as we can see from the example of Jim killing his mother-in-law out of love for her. This begins to look very odd when it is forced into Ryle's format: 'To say that Jim killed his mother-in-law with an over-dose of morphine, out of love, is to say that this action, done in its particular circumstances, was just the sort of thing that he has an inclination to do.' It amounts to saying that '*X* did *Y* out of love' means '*Y* is just the sort of thing that, in the circumstances, he has an inclination to do.' Now the difficulty with Ryle's format is that it appears to be saying that to impute an emotion as a motive for someone's action is to recognise that action as typical of that person's behaviour. But it begins to be a bit bizarre to say that killing his mother-in-law is just the sort of thing that Jim has an inclination to do. If Jim has never killed any-one before, then in what sense can Jim's killing his mother-in-law be said to be behaviour typical of Jim? And, further, if Jim has never before done such an unconventional act out of love for his mother-in-law or for anyone else, or as a result of any emotion, in short, if Jim till now had not been known as an emotional person, how could Jim's killing his mother-in-law out of love be said to be typical of Jim?

One can surely always attribute an emotion as a motive for someone's action without claiming that the person concerned is often given to acting out of this motive in such circumstances. One can surely make a motive claim where a dispositional claim about the person's usual sort of behaviour in such circumstances is impossible. I can say that someone did something kind out of fear and add that it was that person's only known act of kindness and that he had never before been known to have been moved by fear. Dickens' story, 'The Christmas Carol', comes to mind as a ready-made example. This story is about a man, Scrooge, who was mean and miserly all his life till one Christmas, prodded by visions of an alarming nature, he is moved to an act of kindness in regard to the crippled boy, Tiny Tim. Scrooge's action was done under the in-fluence of an emotional state, fear, which had never previously influenced him to actions of this sort. Indeed, part of the charm of the story is the unexpectedness of the action and the motive, the unpredictableness of the desire to help Tiny Tim.

Kenny holds what, at first sight, appears to be a view very similar to that of Ryle's, and differing from it only in that it is an even more generalised version of the workings of an emotion attributed as the motive for some action. He writes:

> This, I think, is the truth behind Ryle's idea that an explanation in terms of motives stated a 'law-like generalization'. Being told that a man acted out of vanity helps us to understand his action

not because (as Ryle thought) we say to ourselves 'Yes, of course, he often acts like that', but because we say to ourselves 'Yes, of course, *men* often act like that' [Kenny, 1963, p. 95].

In other words Kenny's position seems to be that 'X did Y out of love' amounts to saying 'Y is just the sort of thing that, in the circumstances, people often do.' In other words Kenny is saying that to impute an emotion as motive for someone's action is to recognise that action as typical of people's actions in such circumstances.

And such a position would be open to the following sort of objection, namely that it *is* possible to say that x was a result of love in circumstances in which the action in question would be most *un*typical of people caught in such circumstances. A case that would illustrate this objection is that of Padre Kolbe. Unasked and without being forced to, Padre Kolbe took the place of a man in a group destined to be starved to death in a concentration camp, out of love. It can hardly be said that 'men often act like that' or that it was typical of the actions of men in such circumstances. Indeed we remember Padre Kolbe because an action such as his is rare, and we praise him precisely because his action was above and beyond what could be either expected or demanded in such circumstances. On the other hand, it is equally clear that the action can be said to have been done *out of* love and might even be said to have been appropriate to love (where by 'appropriate' is meant 'traceable to the appetitive or want aspect of love').

So, I suggest that what Kenny ought to have said in his correction of Ryle was something like the following: 'Being told that a man acted out of vanity helps us to understand his action not because (as he, Ryle, thought) we say to ourselves "Yes, of course, he often acts like that", but because we say to ourselves "Yes, of course, this is the sort of action which is appropriate to vanity".' To put the point in the context of the emotion love again, I think that what Kenny ought to have put forward is the position: to say 'X did Y out of love' is to say in effect 'Y is just the sort of thing that, in the circumstances, a *person in love* has an *inclination* to do.'

I think that it is correct to say that the imputation of an emotion as the motive for someone's action is very often a result of recognising that action as, if not typical of some emotion, at least appropriate to that emotion. Actions will be *typical* of some emotion if they are not only traceable to that emotion but are also frequently traced to that emotion. Actions will be *appropriate* to some emotion if they are merely traceable to that emotion (as stemming from some part of the appetitive aspect of that emotion).

Thus, in the context of the emotion love, since the appetitive aspect of love seems to entail such desires as a desire to be in someone's company in preference to that of others, and to cherish and please that person, then actions such as constantly seeking out that particular person's company, constantly being protective towards that person and constantly trying to please that person in various ways, will most often be the result of love. Since they are actions that are frequently seen in the context of love, they can be said to be typical of love.

Actions which are merely appropriate to love may not be so easily recognisable as such, at least immediately, and are not to be confused with actions typical of love. My wanting to please the one I love may lead me to accede to her request to go away and never see her again (she may not love me and may find my attentions a nuisance). Taking great pains to avoid going near a person is hardly typical of love because it is not the sort of action which we usually expect in situations of love, because we have not frequently traced such actions to love. Indeed avoiding someone is associated typically with dislike rather than liking or loving. On the other hand, in the context, the action of avoiding the woman in question can be traced to one of the wants associated with the concept of love (the want to please the beloved) and, on this account, can be said to be appropriate to love.

All this leads to the following important point. Not all actions done out of love or vanity (or any other emotion or motive) can be said to be typical of love or vanity (or of some other emotion or motive). I therefore feel that to be absolutely precise, Kenny should have said and is only entitled to say something such as the following:

> Being told that a man acted out of vanity helps us to understand his action not because (as Ryle thought) we say to ourselves 'Yes, of course, he often acts like that', but because either the action is of such a sort that we can say to ourselves 'Yes, of course, this is the sort of action which is typical of vanity' or it is of such a sort that we can say to ourselves 'Yes, now that I have been told all the details, I can see that it stems from vanity and, in that sense, is appropriate to vanity.'

The crux of my reformulation of Ryle and Kenny as regards how motives function as explanations for actions, is this: where they give a more or less behaviouristic account by appealing to typical behaviour patterns, I am arguing that a truer account lies in showing that motives function as explanations of behaviour, whether it be typical or not. This is so, in so far as the behaviour concerned can be shown to be the result of some want which is inherent in the motive under consideration. My account treats the behaviour as a rational result of having a motive, rather than as a mere typical concomitant of it on many occasions.

12

Emotions and purpose

There are at least three possible interpretations of the thesis, 'emotions are purposive':

(1) The first interpretation is that 'emotions are purposive' means 'emotions give rise to purposive behaviour';

(2) The second interpretation is that 'emotions are purposive' means 'emotions are had for a purpose';

(3) The third interpretation is that 'emotions are purposive' means 'emotions can be seen as serving the purpose of or as being useful to the person(s) having them'.

I want to argue that interpretation (1) is acceptable, that (2) is not, but that (3) is with provisos and qualifications. Most of the discussion will be about interpretations (2) and (3) and it will become clear that these are the more interesting theses. Indeed the discussion of (3) will lead on to the discussion of

(4) Whether or not worthwhile distinctions can be made in terms of useful/useless and socially-approved/socially-disapproved-of emotions;

and

(5) The emotions-as-organising and emotions-as-disruptive-of behaviour dispute in psychology.

Emotions give rise to purposive behaviour

The thesis that emotions are purposive in that they give rise to purposive behaviour is, one would think, unexceptional. At least I hope this is so after the discussion in the previous chapters. As we have seen, the concept of particular emotions will involve not merely reference to evaluations about objects but most often also to desires, which imply purposes. Fear is not to be defined merely as a belief that there is something about which is to be evaluated as dangerous but also as including a desire to avoid or be rid of the danger. For it is this desire as part of an occurrent state that typically gives rise to a frightened person's running away, that is, to his purposive behaviour. Besides, as we have seen, it is when this conative or appetitive aspect peculiar to some emotion is seen as the cause or possible cause of behaviour that the emotion can be cited as the motive for the behaviour. Indeed, as we have seen, it is only by including desires as part of emotions that we can explain the connection between emotions and behaviour. And it is because, as a result of assessing or evaluating the world, emotions give rise to desires to achieve some purpose relevant to that evaluation or assessment, and often to engage in the behaviour appropriate to achieving it, that emotions can be seen as giving rise to purposive behaviour. That is, there is no denying that emotions make one want to do things in order to achieve things, because they make one want to achieve things in the first place.

The interesting theses in this area begin when one goes further than this and makes special claims for emotions as a source of purposive behaviour. Claims, for example, that emotions in giving rise to behaviour are to be seen as useful to humans, or that emotions in giving rise to behaviour are to be seen as fulfilling human purposes, conscious or unconscious, or that emotions in giving rise to certain sorts of desires are to be seen as organising and channelling behaviour which might otherwise be disorganised and haphazard. In the succeeding sections I will consider some of these special claims.

Emotions are had for a purpose

The claim that emotions are purposive in the sense that they are had for a purpose, was given its classical expression in Sartre's *Sketch for a Theory of the Emotions* (1939). There, as we saw in chapter 1, Sartre depicted emotions as a deliberate way of retreating into the world of 'the magical' in order to escape from reality, that is emotions are deliberately engendered or adopted as a way of avoiding some unbearable aspect of reality (a thesis that also calls to mind R. D. Laing's later account of madness). The psychologists Magda Arnold and J. A. Gasson espouse the most contentious aspects of this view in their article 'Feelings and emotions as dynamic factors in personality integration', for they also maintain that emotions are to be seen as 'instruments in the pursuit of our purposes' (Arnold and Gasson, 1968, Part 7, p. 212). More recently the philosopher Robert Solomon, in his article 'Emotions and Choice', wrote that 'emotions are purposive, serve the ends of the subject, and consequently can be explained by *reasons* or "in-order-to" explanations'. And there are others who seem to hold a similar view.[1]

There is the first obvious sort of objection to this view, namely that if one loved for a purpose or was angry in order to do or achieve something, then one would not be genuinely angry or in love but would be pretending to be angry or in love. Perhaps this is most clearly seen in the case of love. If one says that X loves Y for a purpose, say in order to get her to marry him so that he will thereby eventually inherit her father's fortune, this implies that X is regarding Y not as a good in herself but merely as a means to some other ulterior good or goal, in this case the father's fortune. This in turn makes nonsense of the behaviour which is most characteristic of love, altruistic behaviour. One of the clues we look for in assessing whether X *really* loves Y or whether X is just pretending to or else is deceiving himself, is any selfless acts of X in regard to Y; that is, acts of X which clearly cannot be of any benefit to X but only to Y.

But it might be thought that this sort of reply relies heavily on the particular examples, love and anger, and that, though false in regard to these particular emotions, the thesis is still true in general. So let us consider another more general argument. If emotions were just means or instruments which we employed to achieve goals and we all possessed these means to some degree, unless deformed or injured, as say we possess and can employ vocal chords for speech, then there is no good reason to believe that we should not be able to employ this instrument, the emotions, deliberately, that is, at will. But we cannot. This point might be put in another way, using grief as our example. While one might say, and make perfectly good sense in saying, 'Try to grieve over the death of your mother-in-law', you cannot sensibly utter the command to someone 'Grieve over the death of your mother-in-law' and expect it to be obeyed. One cannot grieve on demand, though on demand one might be able to induce grief – though not, probably, about just anything one is asked to grieve about – by thinking about suitable scenes or

[1] E.g. Lazarus (1966, esp. pp. 250–3) who describes emotions as a 'coping process', though at times he seems to be referring to what I have referred to as interpretation (3).

getting into a certain frame of mind, but there could be no guarantee that even this would be successful in the way that there could be a guarantee that an attempt to speak by a man who had vocal chords and any other necessary functional items for speech would be successful. Part of the reason for this is that having an emotion is not engaging in an activity and so is not the voluntary mobilising of anything as a means to this activity though, as we have seen, emotions give rise to activities. Another part of the reason is that emotions are complex items involving beliefs, evaluations, wants and physiological reactions to these but that one cannot command someone to genuinely believe something, or sincerely evaluate something as so-and-so, or really want something or other, because believing that something is true, evaluating in a particular way, and wanting something in particular are not things which can be done on demand. One must see the evidence for beliefs or at least have reasons for them, have grounds for evaluating something in one way rather than another, and be drawn to some particular aspect of something if one is to want or desire that thing. Beliefs, evaluations and desires cannot be conjured up just because they are asked for. They are not isolated or empty performances; indeed they are not even performances.[2]

Bernard Williams has put the point above about beliefs with considerable cogency in his article 'Deciding to Believe' (Williams, 1973). He points out that one cannot decide to believe, because this would mean that one could do it at will, and then if one realised the implications of this, one would realise that one could acquire beliefs irrespective of whether they were aimed at the truth or not. But this is contrary to the fundamental nature of belief, which is in part that the believer hold the propositional content of his belief as being true of or about something. If one just adopted beliefs at will, or for some purpose unconnected with their content, one would be believing that *p*, that is, holding *p* to be true, but at the same time realising that one had just decided to adopt *p* irrespective of whether it was true or not. In short, one cannot both decide to believe and realise or be conscious that one's belief is the result of such a decision (Williams, 1973, esp. pp. 148–50).

Deciding to believe would make nonsense of empirical beliefs in particular, for one adopts empirical beliefs, not because one just

[2] On this latter point one might read Penelhum (1967, pp. 245ff.) in *Essays in Philosophical Psychology*.

decides to at will, but because one's observations or evidence-gathering make one believe. Empirical beliefs are useful or functional. They are, as F. P. Ramsey puts it, maps by which we negotiate our way in the world (Ramsey, 1978, p. 134). They could not have this use if they were just adopted at will and had no causal relationship to the world. They would not even be candidates for being called empirical beliefs if there was no causal connection between their adoption and the gathering of evidence by observation or other means.

But it might be argued that neither of these arguments touches the possibility that one could *unconsciously* or *subconsciously* decide to believe and so unconsciously or subconsciously decide to have an emotion. But one must elucidate this possibility very carefully. For a start, I think that one could not obtain genuine empirical beliefs by just deciding to believe something or deciding to believe it for reasons not connected with the content of the belief, even if this were done subconsciously or unconsciously. The necessary causal connection between the content of the belief and reasons for believing this to be the case would be missing. More importantly, it would not even have been given a chance to be present; it would not even have been attempted. So beliefs unconsciously or subconsciously adopted at will are not really even candidates for being given the status of empirical beliefs (even false ones). But it might be argued that one might adopt at will a viewpoint *p*, unconsciously or subconsciously, and that then one might believe this to be a genuine empirical belief, that is, a belief gained in such a way that it is a candidate for being a true empirical belief. In other words – unconsciously or subconsciously – one could be deceived into thinking that *p* is a genuine empirical belief. (It would have to be deception not self-deception, otherwise Williams' argument would count against such a case.) And one could then go on and base an emotion upon this 'belief' that *p*.

This, I think, is a possible scenario for the generation of some emotions but it begins to look implausible if it is made out to be the blueprint for the generation of all or even most emotions. For it would amount to saying that all emotions are malfounded because they are based, not on beliefs, but on things which we are deceived into thinking are genuine beliefs. It would also mean, unless it were added that emotions were adopted for a special purpose, that all emotions or most of them are basically misdirected and so likely to prove useless. While I do not think that *a priori* there is anything against emotions being malfounded and useless states as such, I think that there are facts which suggest that such a thesis is empirically false. There are, for example, many cases of fear which are not merely based on fact but are useful as well. My fear of fire is well-founded and useful, so is my fear of excessive speed in motor cars, of primed but unexploded bombs, of standing on cliff edges when there is no guard rail, and so on. Fear does help us to escape or avoid real dangers. To approach this from another angle, we can and do separate off phobias and other forms of irrationality in regard to emotions from ordinary cases of these emotions because we feel that we have evidence that most or a sizable number of cases of emotions are wellfounded. In other words, we make the malfounded/wellfounded distinction for good factual reasons. And, as I shall go into detail in the next section, we do have good reasons for thinking that emotions are quite often useful.

Robert Solomon's version of this thesis – that emotions are purposive means that emotions are had for a purpose – may be thought to have anticipated and obviated the more obvious sorts of objections to the thesis that emotions are had for a purpose, by bringing in the subconscious. He suggests that the person with an emotion has an 'inability ... to suspect the *purpose* of his emotion', for while an emotion such as anger 'is purposive and intentional in so far as it can be clearly shown to fit into the structure of the subject's purposes and intentions ... these purposes and intentions cannot be known by the subject at the time' (Solomon, 1973, pp. 37–9). In short, Solomon maintains that the thesis only makes sense in the context of subconscious motives which the person having the emotion unknowingly acts in concert with. To put it another way, Solomon's reply is that emotions indeed are had paradigmatically as a result of some purpose or intention, but as a result of some purpose or intention of which the subject of the emotion is unaware (though later on he may become aware of it). As illustration of this more sophisticated version of the Sartrean thesis, Solomon cites the case of 'the husband ... [who] has *used* his anger to manipulate his wife. He has become angry "about" the shirts *in order to* get his wife's mind off the party [for subconsciously the husband does not want to go to the party] and in order to stop her irritating reminders [about the party]', though the husband does not realise why he is angry (Solomon, 1973, p. 33).

For a start, it is not clear in Solomon's thesis whether the husband subconsciously or unconsciously adopts the beliefs and evaluations which generate his anger, or only his purpose in generating the anger. If only the purpose for adopting the emotion is subconscious, then Solomon's thesis would entail *consciously* adopting in pursuance of these purposes – that is, adopting on demand – the beliefs, evaluations and wants which are needed to generate the emotion. Thus his thesis would not be able to meet objections, such as Williams generated, about the impossibility of consciously adopting beliefs on demand or at will. If the beliefs and so on are adopted *unconsciously*, on Solomon's view, then his thesis has to live with the conclusion that emotions are malfounded as such and more than likely to be useless. This conclusion, I have suggested, is contrary to the facts.

Another alternative interpretation of Solomon's thesis is that the beliefs, evaluations and wants are ordinary ones but that they are manipulated to serve a purpose which is subconscious or unconscious. That is, in the example, the husband does believe (and realises that he believes) that his wife laundered his shirts badly, perhaps even burnt them, but normally this would not greatly upset him. However, he sees a purpose in being emotionally angry about it on this occasion; it is a way of causing a 'scene' and so avoiding having to go to the party. So, presumably, he makes himself be emotional about the shirts on this occasion. This interpretation is probably the least plausible because what is done on demand here is the stirring up of the bodily changes and feelings which are not usually causally connected to beliefs, evaluations and wants of the kind and intensity which he now has about the shirts. So the husband has to cause the physiological changes and feelings in some other way. But to do this seems to involve increasing one's heart beat, respiration rate, adrenaline flow, flushing, shaking and tension at will. While it might be possible to do some of this on demand, most of it cannot be so done. But even supposing that the attempt were successful, why should we call the resulting state 'emotional'? The resulting state could not be a genuine emotional one because the unusual physiological changes and feelings are caused, not by the beliefs, evaluations and desires about the wife's laundering of his shirts, but by something else, the husband's will and decision in furthering some purpose.

Leaving aside these difficulties in interpreting the Solomon thesis, and the different difficulties with each of the possible interpretations, let me come back to what does seem central to Solomon's account: that emotions are had or occur on purpose, where the purpose is unconscious or subconscious. For this central aspect of Solomon's thesis has its own difficulties. For a start, there is the basic one of finding evidence in most cases of emotion for the alleged unconscious or subconscious purpose for which, according to Solomon, the emotion is had. If Fred falls in love with his brother's wife, this might seem at a conscious level to be disastrous, for he loves his brother as well and would not want to run the risk of breaking up his brother's happy marriage and giving his children the traumatic experience of having divorced parents. At the conscious level, far from promoting his love as being in keeping with any known purpose or goal of his, he would most likely seek to abort his love for his brother's wife, say, by going away.

Solomon, of course, might reply that the above account may well be the correct one at the conscious level but this does not rule out the possibility of an unconscious or subconscious purpose served by falling in love with his brother's wife. But if Fred himself and no one else could find in his previous behaviour any evidence for inferring such a purpose, what could be the grounds for still maintaining that his falling in love was done for a purpose? In short, if the thesis with or without its modification is ultimately an empirical thesis, that emotions are in fact always adopted or engaged in for a purpose, then the thesis stands or falls according to the evidence for the existence of such purposes. The supporters of the thesis in any form must admit that these overall purposes must ultimately come to light, otherwise the thesis will be vacuous because unfalsifiable and unconfirmable. But where is the evidence for all such purposes, overt or covert? The thesis, being about emotions in general, is only plausible if, in something like the majority of cases, we can see or infer that an emotional occurrence is useful as a means, in the light of what we know about that person's current goals or purposes, and so can be said to be brought about as a means to fulfilling some identifiable goal or purpose.

But in fact the picture seems to be very different. Emotional occurrences are often, for example, unpremeditated reactions. Someone unknown to us elbows us while getting on to the bus, or someone utters a racist remark, and we become angry. All the evidence is that anger of this sort is an instantaneous reaction to something rather than a purposive action or performance to achieve something. Again, emotions are often not merely unpremeditated but also suppressed. In the above case, when someone elbows us out of the way as we board a bus, anger might well up inside us but we fight to control and suppress it, we just fume inwardly. How could one infer that this anger was for a purpose if it is deliberately suppressed, deliberately inhibited from achieving a purpose? Perhaps one could argue that such a person would be at cross purposes – his reason for suppressing the anger cut across his reason for having the anger. But if one always tried to suppress anger because, say, it is an antisocial emotion, we would have the strange picture of a person endlessly at cross purposes with himself!

This thesis, that emotions are done for a purpose, is also precariously close to the old argument that all who do good act benevolently only in pursuance of their own interests, even though they don't admit it or even know it. This argument asserts that even though the benevolent person has no evidence of any ultimate selfish purpose behind his altruism, and even though no one else can see any personal advantage that the benevolent person could achieve by his benevolence, nevertheless there is a hidden or subconscious and self-serving motive behind it all. Indeed such a thesis must keep the motive hidden or subconscious if it is to avoid the risk of refutation by the benevolent person or by others, but if it does do this successfully it also has to admit that no one can bring forward evidence that there *is* any such lurking motive. Likewise this thesis about emotions is in danger of depending for its plausibility on the credibility of positing motives behind emotional occurrences which are forever consigned to our subconscious, or to some other even more shadowy world, so that no evidence can count for or against the positing of such subterranean motives.

Emotions as serving the purposes of the person having them

Unless I was afraid of being burnt I might not avoid putting my hand into the fire. A child has to learn about fire if he is to be able to evaluate it as dangerous, which in turn will lead the child into wanting to avoid it. Emotions are not just registerings or scannings of the world, or even just processes of rating or evaluating what is scanned, *they get us to do things* (or, at least, to want to do them) as a result of our evaluations. Some have thought that this means that emotions should be seen as useful to humans, not as things which are done as a means to furthering basic human interests or instincts – for we have seen that this thesis is false – but as things which lead us to do things which further our interests. Emotional reactions are related to our basic wants such that behaviour stemming from them will also be related to our basic wants. Fear is evaluating something as dangerous and reacting bodily to this evaluation; it is also a reaction which stirs up very strong desires to avoid or be rid of the danger, because one of our basic interests is self-preservation. An emotion such as fear could be called an alerting mechanism in that it stirs up man's physiology, gets the adrenaline going, and drives him to defensive or avoidance action in times of danger (the 'fight or flight' view of fear). This then is a general sketch of that view of the emotions which sees them as useful in furthering man's basic interests or instincts at times when they are threatened and urgent action is required.

The most immediate difficulty with this view of the emotions is that, while it might well fit emotions like fear and anger, it does not seem to fit emotions like envy and malice. Envy is not stirred up in response to any threat to some basic instinct or interest, nor does it seem to promote any instinct or interest. It is stirred up by self-centred resentment at another's good fortune. It is engendered by a failure on our part to enjoy or at least not mind another's good fortune. Malice is even further from any preservation of ourselves from threat or any furtherance of our basic interests as it involves vindictive pleasure in another's misfortune, and is a reaction to a state of affairs which might have no conceivable effect on our own fortunes. Far from seeing envy and malice as useful, we tend to find them regrettable reactions which are hard to get rid of but which we feel we ought to try to eradicate or at least suppress. We feel that they result from a warped personality or at least from a personality which is so self-centred and self-seeking that it cannot bear others' good fortune and positively delights in their misfortune. If such emotions as envy and malice are ever related to interests, they are related to less acceptable and less useful interests than self-preservation.

It is this contrast between emotions such as fear and anger, and emotions such as envy and malice, which partly generates the useful/useless distinction between emotions. Fear is useful in the avoidance of danger, and anger might be useful in stirring up the aggression needed to get us to fight to protect ourselves or others. Other emotions, for example remorse, might be seen as useful, not so much as against immediate threats, as on some longer term basis. Remorse might be seen as useful in helping us to avoid a repetition of some moral wrong, sin or crime about which we now feel remorse. On the other hand no such uses, either long or short term, can be found for envy and malice. Indeed because the latter are not merely not useful, but socially divisive, one could derive a distinction between emotions which are socially useful or socially approved of and those which are socially divisive and so socially disapproved of. Socially approved of emotions would be ones like love, pity and sympathy which promote social cooperation and so could be said to be socially useful. The divisive and socially disapproved of emotions would be ones like envy, jealousy, malice and hate which tend to issue in behaviour which is antisocial. This distinction is probably not exhaustive, because one should probably class emotions such as grief and joy as asocial. They tend to be personal and lead neither to social nor anti-social actions, though one could perhaps make out a case that grief leads one to try to avoid the causes of the tragedies which cause us to grieve. I am not convinced, however, that this is true, or that joy leads us to a better frame of mind and so is more likely to make us pleasant to deal with. But at any rate such explanations are already beginning to look rather strained and implausible. And it is probably less controversial to describe emotions such as embarrassment and depression as asocial and private emotions, though one could conceivably find ways in which they lead to actions which are socially useful or otherwise.

Emotions as organising or disruptive of behaviour

Another outcome of the view of emotions as serving the purposes of or as being useful to the person having the emotions is the theory that looks upon emotions as a mechanism which facilitates and organises behaviour in certain circumstances. On the other hand, there are psychologists who claim that the opposite is the case, namely that emotions are disruptive of behaviour and disorganise it.

Arnold and Gasson claim that emotions 'help us reach the perfection of our personality, the actuation of our potentialities' (Arnold and Gasson, 1968, Part 7, p. 212). Presumably, though they do not make this clear, what is meant by this is that the emotion will bring out in us new levels of daring and, more tangibly, new levels of behavioural response which help us and would not otherwise be possible. Fear, for example, will so stir us up and get the adrenaline going that, in a certain context, it might give fleetness of foot not normal to us; thus fear might be seen as helping us escape from the tiger by enabling us to run away with a speed which is beyond us except in this specially aroused emotional state. So, they claim, emotions are to be seen primarily as 'instruments in the pursuit of our purposes', that is, instruments which enhance and organise our reactions in the pursuit of our purposes, though they do allow that 'emotion can act as a disorganizing factor as well' when it is very intense and when a person is 'inordinately attached to his self-ideal' to the neglect of his 'rational goal and ... final end',[3] by which they mean, I think, when a person is following short-term selfish goals to the neglect of his real ultimate (and unselfish?) goals. R. W. Leeper is more emphatic that emotions are primarily organising processes:

> The stronger the emotional process aroused ... the more certainly will his behavior be governed in a way consistent with his emotional reaction ... If this line of argument is sound, it means that emotional processes operate primarily as motives. It means that they are processes which arouse, sustain, and direct activity.[4]

On the other hand there are psychologists, such as Pradines, who are equally emphatic that 'emotions are disruptive by nature' for 'disorder is emotion itself. It defines and constitutes emotion.'[5] N. L. Munn in his chapter on emotion in his book, *Psychology: The fundamentals of human adjustment*, writes that 'perhaps as satisfactory a definition as can be given at the present time describes emotion as "an acute disturbance of the individual as a whole, psychological in origin, involving behaviour, conscious experience, and visceral functioning"'. He then explains that 'all but the mildest emotions

---

[3] Arnold and Gasson (1968, pp. 212, 216–17). Here one might question the whole notion of man's having a final or ultimate end but to do so would take us far away from the discussion of emotions and purpose.

[4] In Leeper (1948) reprinted in Arnold (1968, p. 185). And Young in 'Affective processes', an extract from Young (1961) and reprinted in Arnold (1968, p. 236), concludes that 'affective arousals [emotions] are motivating in the sense that they evoke action, regulate the course of behavior, and organize patterns of approach and withdrawal. They engender relatively stable systems of value within the organism', though in an earlier book, Young (1943) inclined to the opposite view.

[5] From an extract from Pradines (1958), reprinted in Arnold (1968, p. 197).

disturb or upset whatever activities are in progress at the time of arousal'.[6] This school sees emotions as basically useless and best suppressed or overcome where this is possible.

So emotions are seen by one lot of psychologists as basically good or helpful but by another group as basically bad and disruptive. Since both sides in this dispute have evidence for their view and document cases in which emotions facilitate and organise behaviour, and cases in which emotions disrupt behaviour, the truth is surely, as E. J. Murray writes, that 'the evidence so far suggests that both emotion and motivation can positively organize and facilitate be- havior, at certain times, but they may also disorganize and disrupt behavior' (Murray, 1964, p. 64).[7] For there are, of course, many cases which do illustrate the fact that emotions, when they involve a speeding up of our metabolic processes, such as our breathing, blood-flow and adrenaline supply, are useful. There is the well- known account of a woman who, on seeing her child pinned by the wheels of a heavy truck, lifted the truck and so freed her child; a task which she would not have attempted in a cool unemotional moment and which in such a moment would have been beyond her strength.

There are also clear-cut cases when just this speeding-up proves disruptive. Nervousness, fear or overexcitement can spoil the com- petitor's aim when firing a target pistol or rifle, as his speeded-up metabolism makes it harder for him to keep his arm steady and to put a steady pressure on the trigger at the right moment.

E. J. Murray suggests that we can draw up principles for when emotions are useful and for when they are disruptive.

> Two important factors are involved: the strength of the motive and the difficulty of the task. Behavior is facilitated by a motive up to some strength and then the motive is disorganizing. The exact point of the change depends on the difficulty of the task, with more difficult tasks becoming disorganized at lower levels of motivation [Murray, 1964, p. 64].

I think the matter is more complicated than this. It is not a simple interplay of these two factors on all occasions. In the first place the strength of the physiological changes or upsets can alone be dis- ruptive of even the simplest of tasks. For while fear, by pumping

---

[6] Reprinted in Arnold (1968, p. 173). Others holding a similar view are Dockeray (1942) and Woodworth (1940).

[7] See also Hebb (1949) reprinted in Arnold (1968, pp. 142–4).

adrenaline into the fearful person's system, may lend the fearful person a speed of which he would not otherwise have been capable, it may also render him incapable of running at all, for it may make him shake violently so that his legs tighten up too much or he loses control of his legs. So 'the exact point of the change' from emotion as organising and facilitating to emotion as disrupting may, at least in certain cases, be entirely a function of the strength of the emotion. Secondly, the other factor in interplay with the strength of the emotion would often be more accurately described in terms of the nature and persistence of a situation, and the nature of the person undergoing the emotion, rather than in terms of the difficulty of some task. An extremely dangerous situation persisting for a long time might be just too much for a person, so that he goes beyond the point of controlling and channelling the emotional behaviour. For example, a mountain climber in a dangerous situation, and so in a state of fear, might be able to control his limbs well for two hours but then suddenly 'crack' and succumb. The cause of his succumbing is the persistence of the danger and the fatiguing effect of his persisting fear rather than the difficulty of the task, though this latter might have something to do with it. Again it is often the nature of the emotional person which, in combination with the strength of the emotion, disrupts behaviour. To put it simply, the strength of anything is relative. A mildly dangerous situation might stir up an emotional state of fear which immobilises and disrupts the behaviour of one person but not of another, not because the first person's emotional state involves more intense physiological reactions and feelings but simply because he is less able to cope with the level of physiological reactions and feelings which another might cope with easily.

Furthermore, in so far as the task concerned has an effect on whether the emotion is organising or disruptive of action, it is not always the difficulty of the task to the exclusion of other aspects of the task which renders the emotional effects disruptive. It could be merely the nature of the task, which requires skills not facilitated by the effects which emotions often produce. Emotional states of the speeded-up adrenaline-pumping variety will not help one to do tasks which require coolness, calmness, steadiness and thoughtfulness, but will help one to do tasks which require strength, aggressiveness and speed, at least at times. Nervousness, excitement, anxiety and fear will probably spoil the aim of the marksman but may well help the speed of the man running away from the tiger. Anger may well give one an aggressiveness one would not otherwise have and so enable one to stand up and fight better, but it may well ruin one's debating technique or one's skill at chess. Indeed an emotional state can have both helpful and unhelpful effects on a person at the same time. Anger may make a boxer more aggressive and in that respect make him a better fighter, but anger may also spoil his boxing technique for this requires concentration and coolness in the heat of the contest. Anger may make him want to punch his opponent very hard but it may make him forget to keep his guard up.

Yet there are emotions, the depressant ones, which seem to slow down our responses, dampen our enthusiasm and so render us unfit for what we can normally cope with. Sadness, some forms of depression,[8] and some forms of anxiety seem to slow down our metabolic processes abnormally and so make us listless, which in turn makes us less able to perform things which require our interest, attention, concentration or persistence. A sad tennis player is less likely to play well than one not sad. The sad or depressed player will lack the competitive 'edge' and so lack the will to retrieve the difficult shot or to summon up his ebbing strength for a fast first serve. On the other hand, the calmness and the carefree feeling which comes with some emotional states of happiness or love may make a person persist in tasks which in other moods or in the grip of other emotions he would give up. Calm and happy workers at most jobs are better than edgy and irritable ones.

[8] Clinically speaking, there are agitated and anxiously excited depressions, anancastic depressions which are characterised by compulsions of various sorts, and neurotic depressions that can be manifested in hysterical or aggressive behaviour. But here, and elsewhere, when using the term 'depression', I am referring to the sort of depression which is a reaction to one's disadvantageous or undesirable circumstances and shows itself as a lowering of one's physiological vitality, in an inability to react in any excited way, and in a pessimistic view of one's circumstances. See 'Depression' in Eysenck, Arnold and Meili (1975, Vol. I, pp. 259–60).

13

Blaming the emotions

In this chapter I shall discuss when, if ever, one may blame a person for his emotions. *Prima facie* it might seem that emotions come upon us like gusts of wind and blow us about in one direction and then in another without our having any say in the matter, and that it would be as absurd to blame a person for having emotions as to blame him for being blown about by the wind. But I want to argue that this view of the matter is only superficial for, while it may be useful in some respects to view emotions as gusts of wind over which we have no control, it can also lead us badly astray. For, if we look more closely, we will find that there are a number of ways in which we can control our emotions and so a number of ways in which we can be blamed in respect of our emotions. In the course of this closer look, I will discuss:

(1) The notion of blame which I employ;

(2) The ways in which one can be said to control the emotions; and (3), with (2) above in mind: The ways in which a person could be blamed in regard to his emotions.

Blame

Without being drawn into a protracted discussion as to what blame is, I think that it will help to avoid ambiguities if I declare in what sense I am using the term 'blame'. While I am taking it, to quote J. E. R. Squires, that 'to blame a person is to be of the opinion that he is responsible for an undesired upshot, that he has done what he ought not' (Squires, 1968b, p. 60), I feel that L. C. Holborow is correct in saying that our ordinary and central notion of blame contains an additional element of 'holding it against' the person blamed or of implicit discredit to the person blamed (Holborow, 1971–2, p. 89). And I think Holborow's contention is borne out by the fact that

J. J. C. Smart's notion of blame, which is very similar to Squires',[1] is not, as he frankly admits, the current or ordinary notion.[2]

Holborow has also pointed out that the presumption (made, for example, by Smart (1961, p. 305)), that our ordinary notion of blame would be inappropriate if applied to determined actions, is incorrect. We do in fact blame people for some determined actions, for example those actions that stem from 'psychological inabilities such as tactlessness, social obtuseness, and chronic insensitivity to the feelings of others' (Holborow, 1971–2, p. 91). In the light of this comment, it should be noted that, while the responsibility criterion for blame is usually to be construed widely enough so as to include such determined actions, I will be employing this criterion more narrowly, so as only to be applicable when the agent has some control over his actions. This in turn will mean that my concept of blame is slightly stronger than the usual one and will leave no room for the suggestion that to blame a person in regard to his emotions is to blame in only a very weak sense.

I think that Holborow draws attention to another important and usually overlooked aspect of blame when he argues that to have been responsible for an undesirable upshot is not enough to merit blame, it must be clear that there are no mitigating circumstances (Holborow, 1971–2, pp. 87–8).

I am not so convinced that Holborow is correct in extending the notion of 'undesirable upshot' to actions or states of affairs which are merely the expression of an undesirable character trait or motive (Holborow, 1971–2, p. 100). I am not sure, for instance, that someone's words may be blameworthy merely because they are a revelation of a blameworthy and undesirable character trait rather than blameworthy or undesirable because of some harm or undesirable upshot which they cause. I suspect that Kenny is closer to the truth when he writes that 'we are praised and blamed for what we do, envied or pitied for what happens to us'. Kenny, (1963, p. 179; see also p. 184). I think that we are blamed for character traits and their expression *only* in so far as it is considered that a character trait has given rise to actions which have had an undesirable upshot. If character traits did not ever do anything, they could never do harm.

---

[1] Smart (1961, pp. 304–5) writes that 'to blame a person for an action is not only to grade it (morally) but to imply that it is something for which the person is responsible'.

[2] Smart (1961, p. 305): 'Now most men do not, in my opinion, praise and blame people in this dispassionate and clear-headed way.'

I suspect that what is needed here[3] is a distinction between *moral disapproval* and *blame*. We very often morally disapprove of actions or words in so far as they are expressions of undesirable character traits or motives because, rightly, we believe that sooner or later such traits or motives will lead to some undesirable upshot. But it seems logically odd to blame before there is any proof or even suggestion of any undesirable upshot. We might disapprove of the selfish man but we don't blame him till he has actually done something undesirable. We might blame the malicious man but only because we believe that malicious talk is harmful, for example to reputations. Given that the phrase 'harmless malice' is not a contradiction in terms, it would seem odd to blame harmless malice. On the other hand *schadenfreude*, an enjoyment of another's misfortune, is a type of malice which might not involve any actual harm to another and so not give rise to any undesirable upshot. But this said, it becomes clear that it would therefore be odd to blame someone even for *schadenfreude*, though we might morally disapprove. There just is not anything to blame the person for.

So, on the view of blame which I have adopted, there are four main elements:

(i) The imputation of responsibility to some person for some action or state of affairs brought about wholly or partly by his action, inaction or influence;

(ii) The contention that the action or state of affairs brought about by the action is, according to the criteria of some system (usually moral), harmful in some sense or, in general, undesirable;

(iii) The belief that there are no excusing circumstances;

(iv) The consequent discrediting or disapproval of the person concerned. At times, for (i), (ii) and (iii) above to be true of some person will itself in the context amount to the discrediting of that person. At other times, words of disapproval or faulting, or gestures or tones of voice which amount to the same, may be added.

Controlling one's emotions

Given that the above account of blame is acceptable, then it will follow that, to show that one can legitimately blame people for

[3] As L. C. Holborow has suggested to me in conversation.

having emotions, one must first make out a case that a person can be responsible for his emotions at least in some respects and to some extent. I propose to make out a case that, to some degree at any rate, a person can exercise control over his emotions and to that extent be held responsible for them.

In the previous chapter, when discussing whether emotions could be had on purpose, I argued that they could not. I pointed out that emotions include beliefs, evaluations and wants which cannot be induced at will, as they are not like actions or performances which one can do on demand, but are more like reactions or responses engendered or stirred up in us by conditions which we usually cannot control.

In this section I want to dwell on the ways in which, at least to a certain extent, we can be said to exercise control over our emotions. One can, of course, much more easily induce certain emotions, for example fear, *in others* but a discussion of this would not be germane to a discussion of how much a person can control and so be held responsible for his own emotions.

Inducing an emotion in oneself by manipulating the context

To induce emotions in oneself, one could consider under which conditions the appropriate emotion occurs and then deliberately manufacture or duplicate such a situation. This is not to induce emotions in oneself at will but is an ability to induce some emotions in oneself in certain circumstances with some likelihood of success. In fact this is just what an experimental psychologist interested in studying the emotions does with his subjects. If I know that I am afraid of spiders, I know that to put myself in the vicinity of a spider will be to induce fear. And, given a detailed knowledge of the conditions under which I undergo any of the other emotions, there is no reason to believe that I could not induce those emotions too, in those circumstances.

Avoiding an emotion by manipulating the context

Now, in so far as one can discover the objects or situations which cause the different emotions in us, and in so far as one can manipulate one's environment so as to duplicate or reproduce these objects or situations, which is by no means always possible, one can not only induce an emotion in oneself, but one can also avoid being overcome by an emotion. Very often we cannot control our environment, and cannot control our emotional reactions. But sometimes we can. Take the case of an agoraphobe who avoids open spaces to such an extent that he has never been outside his house since he was married. He may have reflected that going outside causes an emotional state of fear so intense it incapacitates him. So he may have argued to himself, and quite rationally, that since he cannot get rid of his fear of open spaces, he can at least control it by avoiding them. Of course he may be simply, unreflectively afraid and just never go outside. To take another example, part of the point of monastic solitude and enclosure is to make sure that the monk does not meet women, with whom he might fall in love, for that might lead him to break his vow of celibacy and lessen his total commitment to God's service. In voluntarily placing himself under the monastic rules, a monk is voluntarily avoiding certain emotions, such as sexual love.

Aborting an emotion by manipulating the context

One can also exercise control over one's emotions on occasion by deliberately aborting them once they have taken root. If one finds that one is quaking with fear while viewing Paris from the Eiffel Tower then, if one realises that this fear is a fear of heights in general, one can rid oneself of this particular fear – though not of the disposition or liability to be afraid of heights – by simply climbing down to the ground. Or a woman who wants to stop herself loving a colleague who does not return her love but insults and ridicules her might smother her love by getting a new job so as to ensure that she won't see him every day in the office. With love, the adage 'out of sight, out of mind' will work, after a time, for some people. One can see some point in rich Victorian parents sending their love-struck daughter, infatuated with someone quite unsuitable, on a long sea voyage. Her mind occupied with the social life on board and the sights of the Mediterranean ports, the memory of her suitor would be erased, and her love aborted.

Talking oneself or allowing oneself to be talked out of a badly grounded emotion

Our emotions are generated not only by the external situation but also, and indeed chiefly, by our view of the situation, that is, as we have seen, by our evaluation of the situation. This gives us a clue to another way in which emotions can be controlled. It is not inconceivable that the agoraphobe could have talked himself out of his fear; though the very use of the words 'phobia' or 'phobe' usually implies such a tenacious state that only a psychiatrist is likely to succeed. A child might initially be afraid of going outside the house, particularly without his or her mother or father, but once it is explained that there is nothing to fear, that the birds, butterflies, and other denizens of the back garden do not attack children or cause them harm in any way, and she discovers that this is so, the fear will dissolve. The parents initiated the change in the child's evaluation of the back garden, from a dangerous to a not so dangerous place, but there is no reason to think that one could not do this for oneself. The difference between the case of the child and that of the agoraphobe is that the former's fear is rational but the latter's not. An agoraphobe is a person whose fear of open spaces cannot usually be overturned by reasoned explanations to the effect that open spaces as such are not dangerous. For the agoraphobe's fear is based on an incontrovertible evaluation of open spaces as dangerous; he allows no evidence to count for or against his evaluative judgment. His evaluation is simply irrational, that is, not open to being breached by reasons, rather than simply being without reasons.

But leaving aside cases of irrational evaluations, one can change one's own evaluations or allow one's evaluations to be changed, and so any emotions wholly based on them, if the evaluations are based on an undetected mistake of fact or on a deliberate avoidance of the facts or on a deliberate effort to forget them. For all these paths are paths to the generation of malfounded emotions, and such emotions can be aborted when the facts are brought to light and they change the basic evaluation that gave rise to the emotions. One's love for someone might be aborted if one finally agrees to listen to those who have all along pointed out that he or she is only after one's money and is an irredeemably selfish person. One is allowing oneself to be talked out of the love. Al Capone's moll might love him dearly but her love for him might be aborted if she eventually does really listen to and take in the reports of his crimes, given of course that moral values and so moral evaluations play an important part in the evaluation of him. Examples of emotions less subjective than love are probably more convincing. A child might cease to be afraid when she realises that some of the landmarks are familiar, and that in consequence she is not lost. A person might cease to be angry with his rival by finally allowing himself to see that all the evidence points to the fact that it was not he who betrayed him.

Talking oneself into a badly grounded emotion

There are the cases of inducing emotions by self-deception. One might learn, say, to hate a certain race by deliberately concocting and eventually believing what one initially knew to be defamatory lies about the people of that race. But self-deception is usually less obvious. It might begin simply with jokes implying that members of a race are mentally inferior, which are then extended to suggest that they are dangerous or evil. Eventually, by coming to believe the suggestions, one might generate in oneself a fear or hatred of the race concerned.

More usual perhaps are the cases of people deceiving themselves about someone and then reacting to their deceptive image of that person. A person might project his fantasy of an ideal woman onto a woman who possesses few if any of his ideal characteristics and thereby fall in love with her.

Keeping an emotion going

One can protect and promote an emotion by fostering the conditions in which it is likely to prosper. Love, for example, is more likely to prosper if the persons concerned are free from anxiety which tends to cause tenseness, short temper and quarrelling. By taking measures to avoid anxiety, say by taking measures to ensure job security, a reasonable income and non-interference by relatives, a married couple might be said to be taking measures to preserve and protect their love. It is not obvious that there are other emotions which one would try to promote in this way, though conceivably someone with a vested interest in his anger or hate may continually dwell on the facts which give rise to his anger in order to preserve it. Western films sometimes make use of the character of an old gunfighter who continually feeds his hatred or anger, by 'flashback' to some dastardly deed he suffered, to ensure that his desire for revenge, which propels him through the film towards its object, is sustained.

Overcoming an emotion by shock tactics

One way of controlling the emotions is the very direct one of just not giving in to the wants or desires that arise from them. By positively seeking out the occasions of these unwanted emotions, yet not acting in accordance with them, one may eventually overcome them; it is almost a form of inoculation. For example, it used to be thought important to get an apprentice pilot who had had an accident while flying, back into the air immediately in order to conquer the fear of flying produced by the accident. It was a form of shock treatment which made him act in direct opposition to his fear and by reestablishing his confidence overcome it. I suspect that cures weren't always wrought by this method, and that it might have been better to let the pilot's fear subside before getting him to fly again. Be all this as it may, one can transfer this example to contexts in which a person employs similar shock tactics upon himself. To change the example slightly, someone learning to fly might ask to be allowed to get back into an aeroplane and fly immediately after a serious accident. Or a steeplejack, after a fall, might talk himself into going back to work on high buildings despite his fear of falling again. A person might try and overcome his fear of spiders by deliberately allowing them to crawl over his hand, to demonstrate to himself that they do no harm, and so overcome his fear.

Though usually associated with fear, this direct tactic can work with other emotions as well. An adolescent boy embarrassed by girls might deliberately join various mixed clubs so as to overcome his embarrassment. A person may succeed in overcoming a dislike or revulsion by deliberately putting himself in the presence of that which causes it.

This shock tactic of deliberately and suddenly exposing someone to the object of his fear is one of the three main sorts of behaviour therapy for phobias and is called 'flooding'. The other two methods are connected. The second, called 'desensitisation', is essentially the same operation without the shock. The neurotic patient is gradually accustomed to the object of his phobia. The third method involves getting the patient to copy someone who – on film or in situ – is successfully coping with the object of the phobia.[4]

Controlling the behaviour stemming from emotions

While one might not be able or not want to stifle an emotion, one might be able and think it important to stifle the behaviour stemming from it. One might find oneself in a fit of temper and have an urge to hit someone nearby but one might see good reasons for controlling this urge. Often this control will take the form of recognising overriding reasons for not acting on the wants and

[4] H. J. Eysenck, *You and Neurosis*, Fontana-Collins, 1977, Ch. 4.

desires which arise in emotional states. I might stop myself hitting my child in a fit of exasperated anger by telling myself that this would be immoral, or at least illegal and likely to land me before the courts on a charge of child battering. Sometimes this control will take the form of just making oneself realise that to act on the emotion is pointless. If the person who killed my child is now dead, there is little point in raging around trying to do him harm. With some emotions, like envy and jealousy, we might feel that we should always stifle their expression simply because we find them demeaning and believe that they reveal one to be small-minded. We might have more high-minded reasons for always stopping ourselves acting out of hate or anger, feeling that harm often comes from these emotions. With other emotions we might feel that while no harm usually comes of them, no good comes either. For example, self-pity is often regarded as a wasteful indulgence, a self-centred wallowing, which we are better off without.

Controlling the non-purposive expressions of emotion

Finally, to a certain extent one can control or at least hide the non-purposive expressions of emotions. Contrariwise one can wallow in them as well. A grief-stricken person can strive and sometimes succeed in keeping back tears, or at least stemming them. Alternatively they can wallow in having the tears and spend days and months in displays of grief. It is a lot harder to stop oneself blushing out of embarrassment, though one can learn to mask it. Sometimes, too, a fearful person can steel himself and stop trembling. That is, in so far as the physiological effects of emotions affect our muscles, and in so far as ordinarily we exercise considerable control over our muscles, we can exercise control over the physiological expressions of our emotions.[5]

There may, of course, be occasions when we want to exaggerate the expression of our emotions, though this seems to be much more unusual and more difficult. Nevertheless it is not inconceivable that a person might learn, if not to weep, at least not to inhibit his weeping when grief-stricken. This would be important if one moved from a culture where for a man to show grief by weeping was

[5] In physiological psychology there is a growing body of evidence to suggest that we can control visceral changes – such as heart rate and blood pressure – to a much greater extent than was previously imagined. See Richard S. Lazarus (1975b, esp. pp. 62–3).

considered unmanly to one where for a man not to show grief by weeping would be for his grief to be suspect.

In this general section on controlling the emotions I have discussed:

(a) The ways in which one might avoid, abort, or overcome one's own emotion whether it be well-founded or badly grounded;

(b) The ways in which one might induce in oneself a wellfounded or badly grounded emotion or particular emotional state;

(c) The ways in which one might promote or foster an emotion in oneself, or the behaviour and expressions stemming from them;

(d) The ways in which one might curb the behaviour and expression stemming from one's emotions.

I shall now turn to the discussion of the blame that might attach to a person for his emotions, as the corollary of each of these types of control over them.

Blaming the emotions

If each of the ways in which we can be said to exercise control over the emotions can give rise to some undesirable upshot so that the person having the emotion can be held responsible for the undesirable upshot, and if it is presumed that, in the cases exemplifying these ways, there are no mitigating circumstances, then all the conditions for blame have been fulfilled in respect of a person's emotions. It will have been shown when a person can be blamed for his emotions.

Blaming a person for avoiding, aborting or overcoming his own emotion

Though blaming a person for avoiding, aborting or overcoming an emotion might be rare, it is not impossible to conceive of this. The most likely cases, I think, would involve love. One might blame a person for aborting his love for someone for selfish reasons. John, though very much in love with Susan, and *vice versa*, might deliberately stifle his love when, after she is invalided by a car accident, he realises that he is spending all his time and money looking after her. While still loving Susan he may begin to resent the erosion of his savings and social life, which caring for her entails. He might decide that his love for Susan is ruining his enjoyment of life, and take steps to eradicate it. Now, if he succeeds, and abandons

Susan to her own resources, we would, I think, blame him if Susan, without the emotional and monetary support that stemmed from his love, was left without adequate financial or psychological resources. And in such a case I think that it would be clear that John's aborting his love in order to avoid its consequences would not be excused by his reasons for doing so.

Let us take an example which involves another emotion than that of love. Deliberately stifling or aborting one's pity might be blameworthy. If a guard at a concentration camp was moved by pity for his victims to want to ease their lot, but deliberately stifled his feelings of pity so as not to risk losing his job, we would blame the guard. For in smothering his pity he was led to making no attempt to try and save the inmates from torture and death, and there is nothing in the description of the case to make one think that he had any excuses for not helping them.

Blaming a person for inducing an emotion or a particular emotional state in himself

Hatred is the obvious example here. I think we would blame a person for inducing race hatred in himself by, say, seeking out and reading literature which he knew was considered to be racialist in the extreme, if his hatred then led him to commit racial violence. And even before he had acted on his hatred we would morally disapprove of him. Indeed I think we would morally disapprove of a person who deliberately induced in himself any emotion, such as envy or resentment, which is liable to lead to morally undesirable acts, and we would blame him if in fact he did commit such acts.

But I think that one can blame a person for inducing in himself an emotional state of any emotion which we usually approve of or are at least neutral about, if it could be said that he ought to have foreseen that, by inducing such an emotional state in the circumstances, undesirable results would ensue. A person who deliberately puts himself into a situation which he knows reduces him to a state of hysterical fear incurs blame if this leads him to neglect important duties, like caring for his children. We would blame a father who was hysterically afraid of water if he took his children to bathe at a secluded beach and then was unable to overcome his fear to help when one of his children got into difficulties in the water, and drowned.

Blaming a person for promoting or fostering his emotions or the behaviour and expressions stemming from them

If we would be blamed for not aborting an emotion, or for deliberately inducing it, *a fortiori* we would be blamed for promoting or fostering it. If a person's hatred has already led to murder, then for him deliberately to stoke his hatred merits further blame. Such examples are, I think, obvious.

So here I will concentrate on cases where the emotion itself is not blameworthy if it is kept within bounds, but becomes blameworthy if it is not, that is, on cases where what leads to the undesirable upshot is the deliberate fostering of emotional behaviour and emotional expressions. I am not suggesting that we should blame a person for excessive displays of emotion as such, though we might find such inordinate abandonment to an emotion aesthetically displeasing or annoying or just ridiculous, but only for their resulting in an undesirable upshot. For example, for a widow with several children to wallow deliberately in her grief at the death of her husband, to such an extent that she neglected her children's health, would be blameworthy. And the neglect of the children's health is a result of wallowing in grief and not just of the grief. One can grieve quietly and within reasonable bounds, not neglecting at least one's duties to others, or one can grieve with selfish indulgence, dwelling so much on one's loss and with such wild displays that one gives oneself wholly to grief at the expense of all else.

Self-pity is another emotion which may be indulged in to excess, to the neglect of one's duties to others.

There is a further way in which excessive displays of emotion may be deemed blameworthy. If the occurrence of emotional states makes acting on the motives inherent in such emotional states more likely, then deliberately to abandon oneself to an emotional state could be deliberately to abandon what control one does have over one's emotional behaviour. When angry, for example, one might feel like indulging in physical violence, which usually turns out to be morally reprehensible. Now if one fosters anger, savouring the outraged feelings and aggressive impulses, knowing that one normally acts on them quite impulsively, one can be said to be deliberately loosening one's hold on one's aggressive impulses. If something morally undesirable does then result from my fit of anger, I can be blamed, not merely for not controlling my anger, but for deliberately putting myself into a position which I knew from previous experience would lead to uncontrollable behaviour. In a sense, then, I am being blamed for deliberately abandoning what control I do have in these matters by indulging my anger to the point where my control vanishes.

Now of course one need not have fostered or induced an emotion to incur blame for its undesirable consequences. It may just be a strong emotion in any case, with unfortunate effects, in which case one may deserve blame for failing to try and quell the emotion and curb the behaviour stemming from it. One would not be excused from blame for running away and not staying to *try* and defend one's wife from an assailant, by claiming that one was afraid. Because one is deemed to have some control, usually, over one's fear, one is not excused from acting in opposition to one's fear in such circumstances. To give in to fear in such circumstances is reprehensible, for it is not just being afraid, it is also being cowardly.

To revert to an earlier example, it is reprehensible not to try and abort a love which can only lead to tragic consequences for others, and so not to try at least to curb any expression of it or behaviour stemming from it, which helps to keep it going.

Blaming a person for deliberately curbing the behaviour resulting from, and expression of, emotion

Cases where deliberately curbing the expression of one's emotions would give rise to morally reprehensible results, are, I think, less obvious. One that comes to mind is that of a mother deliberately curbing the display of her love for her child to such an extent that the child becomes emotionally disturbed. Here the causal connection seems clearly to be between the curbing of the display or expression and the emotional disturbance, for, in the context, the emotion itself, far from being unworthy in any respect, is especially appropriate. However, it would be difficult to be sure that there were no mitigating circumstances. For the parent who loves her child, but deliberately refrains from showing this love in any way, would usually be following out, I suspect, some unfortunate theory about how showing love or too much of it is bad for the child. But it is possible to imagine circumstances where more sinister motives were at hand. A mother might deliberately refrain from showing her love, in order to punish the child for some real or imagined slight, failure or mishap, or as a way to carry on a quarrel with her estranged husband who dotes on the child.

One can also imagine circumstances in which the curbing of the natural or appropriate expressions of an emotion other than love was blameworthy. For example, for a teacher to show anger at one pupil's bullying but not at another's, say because the teacher was friendly with the latter's father, would, I think, be morally reprehensible. For not only is bias in a teacher reprehensible in itself in most instances, in this case it would clearly amount to condoning the second pupil's bullying and so be a dangerous precedent as well.

It is a little easier to find cases where to curb the behaviour stemming from emotions, rather than the expression of emotions or display of them, is blameworthy. For to curb the behaviour stemming from pity or compassion may be to neglect some natural duty to others. Like the Samaritan, the Levite may have felt compassion for the man lying injured by the wayside. His wrong may have been, not that he felt no compassion, but that he would not allow himself to act out of compassion. Perhaps, selfishly, he did not want to be delayed or 'did not want any trouble'. Through not running away from a bomb that is about to go off, say because of some misguided sense of bravado when there is nothing to be gained by staying in the vicinity of the bomb, one might be killed. And if one is the sole parent of children, this could be seen as a neglect of parental duties. Again, not to act out of anger, because, say, of some misguided view that one should *never* act out of anger, might lead one not to defend someone in danger from an assailant.

14

Looking back: a summary

This book has been an attempt to present a clear step-by-step account of one particular version of a cognitive theory of occurrent emotional states. I began, in the first two chapters, with a brief critical survey of classical theories of emotion and outlined four major theoretical streams, the feeling, the behaviourist, the psycho-analytic and the cognitive. Historically the movement has been from the Aristotelian–Thomistic cognitive accounts to the Cartesian or feeling theories, then, via William James, to behaviourism. Finally, via psychoanalytic and instinct theories, there has been something like a return to cognitivism in both philosophy and psychology. But this outline also brought to light that, both in philosophy, because of the influence of Wittgenstein and the Analytic school, and in psychology, because of the dominance of behaviourism and its conspicuous lack of success in the area of emotion, there has been a marked reluctance to put forward full-blooded theories of emotion. In this book, on the other hand, in keeping with the older tradition in both philosophy and psychology, I have put forward a theory in terms of a model of occurrent emotional states rather than an account of how we use various emotion terms.

I began the third chapter by clarifying what it means to give an account of emotional states rather than emotions considered dis-positionally. Then I explained that I had called the theory I was espousing 'a causal–evaluative theory' because it claimed that the concept of emotion as occurrent state amounted to an evaluation which caused unusual physiological changes in the subject of the evaluation. I pointed out the differences between the concept of emotion as such, the concept of particular emotions, and the factor which differentiates one particular emotional state from another. I concluded by trying to allay the suspicions, particularly of psychologists, that cognitive theories, and in particular this causal–evaluative version, must be intangible or non-objective because the evaluative aspect is intangible and non-objective. Giving the evaluative aspect of occurrent emotional states a dispositional analysis would make it clear that dispositions must have some enduring (at least as enduring as the disposition) physiological or psychological factor as its causal or structural base.

In chapter 4 I concentrated on teasing out the details of the cognitive and evaluative aspects of emotional states, and pointed out how these aspects are severely modified in certain circumstances. I pointed out that the evaluative aspect is parasitic on there being certain beliefs in the subject (though 'in' here may be very weak) about the world or oneself, yet the beliefs need not be true. The beliefs need not even be peculiar to the type of emotion in question, for emotions are not distinguished on the basis of factual beliefs but evaluative ones. But the factual belief part of emotion is none the less important as it is one of the paths by which actual emotions in people can be judged as superficial, irrational or mistaken.

The claim, usually made in connection with 'objectless' fear, that the emotional subject may not in certain cases hold any factual beliefs at all was also discussed. I argued that there were beliefs present in such cases but that they were unusual beliefs, namely claims about one's own ignorance of the situation or helplessness in the face of it, or else a claim about what *could* possibly happen to one rather than what *was* happening. This discussion led in turn to considering what I called reflex or Pavlovian emotions, where the cognitive aspects were embedded, and wishful-thinking emotions, where the cognitive aspects were present but appeared unrelated to reality.

In discussing the evaluative aspect of emotions, I distinguished the more or less objective sort of evaluation which is characteristic of emotions such as fear from the much more subjective evaluation, or appraisal, which is characteristic of emotions such as love. I pointed out that it is because some emotions characteristically have a more or less objective evaluation as their core that we have one sort of basis for saying that in certain cases such emotions – ones where the objective evaluation is missing or unheeded or deviant in some way – are neurotic.

I argued that the obvious objections to cognitive theories which place all the weight on the evaluative aspect – the objections that certain emotions share the *same* evaluative aspect and so are not distinguishable in terms of it, and that some emotions have no evaluative aspect at all – do not hold up under close scrutiny. Emotions appear to share the same evaluative aspect only because philosophers and psychologists have not been sufficiently industrious and subtle in isolating the evaluative aspects in question. Some emotions appear to have no evaluative aspect only because the dispositional nature of evaluations is overlooked.

I also discussed the backward-looking/forward-looking and approval/disapproval distinctions in emotions which, I suggested, are ultimately based on the evaluative aspect of emotion. I gave reasons for thinking that they are not as tight as has been supposed.

In chapter 5 I argued that most, though not all, emotions contain desires as part of their occurrent states, and that, with some emotions, this appetitive aspect is part of their very concept. It is this aspect which explains how emotions can be cited as motives, and how behaviour can reveal the nature of emotions, for the desires generated by the evaluative aspects of emotions are the causes of the behaviour associated with emotion. The appetitive aspect, while it does mingle in practice with the evaluative aspect, can be separated at the theoretical level. They are logically distinct and, besides, certain emotions can exhibit the latter without the former. Finally there was a discussion about distinctions between emotions which were based on the appetitive aspect of emotions, namely emotions which are useful, in various senses, versus those which are not.

In chapter 6 the discussion centred on the various interpretations of the phrase 'object of the emotions'. The concept of 'the formal object of an emotion' was held to be a misleading misnomer, as it was really not an object at all but the general evaluative category under which an emotional subject's particular appraisal or evaluation of a particular object falls. This led in turn to a discussion of the two sorts of particular object or target of the cognitive, evaluative and appetitive aspects of emotion, namely the material object and, that bane of philosophers of mind, the intentional object. I tried to avoid an unnecessarily obscure and so unhelpful distinction between the material and intentional object by reducing the material/intentional object distinction to one about the existential status of the object of psychological or intentional activities. The distinction between particular objects of emotion with regard to the correctness or otherwise of the subject of the emotion's beliefs, and with regard to the subsequent effect of this on some wider intentional or psychological activity or state, I built into a separate non-illusory/illusory object distinction. That is, I separated off talk about the grounding of emotions in relation to their object or target from talk about the existential status of the focussed-on object or target of emotion. As regards understanding the nature and development of emotions, I argued that it was the illusory/non-illusory object distinction (which is to do with the grounding of emotions) which was the important one, and that philosophers had rather pointlessly been taken up with discussing the material/intentional object distinction in the context of emotions.

Then I went on to discuss the limits imposed by the formal object of an emotion on the possible range of objects that that emotion can have. It amounted to a discussion of the limits on the possible range of objects that a particular emotional state can have if it is to continue to be *called* that particular sort of emotion.

In chapter 7 I analysed what, among philosophers, is a particularly neglected area, namely the relation between physiological changes and emotions. Still influenced by Cartesian views of emotion, philosophers tend mainly to discuss the cognitive aspects of emotion and the nature of the object of emotion, but neglect the bodily motions side. This stems, too, from the fact that philosophers tend now to approach the study of emotions via emotion language rather than via a study of occurrent emotional states.

As in chapter 3, I again emphasised that the term 'physiological changes' referred chiefly to those changes associated with a discharge of the sympathetic or parasympathetic nervous system, and to those which could be termed 'abnormal' in that they are an upsetting of the usual equilibrium levels of physiological states. I cautioned, too, that these abnormal physiological changes should not be thought of as always of a disturbing, alarming or speeded up variety. There are the calm emotions which lower the rate and level of physiological activity. In regard to the physiological changes associated with emotion, I made a further distinction between those which we are subjectively aware of and necessarily so, those which we are necessarily not aware of, and those of which we may or may not be aware of depending on the circumstances. I explained why the discussion in the rest of this chapter should be confined to the part in emotional states played by changes of the third type.

Theories of emotion which claimed that the differentiating factor of emotions was distinct patterns of physiological changes were distinguished from those in which these patterns were the emotions as well as the means of differentiating them. I suggested that these were empirical theories which stood or fell according to the empirical evidence for them, and that the empirical evidence available, while inconclusive, gave little or no comfort to these views.

I examined in particular the very interesting experiments conducted by Schachter and Singer. These psychologists found that their subjects only claimed to have emotions if they believed that their abnormal physiological changes were caused by 'cognitions' concerning their situation. These experiments are not, of course, clinching, as they pivot upon people being prepared to claim that they are having emotions, and so on their intuitions about what is to count as emotion. But the findings from these experiments do accord well with the theory argued for in this book.

In this chapter the question was broached as to whether the feelings associated with emotion are the subjective registering of some of the physiological changes which form part of emotional states or not. I gave reasons for concluding that the feelings should be so considered, and also suggested that physiological changes, while not differentiators of the emotions, do serve as a reflex indicator that some emotional state is probably present. If one can establish, or has strong evidence for proposing, that there is a causal link between the subject of the physiological change's beliefs or attitudes and the physiological changes themselves, then one can say with good reason that an emotional state is in question. Given that we have established that the physiological changes are emotional, then they can serve as an indicator of the genuineness of the emotion, for these changes cannot usually be produced on demand.

The connection between feelings and emotions was discussed in chapter 8. This was to be read against the background of the discussion of the feeling theory of emotions in chapter 1, for it was there that I set out some of the reasons why we should not equate feelings with emotions.

I argued that one labels a feeling as of some particular emotion only after causally correlating it with the core or defining aspect of that emotion, namely the evaluation and, usually, wants peculiar to that emotion, though one can attach labels to feelings – labels such as 'twinge' or 'itch' – just by reference to the content or qualities of the feeling itself. The empirical evidence available tends to show that no set pattern of physiological changes is found invariably with any particular emotion, and that emotions cannot be differentiated in terms of physiological changes. Since it seems likely that the feelings to be associated with emotions are the subjective registering of the physiological changes, one cannot differentiate emotions by reference to feelings. I argued, too, that introspection bore this out, for we do not experience any unvarying 'lovey feeling', for example, whenever we are in love.

I suggested that we can be misled into taking the opposite view by failing to realise that feeling terms are not really as neutral as they might appear to be. They are often loaded not merely with evaluative connotations but with causal ones as well. Even an apparently neutral content-labelling label, such as 'twinge', is really 'loaded'. It has overtones of being an unwelcome and unpleasant feeling which suggests that the person with the feeling thinks it is caused by something disagreeable. And it would not follow from the fact that we label our feeling of remorse as a twinge but our feeling of joy as something else, that they are in fact qualitatively different. They might be the same. The label may only express what we think of the feeling and what we think caused it.

In chapter 9, I discussed the relation between emotions and behaviour. I argued, negatively, that the behaviour typical of an emotion is typical in a much looser sense than an equivalent claim about behaviour being typical of an appetite. Positively, I suggested that behaviour may be related to emotions as a natural concomitant, a statistically frequent concomitant, an appropriate or rational response to, or a conventional expression of them. But, while none of these relations implies a conceptual link between emotions and behaviour, as some have claimed, all imply a causal connection, and most imply a rational link as well.

As an addendum to the discussion of emotions and behaviour, I included a short discussion about the ways in which emotion statements are related to emotions. I suggested that sometimes emotion statements report the presence of an emotion, that at other times they form part of the expression of occurrent emotional states, and that, finally, they can amount to interpretations or explanations of behaviour by relating the behaviour to emotion. Besides emotion statements being able to perform more than one of these functions at any one time, the interpretative use can have other functions parasitic upon it. For example, one might interpret behaviour by linking it to emotion in order to denounce it or excuse it.

In chapter 11, I discussed emotions in so far as they can be cited as motives for action. After suggesting that the term 'motive' should not be limited to contexts where we expect that the motivation does not fall within the standard range, I proposed a distinction between 'motives' as 'deliberate causes, or candidates for being such causes, of human action' and 'motivation' as 'all other sorts of causes of uncoerced human behaviour'.

I went on to fill out the account of motives, suggesting that the motive behind an actual action is to be construed as a want which is the cause or part cause of the action, though this does not imply that all actions which can be said to be done out of some motive can be said to be actions which the agent wanted to do. For one might not want, but feel impelled to do, what presents itself as the only means to obtaining what one does really want and so has a motive for. One could also have a motive for something one did not do or that was at most a possibility, for a motive is not just a want which actually causes an action but also can be one which could be or could have been the cause of some action. Poirot can say that everyone in the room had a motive for murdering the heiress though in fact only one person in the room did murder the heiress.

I then translated all this into the context of emotions, explaining that an emotion can function as a motive in so far as it includes a want which could have been, is or could become the deliberate cause of an action, and that this was so irrespective of whether the want was conscious or unconscious. It was also made clear that, while emotions cited as motives can function as reasons for action, they cannot be construed as intentions or aims.

I concluded this chapter by arguing that my account of emotions as motives made better sense of the connection between emotions and behaviour than did rival accounts such as those of Ryle and Kenny.

Chapter 12 was a discussion of the three theses which emerge as possible interpretations of the claim that emotions are purposive. The first thesis, that emotions are purposive in that they give rise to purposive behaviour is, one would think, unexceptional. For, in so far as emotions make one want to do things in order to alter or maintain the situation *vis-à-vis* oneself, so emotions clearly give rise to purposive behaviour. On the other hand, the thesis that emotions are purposive in that they are done for a purpose is both far more interesting and more problematic. I argued that the thesis was false because emotions were not activities and so were not things which could be done, for a purpose or otherwise, and because emotions were complex items involving in a central way such things as beliefs, evaluations and wants which cannot be done on demand. Finally the third thesis, the richest one and of particular interest to psychologists, namely that emotions are purposive in so far as they serve the purposes of or are useful to the person having them, was, I argued, correct given certain provisos and qualifications.

In chapter 13 I discussed when, if at all, one might blame a person for his emotions. To do this adequately, I first gave an account of what it is to blame someone and what the grounds for blame are. Then I discussed the circumstances under which a person might be held responsible for his emotions. Finally I argued that a person can be blamed for his emotions in so far as he could be said to have been able to exercise some control over an emotion, and in so far as it gave rise to some undesirable upshot, and in so far as there were no mitigating circumstances. Thus, in certain circumstances, a person could be blamed for deliberately avoiding, aborting, overcoming or curbing his own emotion, for failing to try to, or for deliberately inducing, fostering or promoting his emotion or the behaviour and expressions stemming from it.

Against the background of the early chapters of this book, I have tried to show that the causal–evaluative theory of emotion can be advanced, when one teases out its implications, to cover the many facets and functions of emotion.

Bibliography

Ahumada, R. 1969. 'Emotion, Knowledge and Belief', *The Personalist* vol. 50.

Alston, William. 1965. 'Expressing'. In *Philosophy in America*, Max Black (ed.), George Allen & Unwin.

    1967a. 'Emotion and Feeling'. In *The Encyclopedia of Philosophy* vol. 2, P. Edwards (ed.), Macmillan and The Free Press.

    1967b. 'Motives and Motivation'. In *The Encyclopedia of Philosophy* vol. 5, P. Edwards (ed.), Macmillan and The Free Press.

    1967c. 'Wants, Action and Causal Explanations'. In *Intentionality, Minds and Perception*, H. N. Castañeda (ed.), Wayne State University Press.

    1969. 'Feelings', *Philosophical Review* vol. 78.

    1971–72. 'Dispositions and Occurrences', *Canadian Journal of Philosophy* vol. I.

Anscombe, G. E. M. 1965. 'The Intentionality of Sensation: A Grammatical Feature'. In *Analytical Philosophy*, 2nd Series, R. J. Butler (ed.), Blackwell.

Aquila, R. 1974. 'Emotions, Objects and Causal Relations', *Philosophical Studies* vol. 26.

Aquinas, 1967. *Summa Theologiae*, vol. 19, 'The Emotions', edited and translated by Eric D'Arcy, Blackfriars and Eyre and Spottiswoode.

Aristotle, 1941. 'Rhetoric'. In *The Basic Works of Aristotle*, R. McKeon (ed.), Random House.

    1968. *De Anima* Books II and III (with certain passages from Book I), translated by D. W. Hamlyn, Clarendon Press.

Armstrong, D. 1968. *A Materialist Theory of the Mind*. Routledge and Kegan Paul.

    1969. 'Dispositions are Causes', *Analysis* vol. 30.

Arnold, M. B. 1945. 'Physiological Differentiation of Emotional States', *Psychological Review* vol. 52.

    1950. 'An Excitatory Theory of Emotion'. In *Feelings and Emotions: The Mooseheart Symposium*, M. L. Reymert (ed.), McGraw-Hill.

    1960. *Emotion and Personality* (2 vols.), Columbia University Press.

    (ed.) 1968. *The Nature of Emotion*, Penguin.

    1970. *Feelings and Emotions: The Loyola Symposium*, Academic Press.

Arnold, M. B. and Gasson, J. (eds.) 1954. *The Human Person*, Ronald.

    1968. 'Feelings and Emotions as Dynamic Factors in Personality Integration'. In *The Nature of Emotion*, Arnold (ed.), Penguin.

Aune, Bruce. 1963. 'Feelings, Moods and Introspection', *Mind* vol. 72.

Austin, J. L. 1961. 'Pretending'. In *Philosophical Papers*, J. O. Urmson and G. Warnock (eds.), Clarendon Press.

Ax, A. F. 1953. 'The Physiological Differentiation between Fear and Anger in Humans', *Psychosomatic Medicine* vol. 15.

1971. 'Review of Neurophysiology Discovers the Mind', *Contemporary Psychology* vol. 16.

Bard, P. 1934. 'On Emotional Expression after Decortication with some Remarks on certain Theoretical Views', *The Psychological Review* vol. 41.

Bedford, Errol. 1956–57. 'Emotions'. *Proceedings of the Aristotelian Society* vol. 57; also in *The Philosophy of Mind*, V. C. Chappell (ed.), Prentice-Hall, 1962; and in *Essays in Philosophical Psychology*, Gustafson (ed.), Macmillan, 1967.

1959. 'Pleasure and Belief', *Proceedings of the Aristotelian Society*, Supp. vol. 33.

Benson, J. 1967 'Emotion and Expression', *Philosophical Review* vol. 76.

Black, P. (ed.) 1970. *Physiological Correlates of Emotion*, Academic Press.

Brady, J. V. 1959. 'Emotional Behavior'. In *Handbook of Physiology* vol. 3, J. Field (ed.), American Physiological Society.

1970. 'Emotion: Some Conceptual Problems and Psychophysiological Experiments'. In *Feelings and Emotions: The Loyola Symposium*, M. B. Arnold (ed.), Academic Press.

Brandt, R. and Kim, J. 1963. 'Wants as Explanations of Actions', *Journal of Philosophy* vol. 60.

Broad, C. D. 1954–55. 'Emotion and Sentiment', *Journal of Aesthetics and Art Criticism* vol. 13.

Candland, D. K. (ed.) 1962. *Emotion: Bodily Change; An Enduring Problem in Psychology – Selected Readings*, Van Nostrand.

Cannon, W. B. 1927a. *Bodily Changes in Pain, Hunger, Fear and Rage*, Appleton-Century.

1927b. 'The James-Lange Theory of Emotions: A Critical Examination and an Alternative Theory', *American Journal of Psychology* vol. 39, reprinted in part in Arnold (1968).

1931. 'Again the James–Lange and the Thalamic Theories of Emotion', *Psychological Review* vol. 38.

Cantril, H. and Hunt, W. A. 1932. 'Emotional Effects produced by the Injection of Adrenalin', *American Journal of Psychology* vol. 44.

Cassin, C. E. 1968. 'Emotions and Evaluations', *The Personalist* vol. 49.

Chisholm, R. 1966. 'Brentano's Theory of Correct and Incorrect Emotion', *Revue Internationale de Philosophie* vol. 78.

Coder, D. 1969. 'Some Misconceptions about Dispositions', *Analysis* vol. 29.

Cofer, C. N. 1972. *Motivation and Emotion*, Scott Foresman.

Darwin, Charles. 1965. *The Expression of the Emotions in Man and Animals*, University of Chicago Press.

Davidson, Donald. 1963. 'Actions, Reasons and Causes', *Journal of Philosophy* vol. 60.

1976. 'Hume's Cognitive Theory of Pride', *Journal of Philosophy* vol. 73.

Day, J. P. 1970. 'The Anatomy of Hope and Fear', *Mind* vol. 78.

Delgado, J. M. R., Rosvold, H. E., and Looney, E. 1956. 'Evoking Conditioned

Fear by Electrical Stimulation of Subcortical Structures in the Monkey Brain', *Journal of Comparative and Physiological Psychology* vol. 49.

Descartes, René. 1911–12. 'The Passions of the Soul'. In *The Philosophical Works of Descartes*, edited and translated by E. L. Haldane and G. R. Ross, Cambridge University Press, as reprinted in *Descartes Selections*, R. M. Eaton (ed.), Scribners, 1927.

Dewey, J. 1894. 'The Theory of Emotion. I. Emotional Attitudes', *Psychological Review* vol. 1.

Dilman, I. 1963. 'An Examination of Sartre's Theory of Emotions', *Ratio* vol. 5.

Dockeray, F. 1942. *Psychology*, Prentice-Hall.

Donnellan, Keith. 1967. 'Reasons and Causes'. In *The Encyclopedia of Philosophy*, vol. 7, P. Edwards (ed.), Macmillan and The Free Press.

1970. 'Causes, Objects, and Producers of the Emotions', *Journal of Philosophy* vol. 67.

Duffy, E. 1934. 'Emotion: An Example of the Need for Reorientation in Psychology', *Psychological Review* vol. 41.

1941. 'An Explanation of "Emotional" Phenomena without the Use of the Concept "Emotion"', *Journal of General Psychology* vol. 25.

1948. 'Leeper's "Motivational Theory of Emotion"', *Psychological Review* vol. 55.

1962. *Activation and Behavior*, Wiley.

Dumas, G. 1948a. *La Vie Affective: Physiologie, Psychologie, Socialisation*, Presses Universitaires de France.

1948b. 'Emotional Shocks and Emotions', extract from *La Vie Affective*, translated by Bégin and Arnold, in *The Nature of Emotion*, Arnold (ed.), Penguin, 1968.

Eidelberg, L. (ed.) 1968. *Encyclopedia of Psychoanalysis*, Macmillan and the Free Press.

Ellis, A. J. 1970. 'Causes and Objects of Emotions', *Analysis* vol. 30.

Ewing, A. C. 1957. 'The Justification of the Emotions', *Proceedings of the Aristotelian Society, Supp.* vol. 31.

Eysenck, H. J. 1977. *You and Neurosis*, Fontana-Collins.

Eysenck, H. J., Arnold, W. J. and Meili, R. (eds.) 1975. *Encyclopedia of Psychology*, Fontana Collins.

Fehr, F. S. and Stern, J. A. 1970. 'Peripheral Physiological Variables and Emotion: The James–Lange Theory Revisited', *Psychological Bulletin* vol. 74.

Feinstein, H. 1970. 'William James on the Emotions', *Journal of the History of Ideas* vol. 31.

Fodor, J. H. 1968. *Psychological Explanation*, Random House.

Fortenbaugh, W. W. 1975. *Aristotle on Emotion*, Duckworth.

Fox, M. 1973–74. 'On Unconscious Emotions', *Philosophy and Phenomenological Research* vol. 34.

Frankenhaeuser, Marianne. 1975. 'Experimental Approaches to the Study of Catecholamines and Emotion'. In *Emotions: Their Parameters and Measurement*, L.Levi (ed.), Raven Press.

Freud, Sigmund. 1953– . *Complete Psychological Works of Sigmund Freud*,

J. Strachey (ed.), in collaboration with Anna Freud *et al.*, Hogarth. Vol. XVI (1959a). *Inhibitions Symptoms and Anxiety* (1926). Vol. XX (1959b).

1971. *Group Psychology and the Analysis of the Ego*, translated by J. Strachey, Bantam Books.

Frijda, Nico H. 1970. 'Emotion and Recognition of Emotion'. In *Feelings and Emotions: The Loyola Symposium*, M. B. Arnold (ed.), Academic Press.

Fromm, E. 1957. *The Art of Loving*, George Allen and Unwin.

Fulton, J. F. 1951. *Frontal Lobotomy and Affective Behaviour*, Chapman and Hall.

Funkenstein, D. H. 1955. 'The Physiology of Fear and Anger', *Scientific American* vol. 192.

Gardiner, H. M., Metcalf, R. C. and Beebe-Center, J. G. 1937. *Feeling and Emotion, A History of Theories*, American Book Co.

Geach, P. 1957. *Mental Acts*, Routledge and Kegan Paul.

Goldberg, B. 1965. 'Can a Desire be a Cause?', *Analysis* vol. 25.

Goldstein, D., Fink, D. and Mettee, D. 1972. 'Cognition of Arousal and Actual Arousal as Determinants of Emotion', *Journal of Personality and Social Psychology* vol. 21.

Goldstein, M. L. 1968. 'Physiological Theories of Emotion: A Critical Historical Review from the Standpoint of Behavior Theory', *Psychological Bulletin* vol. 69.

Gordon, R. 1969. 'Emotions and Knowledge', *The Journal of Philosophy* vol. 66.

1973–74. 'Judgmental Emotions', *Analysis* vol. 34.

1974. 'The Aboutness of Emotions', *American Philosophical Quarterly* vol. 11.

Goshen, C. 1967. 'A Systematic Classification of the Phenomenology of Emotions', *Psychiatric Quarterly* vol. 41.

Gosling, J. 1965. 'Emotion and Object', *Philosophical Review* vol. 74.

1969. *Pleasure and Desire*, Clarendon Press.

Gray, Jeffrey. 1971. *The Psychology of Fear and Stress*, Weidenfeld and Nicolson.

Green, O. H. 1970. 'The Expression of Emotion', *Mind* vol. 79.

1972. 'Emotions and Belief'. In *Studies in the Philosophy of Mind*, American Philosophical Quarterly Monograph Series no. 6, N. Rescher (ed.), Basil Blackwell.

Grice, G. R. 1967. *The Grounds of Moral Judgement*, Cambridge University Press.

Grossman, R. 1969. 'Non-Existent Objects; Recent work on Brentano and Meinong', *American Philosophical Quarterly* vol. 6.

Grossman, S. P. A. 1967. *A Textbook of Phsyiological Psychology*, Wiley.

Hampshire, Stuart. 1972. 'Feeling and Expression'. In Hampshire *Freedom of Mind and Other Essays*, Oxford University Press.

Harlow, H. F. and Stagner, R. 1933. 'Psychology of Feelings and Emotions: II Theory of Emotions', *The Psychological Review* vol. 40.

Hebb, D. O. 1949. 'Emotional Disturbance'. In *The Organization of Behavior*, Wiley, 1949; reprinted in *The Nature of Emotion*, Arnold (ed.), Penguin Books, 1968.

1949. *The Organization of Behavior*, Wiley.

1966. *A Textbook of Psychology* (2nd ed.), Saunders.

Hegel, G. W. F. 1942. *The Philosophy of Right*, trans. T. M. Knox, Clarendon Press.

Hepburn, R. W. 1965. 'Emotions and Emotional Qualities: Some Attempts at Analysis'. In *Collected Papers on Aesthetics*, Barrett (ed.), Basil Blackwell.

Hillman, J. 1961. *Emotion: A Comprehensive Phenomenology of Theories and their Meanings for Therapy*, Northwestern University Press.

Hodge, T. R., Wagner, E. E., and Schreiner, F. 1966. 'The Validity of Hypnotically Induced Emotional States: Part II', *The American Journal of Clinical Hypnosis* vol. 9.

Holborow, L. C. 1971–72. 'Blame, Praise and Credit', *Proceedings of the Aristotelian Society* vol. 72.

Hume, David. 1978. *A Treatise of Human Nature*, ed. L. A. Selby-Bigge, 2nd ed. revised by P. H. Nidditch, Clarendon Press.

Huxley, Aldous. 1946. *The Perennial Philosophy*, Chatto and Windus.

Izard, Carroll E. 1972. *Patterns of Emotions: A New Analysis of Anxiety and Depression*, Academic Press.

James, William. 1884. 'What is an Emotion?', *Mind* vol. 9.

1890. *The Principles of Psychology* (2 vols.), Macmillan.

James, William and Lange, Carl, 1922. *The Emotions*, Dunlap Knight.

Johann, R. 1954. *The Meaning of Love*, Geoffrey Chapman.

Jones, J. R. 1958–59. 'The Two Contexts of Mental Concepts', *Proceedings of the Aristotelian Society* vol. 59.

Jung, C. J. 1960. *The Collected Works of C. J. Jung*, vol. 8, 'The Structure and Dynamics of the Psyche', Read, Fordham and Adler (eds.), Routledge and Kegan Paul.

Kenner, L. 1967. 'On Blaming', *Mind* vol. 76.

Kenny, Anthony. 1963. *Action, Emotion and Will*, Routledge and Kegan Paul.

Lader, Malcolm, and Tyrer, Peter. 1975. 'Vegetative System and Emotion'. In *Emotions: Their Parameters and Measurement*, L. Levi (ed.), Raven Press.

Lashley, K. 1938. 'The Thalamus and Emotion', *The Psychological Review* vol. 45.

Lazarus, R. S. 1966. *Psychological Stress and the Coping Process*, McGraw-Hill.

1975a. 'A Cognitively Oriented Psychologist Looks at Biofeedback', *American Psychologist* vol. 30.

1975b. 'The Self-Regulation of Emotion'. In *Emotions: Their Parameters and Measurement*, L. Levi (ed.), Raven Press.

Leeper, R. W. 1948. 'A Motivational Theory of Emotion to Replace "Emotion as Disorganized Response"', *Psychological Review* vol. 55; reprinted in abridged form in *The Nature of Emotion*, Arnold (ed.), Penguin, 1968.

1970. 'The Motivational and Perceptual Properties of Emotions as Indicating their Fundamental Character and Role'. In *Feelings and Emotions: The Loyola Symposium*, Arnold (ed.).

Levi, L. (ed.) 1975. *Emotions: Their Parameters and Measurement*, Raven Press.

Lewin, B. D. 1968. 'Phobias'. In the *International Encyclopaedia of the Social Sciences*, vol. 12, Sills (ed.), Macmillan and The Free Press.

Lindsley, D. B. 1951. 'Emotion'. In *Handbook of Experimental Psychology*, Stevens (ed.), Wiley.

London, H. and Nisbett, R. E. (eds.) 1974. *Thought and Feeling: Cognitive Alteration of Feeling States*, Aldine Press.

Lycan, W. Gregory. 1969. 'On Intentionality and the Psychological', *American Philosophical Quarterly* vol. 6.

Lyons, William. 1973a. 'A Note on Emotion Statements', *Ratio* vol. 15.

1973b. 'Ryle and Dispositions', *Philosophical Studies* vol. 24.

1973c. 'A Note on Wanting to do some Purposeful Action', *Logique et Analyse* vols. 63–4.

1974. 'Physiological Changes and the Emotions', *Canadian Journal of Philosophy* vol. 3.

1976. 'Emotions and Motives', *Canadian Journal of Philosophy* vol. 6.

1977. 'Emotions and Feelings', *Ratio* vol. 19.

1977–78. 'Emotions and Behavior', *Philosophy and Phenomenological Research* vol. 38.

McCleary, R. A. and Moore, R. Y. 1965. *Subcortical Mechanisms of Behavior*, Basic Books.

McDougall, William. 1908. *An Introduction to Social Psychology*, Methuen.

Mace, C. A. 1961–62. 'Emotions and the Category of Passivity', *Proceedings of the Aristotelian Society* vol. 62.

MacIntyre, A. 1971. 'Emotion, Behavior and Belief'. In MacIntyre, *Against the Self-Images of the Age*, Duckworth.

MacLean, Paul D. 1975. 'Sensory and Perceptive Factors in Emotional Functions of the Triune Brain'. In *Emotions: Their Parameters and Measurement*, L. Levi (ed.), Raven Press.

Mandler, G. 1962. 'Emotion'. In *New Directions in Psychology*, R. Brown et al. (eds.), Holt Rinehart and Winston.

1975a *Mind and Emotion*, Wiley.

1975b. 'The Search for Emotion'. In *Emotion: Their Parameters and Measurement*, L. Levi (ed.), Raven Press.

Marañon, G. 1924. 'Contribution à l'étude de l'action émotive de l'adrénaline', *Revue Française d'Endocrinologie* vol. 2.

Melden, A. I. 1961. *Free Action*, Routledge and Kegan Paul.

1969. 'The Conceptual Dimensions of Emotions'. In *Human Action: Conceptual and Empirical Issues*, Mischel (ed.), Academic Press.

Morgan, C. T. 1965. *Physiological Psychology*, McGraw-Hill.

Munn, N. L. 1961. *Psychology: The Fundamentals of Human Adjustment*, Harrap.

Murdoch, Iris. 1970. *The Sovereignty of Good*, Routledge and Kegan Paul.

Murray, E. J. 1964. *Motivation and Emotion*, Prentice-Hall.

Nagel, Thomas. 1970. *The Possibility of Altruism*, Clarendon Press.

Neu, Jerome. 1977. *Emotion, Thought and Therapy*, Routledge and Kegan Paul.

Pátkai, P. 1971. 'Catacholamine Excretion in Pleasant and Unpleasant Situations', *Acta Psychologica* vol. 35.

Pears, David. 1962. 'Causes and Objects of Some Feelings and Psychological Reactions', *Ratio* vol. 4; reprinted in *Philosophy of Mind*, Hampshire (ed.), Harper and Row, 1966.

    1968. 'Desires as Causes of Actions'. In *The Human Agent: Royal Institute of Philosophy Lectures, Vol. 1, 1966–67*, Macmillan.

Penelhum, Terence. 1956–57. 'The Logic of Pleasure', *Philosophy and Phenomenological Research* vol. 17; reprinted in *Essays in Philosophical Psychology*, Gustafson (ed.), Macmillan, 1967.

    1964. 'Pleasure and Falsity', *American Philosophical Quarterly* vol. 1; reprinted in *Philosophy of Mind*, Hampshire (ed.), Harper and Row, 1966.

Perkins, Moreland. 1965. 'Seeing and Hearing Emotions', *Analysis* vol. 26.

    1966. 'Emotion and Feeling', *Philosophical Review* vol. 75.

    1972. 'Meaning and Feeling'. In *Studies in the Philosophy of Mind*, American Philosophical Quarterly Monograph Series no. 6, N. Rescher (ed.), Basil Blackwell.

Perry, D. 1970. 'Pleasure and Justification', *The Personalist* vol. 51.

Peters, R. S. 1960. *The Concept of Motivation*, Routledge and Kegan Paul.

    1961–62. 'Emotions and the Category of Passivity', *Proceedings of the Aristotelian Society* vol. 62.

    1965. 'Emotions, Passivity and the Place of Freud's Theory in Psychology'. In *Scientific Psychology*, Wolman and Nagel (ed.), Basic Books.

    1966. *Ethics and Education*, George Allen and Unwin.

    1969. 'Motivation, Emotion, and the Conceptual Schemes of Common Sense'. In *Human Action*, Mischel (ed.), Academic Press.

    1970. 'The Education of the Emotions'. In *Feelings and Emotions: The Loyola Symposium*, Arnold (ed.), Academic Press; reprinted in *Psychology and Ethical Development*, George Allen and Unwin, 1974.

Pick, J. 1970. *The Autonomic Nervous System*, Lippincott.

Pitcher, George. 1965. 'Emotion', *Mind* vol. 74.

Plutchik, R. 1962. *The Emotions: Facts, Theories, and a new Model*, Random House.

Plutchik, R. and Ax, A. F. 1967. 'A Critique of "Determinants of Emotional State" by Schachter and Singer (1962)', *Psychophysiology* vol. 4.

Pradines, M. 1958. *Traité de Psychologie Generale*, vol. 1, 6th ed., Presses Universitaires de France.

Quinton, Anthony. 1973. *The Nature of Things*, Routledge and Kegan Paul.

Rachels, J. 1968. 'Wants, Reasons and Justifications', *Philosophical Quarterly* vol. 18.

Ramsey, F. P. 1978. 'Law and Causality: B: General Propositions and Causality'. In F. P. Ramsey, *Foundations: Essays in Philosophy, Logic, Mathematics and Economics*, D. H. Mellor (ed.), Cambridge University Press.

Rapaport, D. 1950. *Emotions and Memory*, International Universities Press.

    1967. *The Collected Papers of David Rapaport*, Gill (ed.), Basic Books.

Reymert, M. L. (ed.) 1928. *Feelings and Emotions: The Wittenberg Symposium*, Clark University Press.

(ed.) 1950. *Feelings and Emotions: The Mooseheart Symposium*, McGraw-Hill.

Rorty, A. O. 1978. 'Explaining Emotions', *The Journal of Philosophy* vol. 75.

Ruckmick, C. A. 1936. *The Psychology of Feeling and Emotion*, McGraw-Hill.

Russell, Bertrand. 1921. *The Analysis of Mind*, George Allen and Unwin.

Rycroft, Charles. 1968. *Anxiety and Neurosis*, Penguin.

Ryle, Gilbert. 1949. *The Concept of Mind*, Hutchinson.

   1951. 'Feelings', *The Philosophical Quarterly* vol. 1.

   1954. 'Pleasure', *Proceedings of the Aristotelian Society Supp. Vol. 28*; reprinted in *Essays in Philosophical Psychology*, Gustafson (ed.), Macmillan, 1967.

Sachs, D. 1974. 'On Freud's Doctrine of Emotions'. In *Freud: A Collection of Critical Essays*, R. Wollheim (ed.), Anchor Books.

Sankowski, Edward. 1977. 'Responsibility of Persons for their Emotions', *Canadian Journal of Philosophy* vol. 7.

Sartre, Jean-Paul. 1971. *Sketch for a Theory of the Emotions*, translated by Mairet, Methuen.

Schachter, S. 1970. 'The Assumption of Identity and Peripheralist–Centralist Controversies in Motivation and Emotion'. In *Feelings and Emotions: The Loyola Symposium*, M. B. Arnold (ed.), Academic Press.

   1971. *Emotion, Obesity and Crime*, Academic Press.

Schachter, S. and Singer, J. 1962. 'Cognitive, Social and Physiological Determinants of Emotional State', *Psychological Review* vol. 69.

Schild, W. 1971. 'Wants and Causes', *Logique et Analyse* vol. 55.

Shand, Alexander. 1914. *The Foundations of Character*, Macmillan.

Sherrington, C. S. 1900. 'Experiments on the Value of the Vascular and Visceral Factors for the Genesis of Emotion', *Proceedings of the Royal Society* vol. 66.

Shibles, Warren. 1974. *Emotion: The Method of Philosophical Therapy*, The Language Press.

Shiner, Roger. 1971. 'Classifying Objects of Acts and Emotions', *Dialogue* vol. 10.

   1975. 'Wilson on Emotion, Object and Cause', *Metaphilosophy* vol. 6.

Shoemaker, S. 1960. 'Review of R. S. Peters' *The Concept of Motivation*'. In *Philosophical Review* vol. 69.

Sigg, E. B. 1975. 'The Organization and Functions of the Central Sympathetic Nervous System'. In *Emotions: Their Parameters and Measurement*, L. Levi (ed.), Raven Press.

Simmel, Georg. 1957. 'Fragments über die Liebe'. In *Brücke und Tur: Essays des Philosophen zur Geschicte, Religion, Kunst und Gesellschaft*, Koehler.

Skinner, B. F. 1974. *About Behaviourism*, Cape.

Skinner, B. F. and Holland, J. G. 1961. *The Analysis of Behavior*, McGraw-Hill.

Smart, J. J. C. 1961. 'Free-Will, Praise and Blame', *Mind* vol. 70.

Solomon, R. C. 1973. 'Emotions and Choice', *The Review of Metaphysics* vol. 27.

   1976. *The Passions*, Doubleday-Anchor Books.

   1977. 'The Logic of Emotion', *Nous* vol. 11.

Spielberger, C. D. (ed.) 1972. *Anxiety: Current Trends in Theory and Research*, 2 vols., Academic Press.

Spinoza, B. 1883. *The Ethics*. In *The Chief Works of Benedict de Spinoza* vol. II, translated by R. H. M. Elwes, George Bell & Sons.

Squires, Roger. 1968a. 'Are Dispositions Causes?', *Analysis* vol. 29.

1968b. 'Blame', *The Philosophical Quarterly* vol. 18.

Stacey, C. and De Martino, M. (eds.) 1963. *Understanding Human Motivation*, Howard Allen.

Stanley-Jones, D. 1970. 'The Biological Origin of Love and Hate'. In *Feelings and Emotions: The Loyola Symposium*, M. B. Arnold (ed.), Academic Press.

Stevenson, L. 1968. 'Are Dispositions Causes?', *Analysis* vol. 29.

Strongman, K. T. 1973. *The Psychology of Emotion*. Wiley.

Taylor, G. 1975. 'Justifying the Emotions', *Mind* vol. 84.

1975–76. 'Love', *Proceedings of the Aristotelian Society* vol. 76.

Taylor, G. and Wolfram, S. 1970–71. 'Virtues and Passions', *Analysis* vol. 31.

Thalberg, Irving. 1964. 'Emotion and Thought', *American Philosophical Quarterly* vol. 1; reprinted in *Philosophy of Mind*, Hampshire (ed.), Harper and Row, 1966.

1973. 'Constituents and Causes of Emotion and Action', *The Philosophical Quarterly* vol. 23.

1974. 'Evidence and Causes of Emotion', *Mind* vol. 83.

1977. *Perception, Emotion & Action*, Basil Blackwell.

Titchener, E. B. 1902. *An Outline of Psychology* (3rd ed.), Macmillan.

1908. *Lectures on the Elementary Psychology of Feeling and Attention*, Macmillan.

Trigg, Roger. 1970. *Pain and Emotion*, Clarendon Press.

Warnock, Mary. 1957. 'The Justification of Emotions', *Proceedings of the Aristotelian Society, Supp. Vol. 31*.

Waters, W. F. and Fried, F. E. 1976. 'A General System Analysis of Emotion: I. An Integrative Model', *Journal of Operational Psychiatry* vol. 7.

Watson, J. B. 1919. *Psychology from the Standpoint of a Behaviorist*, Lippincott.

1925. *Behaviorism*, Norton.

Webb, W. B. 1948. 'A Motivational Theory of Emotions . . .', *Psychological Review* vol. 55.

Weil, John L. 1974. *A Neurophysiological Model of Emotional Intentional Behavior*, Charles C. Thomas.

West, L. and Greenblatt, M. (eds.) 1960. *Explorations in the Physiology of Emotions*, Psychiatric Research Report No. 12, American Psychiatric Association.

White, A. R. 1967. *The Philosophy of Mind*, Random House.

Wilkins, B. T. 1971. 'Concerning "Motive" and "Intention"', *Analysis* vol. 31.

Williams, B. A. O. 1959. 'Pleasure and Belief', *Proceedings of the Aristotelian Society, Supp. Vol. 33*; reprinted in *Philosophy of Mind*, Hampshire (ed.), Harper and Row, 1966.

1965. 'Morality and the Emotions', Inaugural lecture, Bedford College, London University; reprinted in *Morality and Reasoning*, Casey (ed.),

Methuen, 1971, and in Williams, *Problems of the Self*, Cambridge University Press, 1973.

1973. 'Deciding to Believe'. In Williams, *Problems of the Self*, Cambridge University Press.

Wilson, J. R. S. 1972. *Emotion and Object*, Cambridge University Press.

Wolf, S. and Wolff, H. 1943. *Human Gastric Function: An Experimental Study of a Man and his Stomach*, Oxford University Press.

Wolff, H. G. 1950. 'Life Situations and Bodily Disease'. In *Feelings and Emotions: The Mooseheart Symposium*, M. L. Reymert (ed.), McGraw-Hill.

Wollheim, Richard. 1967–68. 'Thought and Passion', *Proceedings of the Aristotelian Society* vol. 68.

1971. *Freud*, Fontana Modern Masters, Collins.

Woodworth, R. S. 1940. *Psychology* (4th ed.), Methuen.

Woodworth, R. S. and Schlosberg, H. 1955. *Experimental Psychology* (3rd ed.), Methuen.

Wundt, W. 1901. *Human and Animal Psychology*, Swan Sonnenschein.

Wylie, Ruth C. 1968. 'The Present Status of Self Theory'. In *Handbook of Personality Theory and Research*, Borgatta and Lambert (eds.), Rand McNally and Co., Ch. 12.

Young, P. T. 1943. *Emotion in Man and Animal*, Chapman and Hall.

1961. *Motivation and Emotion*, Wiley.

Zangwill, O. L. 1950. *An Introduction to Modern Psychology*, Methuen.

Index